Ulrike Brunotte
The Femininity Puzzle

Ulrike Brunotte (Prof. Dr.) worked as an associate professor for gender and diversity at Maastricht University (NL) until she retired in October 2021. Her research focuses on the role of gender and sexuality in cultural discourse, Orientalism, theories of performativity, aesthetics of religion, psychoanalysis, and literary studies.

Ulrike Brunotte

The Femininity Puzzle

Gender, Orientalism and the »Jewish Other«

[transcript]

Bibliographic information published by the Deutsche Nationalbibliothek

The Deutsche Nationalbibliothek lists this publication in the Deutsche National-bibliografie; detailed bibliographic data are available in the Internet at http://dnb.d-nb.de

Cover layout: Maria Arndt, Bielefeld
Printed by Majuskel Medienproduktion GmbH, Wetzlar
Print-ISBN 978-3-8376-5821-7
PDF-ISBN 978-3-8394-5821-1
https://doi.org/10.14361/9783839458211
ISSN of series: 2627-1907
eISSN of series: 2703-0512

Printed on permanent acid-free text paper.

Contents

Introduction

In a broadest sense, this book is inspired by the context and follow-up initiatives that have emerged as part of my international research network with the title: "Gender and Sexuality in (Neo-)Orientalism: An Entangled History of European and Middle Eastern Identity Discourses." The network was funded by the NWO Netherlands Research Association from 2013 to 2017 and treated the role of gender in the context of Orientalism and Antisemitism through conferences, workshops and publications. Following the International Holocaust Remembrance Alliance, I decided for the unhyphenated spelling of Antisemitism.

The research network which was a decisive inspiration for the present volume originally focused on questions that arise from dealing with historical continuities and changes, similarities and differences of Orientalism, Antisemitism and Islamophobia. During our five-years cooperation, however, my research interest, shifted from a comparison of Islamophobia and orientalized Allosemitism to a broader focus on the role of gender and sexuality in the "Jewish Question" discourse and especially on the study of how the Jews were made into the European prototype of an "internal Other" (Brunotte et al. 2017). As it is also documented in our first programmatic publication from 2015 "*Orientalism, Gender, and the Jews*", I then examined the ways in which orientalized stereotypes of the external and internal Other intertwine in 19th century European national discourse. Our joint research further focused on how orientalist self-fashioning demarcated and transgressed these borders in Jewish cultural production.

I started the research network in October 2013 by inviting the network members to an inaugural conference at Maastricht University. This meeting was followed by a conference in 2014 at the Humboldt University Berlin with the theme "The Homophobic Argument. National Politics and Sexuality in Transregional Perspective" and a further conference in 2015 at the University of Antwerp with the focus: "Colonialism, Orientalism and the Jews: The Role of Gender and Postcolonial Approaches". The official work of the network was concluded with a conference at the University of Fribourg (Switzerland) in 2016 that was organized by Damir Skenderovic and Christina Späti on the topic "From Orientalism to Islamophobia?"; the last joint publication, a result of this conference, appeared in 2019.

Of particular relevance for my research approaches, which combine gender studies with an emphasis in masculinity studies with studies in Allosemtism and Orientalism, were the discussions and meetings with research groups at the University of Tel Aviv and Humboldt University Berlin, especially Christina von Braun, Claudia Bruns, Ofer Nur and Ofri Ilany, and with my American colleague Jay Geller from Vanderbilt University Nashville. With its interrogation of the roles assumed in its interplay by gender, processes of sexualization, as well as attempts of a "heroic" masculine "revolt" of the colonized in scholarly and aesthetic formations the present book takes up the red thread of my special contribution within the research network I chaired from 2013-2017.

One focus of the present book, on the role of masculinities, especially in their relevance in the modern Antisemitism, is further indebted to my long-term work in the field of masculinity studies as an Associate Professor at the *Institute for Cultural Studies* at the Humboldt University Berlin and my collaborations with the *Selma Stern Center for Jewish Studies Berlin-Brandenburg* as well as the *Center for Transdisciplinary Gender Studies* at Humboldt University Berlin. Equally significant for this focus were the discussions that I organized and teaching that I did as Associate Professor and Fellow at the *Center for Gender and Diversity* at the Faculty for Arts and Social Sciences of the University of Maastricht from 2010 until my retirement in September 2021.

The term "puzzle" in the book's title encompasses a multi-layered radius of meaning. It may suggest a confused totality whose pieces must be put together in the right places by a long and careful investigation. "To be puzzled" by something, however, need imply neither a totality nor piecemeal aspects. In this sense "puzzle" can also designate the state of being puzzled and thus characterize a phenomenon which, owing to its puzzle-like transformations, can bewilder, shock, perplex or confound. In this book, these disturbing qualities of ambivalence, incoherence, plurality, fluidity, slipperiness and the like attach themselves to "femininity" as a "puzzle" and to the discursive figure of the "Jew" in the European imagination. Framed by a gender-analytical view, the qualities become carriers of uncertainty and transgressors of boundaries, "perplexing matters" or "figures of the third" (see Holz 2004; Bauman 1991) all the more so when "femininity" and "Jewishness" come together and mix in a puzzle-like manner.

The "femininity puzzle" of the book's title is then unraveled in two ways: first, by an analysis of the effeminization of the male Jew and his modern queer sexualization in racialized discourse, and then by an examination of the transgressive and liminal forms of femininity that were attributed to Jewish women, especially in their allosemitic orientalization as "Beautiful Jewess" in 19th century art, opera and literature. The term "allosemitism" was coined by the Polish-Jewish critic Artur Sandauer and given its theoretical shape by Zygmunt Bauman (1998). It goes beyond the reductive, binary terms of Antisemitism and philosemitism to better represent the "radically ambivalent" (Bauman, ibid: 143) attitude towards Jews that combines both antisemitic and philosemitic elements. This term and analytical tool is especially useful in the analysis of literature because it is flexible enough to do justice to the complexity of a literary text. The allosemitic approach of the present book takes into account the "ambivalent and hybrid" (Bauman 1991: 80) social position of the "Jew" and the "protean instability of the 'the Jew' as signifier" (Cheyette 1993: 8), "including the horror and fascination towards a plural, transgressive and liminal Other who defies clear-cut categories" (ibid.). Particularly the figure of the "Jewess" was often not marked antisemitically but represented as an idealized form of femininity and faith. Thus the book analyzes the figure of the "Beautiful Jewess" as a liminal and hybrid figure between different cultures and religions.

The historical focus of the present book is on the Hobsbawmian long 19th century and the fin de siècle. As John C. Fout has emphasized, "a 'new', historically specific stage in the history of sexuality" (Fout 1992: 389) occurred around 1890. The time saw not only the founding of psychoanalysis and sexology but also the production of multiple "sexualities, including the 'homosexual,' the racialization/gendering of antisemitism, and the sharp increase in contemporary Christian homophobic discourse" (Boyarin 1997: 208-209). Connecting the intellectual worlds of Berlin, London and Vienna, the geographical focus of the book lies on Germany, Austria and the UK. Employing an intersectional approach, it explores how gender, processes of sexualization and feminization have been crucial in the construction of the "Jewish Other." It addresses imaginative, aesthetic and epistemological rather than sociological or empirical questions. It analyzes how literature, performing art, psychoanalysis and sexology probe and respond to the ambivalence of racialized gender stereotypes, especially against the backdrop of modern hegemonic masculinity and contested patterns of femininity. The book also reconstructs how third spaces of reflection are opened up in science, literature and "new dance." The analysis further focuses on the influence of gendered homophobic antisemitism in selected works of Jewish scholars, in particular of Sigmund Freud and Otto Weininger, asking how they responded to and in what ways they internalized and resisted antisemitic attributions.

To demonstrate the peak of this process of orientalist sexualization, I chose as one of my examples the figure of the Jewish princess Salome, the related narrative about her, and her modern re-invention. The German scholar Florian Krobb thinks that in the 19th century the "Beautiful Jewess" already became a pan-European obsession, in which her characterization does not always distinguish clearly between "the Jewish and the feminine" (Krobb 1993: 192). The "femininity puzzle" thus also includes speculations on the paradox and confusion surrounding the ambivalent figure of the Jewess. Taking into account that the Jewish minority in 19th century culture was generally seen as half-occidental and half-oriental, modern and medieval, degenerate and regenerate, as well as a European and a non-European people, a general goal of my study is to look for the evidence that gender makes a difference in the visibility and characterization of the "Jewish Other" and what role projections and fantasies of "femininity" and "effeminization" play therein.

Summary of the Chapters

Chapter One "The Femininity Game of Deception: *Female, Jew, femme fatale Orientale* and *belle Juive*" starts reconstructing how the focus on gender and sexuality characterized the field of Jewish cultural studies in the late 1990s and looks at the dominant role played therein by the historical and postcolonial readings of Sigmund Freud's theory of sexuality. It asks about the extent to which these epistemological intentions offered an opportunity that "grants theorizations about Jewishness a place in ongoing discussions about race, ethnicity, nationness, diaspora, memory, religion, gender and sexuality" (Bunzl 2000: 323). The first chapter further examines the surprising impact of androcentrism in these earlier approaches and points out the emphasis on "female" Jewish masculinity, especially the overdetermined significance that femininity – in Boyarin's spelling "effemminization" (Daniel Boyarin 1997) – is given in antisemitic and, as a response, also in inner-Jewish identity discourses. It analyses the role of orientalization in European constructions of an "Orient Within," based on the figure of the orientalized Jewish princess Salome.

Chapter Two "Queering Judaism and Masculinist Inventions: German Homonationalism around 1900" starts from today's homonationalism and its masculinist discourse. It argues that current homonationalism must be placed in a historical genealogy. The case study focuses on the Second German Empire, in which the discourse of political crisis was represented by a "male gender crisis" that revolved round the Kaiser and his alleged "homosexual" circle. Just as with debates within the incipient gay movement, the discourse centered in the dispositive of "normal masculinity" as representative of the nation/state. The chapter addresses a religious contour of this discursive constitution of homosexualities and a possible Jewish inflection to be found therein.

Chapter Three "Modern Masculinity as Battleground of Identity Politics and Otto Weininger's *Sex and Character*" further contextualizes the discursive intertwinement of antisemitism and modernity. As Jacques Le Rider and others have noted, in both Berlin and Vienna the "crisis of modernity" (Le Rider 1993: 17) discourse condensed the political-cultural crisis into a perceived "crisis of masculinity." No other turn-of-the-century work shows more emphatically than Otto Weininger's *Sex and Character* the at once pathographic and seismographic insights of the simultaneously misogynous and antisemitic elements of the then current discourse on the crisis of modernity. In Weininger's bestseller from 1903, antisemitism and misogyny come together inextricably in the thesis of the femininity of the Jews. According to Christine Achinger, "Weininger was not [only] defending the 'male' rational, bounded subject against the threat arising from sexual urges associated with 'woman,' but also against a threat to the autonomous subject emanating from modern society itself, associated in Weininger's work particularly clearly with the 'Jewish mind'." (Achinger 2013: 122).

Chapter Four "Against Effeminization. Sigmund Freud's Theory of Culture between Male Band Discourse and Antisemitism," examines the influence of the growing antisemitism on Sigmund Freud's theory of the founding of culture with its "band of brothers" in its centre as well as basic psychoanalytical theories of homosexuality, masculinity and femininity. The chapter is based on the groundbreaking postcolonial reading of Freud's psychoanalysis by American scholars such as Daniel Boyarin, Sander Gilman, Ann Pellegrini and Jay Geller. The scientific Antisemitism prominent in medicine at the time aimed, among other things, at portraying male Jews as effeminate and diseased. It denied them the possession of masculinity and thus too the aptitude to be a scientist. Freud's personal and scientific struggle to define a "heroic" Jewish masculinity was therefore closely linked throughout his life, up to and including his late work *Moses and Monotheism* (*Der Mann Moses*, 1939), to his fight against the dominant antisemitism.

Chapter Five "The Jewess Question. The *"Beautiful Jewess"* as Liminal Figure in European Culture" concentrates on the "Beautiful Jewess" in general as a central trope in the discourse of the Jewess as a cultural "figure of the third." Starting from the presupposition of her situatedness in a frontier zone between religions and cultures, the chapter focuses on the depiction of the "Beautiful Jewess" in literature. It uses examples from English and German 19th century novels to analyze how literature explores the ambivalences of the stereotype and opens up third spaces of reflection. Narrative and scenic discourses on the "Orient" are examined as a multilayered and ambivalent ensemble of relational references.

Chapter Six "Seeing, hearing and narrating Salome. Modernist sensual Aesthetics and the role of narrative Blanks" focuses on the narrative construction, beginning with the biblical text, of the figure of Salome and on the modern aesthetic obsession with that figure. In 19th century the revival of the figure of Salome was increasingly effected through narrative media, folk stories and literature; around the fin-de-siècle, dance, paintings and opera made her an popular intermedia icon. Only Wilde's play, and then Richard Strauss's opera, however, aestheticized visual desire and produced an aesthetic spectacle abounding in symbolist and biblical metaphors. In the opening scene of Strauss's opera, Salome's visual–physical attraction is contrasted with the fascination of the disembodied "holy" voice of the prophet, proclaiming God's new Christian message from the depths of the cistern. There is a tension between the description of a stereotypical Jewishness of Herod's court and the depictions of the five argumentative Jews on the one hand and beautiful girl Salome on the other:

> The stark doubleness of the Semitic discourse in *Salome* constructed the Jew as the unchanging racialized Other as well as one who encompassed the possibility of a new redemptive order. [...] Caught between the spheres of Judaism and Christianity, the figure of Salome portrayed the plight of the Jews and served as a metaphor for the Jewish question. (Seshadri 2006: 43-44)

This chapter proposes the hypothesis that it is from the "absence" – the "blank space" within the biblical narratives – that modern, multimedia aesthetics draws its formula of self-reflection as "purely aesthetic" and its sacralization of the aesthetic. The guiding question is how narrative gaps and specific narrative strategies have opened a virtual space of imagination in the process of aesthetic response.

Chapter Seven "Dancing on the Threshold. Maud Allan and the English Salome Scandal (1918)," examines the most famous European fin-de-siècle Salome, the Canadian dancer Maud Allan, analyzing the interconnections of Allan's dance, a libel suit and the juridical production of sexualities. On 16 February 1918, the right-wing London journal *Vigilante* published an article under the insinuating title "The Cult of the Clitoris" (quoted in Hoare 1998: 90). The text warned against the harmful effects of a private performance of Wilde's prohibited play *Salomé*, starring the most famous Salome dancer of the time, Maud Allan, in the role of the Jewish princess. Skillfully blending political and sexual phobias, the conservative and patriotic Movement for Purity in Public Life fanned the ensuing public uproar once news of the performance broke on 10 February 1918, a time when catastrophic Allied defeat still seemed possible and England was in the grip of war hysteria. The chapter focuses on how the intrigue of a right-wing member of parliament, Noel Pemberton-Billing, a leading figure in the Purity Movement, succeeded in bringing Allan before the court of the Old Bailey in May 1918. The trial serves as a window into the sexual obsessions, conspiracy theories and politics of the war era. Examination of the court records of the Pemberton-Billing trial show how religious, juridical and medical discourses interacted to produce the so-called sexual "pervert" in normalizing society. The prosecution used new developments and terms in sexology, mainly from Richard Krafft-Ebing's *Psychopathia Sexualis*, to cement the assumption that "perverse" art mirrored "perverse" minds and bodies, and *vice versa*.

Chapter Eight "'Where there is Dance, there is the Devil'. Femininity and Violence: Salome as Maenad" concentrates again on the multifaceted birth of "modern dance" in female exoticism, in which early 20th century dancers exploited the gestural repertoire of ancient or exotic ritual for their own aesthetic and emancipatory efforts. The chapter connects this artistic avant-garde dance of which Maud Allan was a prominent representative to a critical theory in the study of religion that reflected and accompanied the art form in a unique way. The Chapter's focus is Jane E. Harrison (1850-1928), a well-known scholar in archaeology and classics who drew cultural-historical connections between Salome's "Dance of the Seven Veils" and the then very popular dance of the Dionysian Maenads. For her, the wild followers of the god of wine, theater and orgies, represented female transgressions of the public order and public gender division. Many contemporaries, however, saw the maenads, who penetrated more and more into the cultural awareness thanks to the *Dionysian* turn in the discourse about antiquity inspired by Friedrich Nietzsche and Walter Pater, as the very embodiment of violent feminine rebellion and women's fight for suffrage. Harrison interpreted the Jewish Princess *Salome* as a sister of the maenads.

Bibliography

Achinger, Christine (2013): "Allegories of Destruction: 'Woman' and the 'Jew' in Otto Weininger's *Sex and Character*." In: *German Review*, 88, pp. 121-149.

Aschheim, Steven (2010): The Modern Jewish Experience and the Entangled Web of Orientalism, Amsterdam: Amsterdam University Press.

Baader, Benjamin Maria/ Gillerman, Sharon/Lerner, Paul (eds.) (2012): Jewish Masculinities: German Jews, Gender, and History, Bloomington: Indiana University Press.

Bauman, Zygmunt (1991): Modernity and Ambivalence. Ithaka: Connell University Press.

Baumann, Zygmunt (1998): "Allosemitism: Premodern, Modern, Postmodern." In: Cheyette, Brian/Marcus/Laura (eds.): Modernity, Culture and the 'Jew', Cambridge (UK): Polity Press, pp. 143-156.

Blumenberg, Hans (1985): Arbeit am Mythos, Frankfurt/M.: Suhrkamp Verlag.

Boyarin, Daniel (1997): Unheroic Conduct. The Rise of Heterosexuality and the Invention of the Jewish Man, Berkely/Los Angeles/London: University of California Press.

Boyarin, Daniel/ Itzkovitz, Daniel/ Pellegrini, Ann (eds.) (2003): Queer Theory and the Jewish Question, New York: Columbia University Press.

Braidotti, Rosi (2002): metamorphoses. Towards a Materialist Theory of Becoming, Cambridge (UK): Politiy Press.

Brunotte, Ulrike (2015): Helden des Todes: Studien zu Religion, Ästhetik und Politik moderner Männlichkeit, Würzburg: ERGON.

Brunotte, Ulrike/ Mohn, Jürgen/ Späti, Christina (eds) (2017): Internal Outsiders – Imagined Orientals? Antisemtism, Colonialism, and Modern Constructions of Jewish Identity, Würzburg: ERGON.

Bunzl, Matti (2000): "Jews, Queers, and Other Symptoms: Recent Work in Jewish Cultural Studies." In: GLQ: A Journal of Lesbian and Gay Studies 6 (2), pp. 321-41.

Cheyette, Brian (1993): Constructions of 'the Jew' in English literature and society. Racial representations, 1875-1945, Cambridge/New York/Melbourne/Madrid/Cape Town: Cambridge University Press.

Eilberg-Schwartz, Howard (ed.) People of the Body: Jews and Judaism from an embodied Perspective, Albany: State University of New York Press.

Evangelista, Stefano/ Stedman, Gesa (2021): "Happy in Berlin". In: Evangelista, Stefano/Stedman, Gesa (eds.): Happy in Berlin? English Writers in the City, The 1920s and Beyond, Göttingen: Wallstein Verlag, pp. 15-52.

Fournier, Éric (2011): La 'Belle Juive'. D' Ivanhoé à la Shoah, Seyssel : Champ Vallon.

Fout, John (1992): "Sexual Politics in Wilhelmine Germany: The Male Gender Crisis, Moral Purity, and Homophobia." *Journal of the History of Sexuality* 2.3. pp. 388-421.

Freud, Sigmund: The Question of Lay Analysis, SE (1948), 20, London: Hogarth Press, pp. 142.

Garber, Majorie (1997): Vested Interests. Cross-Dressing and Cultural Anxiety, New York: Routledge.

Geller, Jay (2007): On Freud's Jewish Body. Mitigating Circumcision, New York: Fordham University Press.

Gilman, Sander L. (1993a): Freud, Race and Gender, Princeton (New Jersey): Princeton University Press.

Gilman, Sander L.(1993b): The Case of Sigmund Freud: Medicine and Identity at the Fin de Siècle, Baltimore (US): The John Hopkins University Press.

Gilman, Sander L. (1998): "Salome, Syphilis, Sarah Bernhardt and the 'Modern Jewess'." In: Gilman, Sander L.: Love + Marriage = Death, and other Essays on Representing Difference, Stanford: Stanford University Press, pp. 65-90.

Hahn, Barbara (2005): The Jewess Pallas Athena: This is Too a Theory of Modernity. (trans. by McFarland, James), Princeton, N.J. and Oxford: Princeton University Press.

Hausen, Karin (1981): "Family and Role-Division. The Polarization of Sexual Stereotypes in the Nineteenth Century. An Aspect of the Dissociation of Work and Family Life." In: Evens, Richard J./ Lee, W.R. (eds.): The German Family. Essays on the Social History of the Family in Nineteenth and Twentieth Century Germany, London:Croom Helm, pp. 51-83.

Hoare, Philip (1998): Oscar Wilde's Last Stand: Decadence, Conspiracy, and the Most Outrageous Trial of the Century, New York: Arcade Publishing.

Holz, Klaus: "Die antisemitische Konstruktion des "Dritten" und die nationale Ordnung der Welt." In: von Braun, Christina/ Ziege, Eva- Maria (eds.): "Das bewegliche Vorurteil". Aspekte des internationalen Antisemitismus, Würzburg: Königshausen & Neumann, pp. 43-62.

Khanna, Ranjana (2003): Dark Continents. Psychoanalysis and Colonialism, Durham (USA): Duke University Press.

Krishnaswamy; Revathi (1998): Effeminism. The Economy of Colonial Desire, Michigan: University of Michigan Press.

Kristeva, Julia (1982): Powers of Horror. An Essay on Abjection, New York: Columbia University Press.

Krobb, Florian (1993): Die schöne Jüdin. Jüdische Frauengestalten in der deutsch-sprachigen Erzählliteratur vom 17. Jahrhundert bis zum Ersten Weltkrieg, Tübingen: Max Niemeyer Verlag.

Le Rider, Jacques (1993): Modernity and Crisia of Identity: Culture and Society in Fin-de- Siècle-Vienna, New York: Continuum.

Mc Clintock, Ann (1995): Imperial Leather. Race, Gender and Sexuality in the Colonial Contest, New York/ London: Routledge.

Mosse, George (1985): Nationalism and Sexuality: Respectability and Abnormal Sexuality in Modern Europe, New York: Howard Fertig.

Mosse, George (1996): The Image of Man: The Creation of Modern Masculinity. Oxford: Oxford University Press.

Peretz, Neta (2021): La Jewess in Nineteenth Century French Visual Culture. Thesis for the Degree of "Doctor Phil", Hebrew University of Jerusalem, submitted March 2021.

Pieterse Nederveen, Jan (1992): White on Black. Images of Africa and blacks in Western popular Culture, New Haven/Conn. London: Yale University Press.

Rohde, Achim (2015): "Asiens in Europe. Reading German-Jewish History through a Postcolonial Lens." In: Brunotte, Ulrike/Ludewig, Anna-Dorothea/Stähler, Axel (eds.): Orientalism, Gender and the Jews. Literary and Artistic transformations of European National Discourses, Berlin/ Munich/Boston: de Gruyter, pp.17-32.

Sedgwick, Eve Kosofsky (1994): Tendencies, London: Routledge.

Seshadri, Anne L.: "The Taste of Love: Salome's Transfiguration. " In: Women and Music: A Journal of Gender and Culture, Volume 10, 2006, pp. 24-44.

Sicher, Efraim (2017): *The Jew's Daughter.* A Cultural History of a Conversion
   Narrative, London: Lexington Books.
Stoler, Ann Laura (1995): Race and Education of Desire: Foucault's History
   of Sexuality and the Colonial Order of Things, Durham: Duke University
   Press.
Valman, Nadia (2007) The Jewess in Nineteenth-Century British Literary Cul-
   ture, Cambridge/New York/Melbourne/Madrid/Cape Town: Cambridge
   University Press.

1. "All Jews are womanly, but no women are Jews."[1] The Femininity Game of Deception: *Femme fatale Orientale,* and *belle Juive*[2]

This chapter surveys how the focus on gender and sexuality changed the field of Jewish cultural studies in the late 1990s. It asks to what extent these epistemological intentions, which were enriched by postcolonial and diaspora-studies, offered an opportunity that "grants theorizations about Jewishness a place in ongoing discussions about race, ethnicity, nationness, diaspora, memory, religion, gender, and sexuality." (Bunzl 2000: 323) The chapter starts by examining the surprising impact of "androcentrism" (Boyarin/Itzkovitz/Pellegrini 2003: 3) in these earlier approaches. It further points out the emphasis on the male Jew, Jewish masculinity, and homosexuality, especially the overdetermined significance that the trope of the effeminized male Jew is given in antisemitic discourse as well as in early Jewish cultural studies. Following Ann Pellegrini, the texts analyzes the absence of the Jewish woman from initial scholarly discussions and places an analytical focus on the intersections of race and gender in the construction of the Jewish female body. By taking up the role of "orientalization" in European constructions of the "Orient Within" (Rohde 2005) the second part concentrates on the figure of the "Beautiful Jewess" as a cultural "figure of the third" (Eßlinger et al. 2010). As Ann Pellegrini states, "In the collapse of Jewish masculinity into an abject femininity, the Jewish female seems to disappear." (1997a: 109; see also Pellegrini 1997b: 18) She clearly directs this statement and problem also to her male colleagues,

---

1   Pellegrini (1997a: 118); see also Pellegrini (1997b: 28), *Performance Anxieties,* p. 28. The book *Performance Anxieties* by Pellegrini (1997b) includes portions of the article "Whiteface Performances" (Pellegrini 1997a) but in a revised and expanded form.

2   Translated by Allison Brown.

who largely focus on the Jewish male when speaking of the cultural production of Jewishness. In its concluding sections the chapter returns to the great significance of Sigmund Freud's psychoanalysis for the early gender/sexuality discussions in Jewish cultural studies.

Jewish Cultural Studies, Feminism, and Queer Theory

In Miriam Peskowitz and Laura Levitt's 1997 anthology with the provocative title *Judaism Since Gender*, feminist authors had already suggested a shift in emphasis in Jewish studies from "women" to "gender." The authors of the articles in the book, including Susan Shapiro and Susannah Heschel, argued the case using a more or less constructionist approach in considering Jewish religious history with respect to gender. This meant following Joan Scott and using gender as a "useful category of historical analysis" (1986: 1067) and "the primary way of signifying relationships of power," (ibid) and thus understanding it as a basic category of knowledge.

In a way, the issue of Jewish masculinity occasionally arose out of historical antisemitism around the end of the nineteenth century, when "non-Jewish commentators began to express serious concern about gender expressions among Jewish men and women, and [when] the trope of the effeminate Jewish man became the target of persuasive and vicious anti-Semitic critique." (Baader/Gillerman/Lerner 2012: 2) The surprising impact of "androcentrism" (Boyarin/Itzkovitz/Pellegrini 2003: 3) in the connection drawn in the 1990s between Jewish studies and gender and queer studies and the emphasis on antisemitic constructions of "deviant" and "female" Jewish masculinity, homosexuality, and homophobia in the initial discussions were partially caused by the historical discourse itself. These scholars were interested "in exploring the complex of social arrangements and processes through which modern Jewish and homosexual identities emerge as traces of each other" (ibid). Jewish studies and queer studies were first brought together in the 1997 anthology *Jews and Other Differences*. Following Jay Geller (1991, 1993) and Sander Gilman (1991, 1993a), here the editors Daniel and Jonathan Boyarin postulated an entangled history of modern constructions of gender/sexuality and antisemitism. In addition to taking up the approaches to the history of sexualities of Michel Foucault (1978), Eve Kosofsky Sedgwick (1985), and Marjorie Garber (1992), they also particularly address the pioneering studies of George Mosse (1985) on nationalism, gender, sexuality, and antisemitism.

In *Unheroic Conduct: The Rise of Heterosexuality and the Invention of the Jewish Man*, Daniel Boyarin (1997) claimed that the antisemitic stereotype of the
"feminized Jewish male" is also a product of the hegemonic concept of Western European heterosexuality. This book in particular "helped open up such
new interpretative possibilities with [Boyarin's] provocative and controversial claim that Jewish mode of culture has fostered a distinct Jewish gender
order and a unique mode of masculinity that resonated from ancient times
into the twentieth century." (Baader/Gillerman/Lerner 2012: 3) He puts Jewish
constructions of the "female masculinity" in a postcolonial perspective, beginning with the Roman Empire and the Jewish diaspora. Moreover, he links
the rhetorical and theoretical constructions of the "homosexual" to the discursive development of modern sexuality. Boyarin's point of reference is the
modern construction of heterosexuality, which he asserts is homophobic at its
roots and which, since its emergence in the nineteenth century, no longer allows any latitude or ambivalence whatsoever: "'Heterosexuality,' as its tenets
have been ventriloquized by David Halperin, involves the strange idea that
a 'normal' man will never feel desire for another man." (Boyarin 1997: 212;
see also Halperin 1986: 44) Historian Wolfgang Schmale, who, like Boyarin,
refers to Foucault's concept of a regime (*dispositif*) of sexuality in his book
Geschichte der Männlichkeit in Europa (1450–2000) (History of Masculinity in Europe, 1450–2000), shifts "the norming of the man as heterosexual," (2003: 207)
which he says necessarily implies homophobia, all the way back to the eighteenth century.

If the Jewish man was then characterized as "female" because he was circumcised, as occurred in the antisemitic discourse of the late nineteenth century (cf. Geller 1992; Gilman 1993a), then he was also placed in close proximity
to a pathologicalized homosexuality, even though he was simultaneously said
to be fixated on the family (Mosse 1985). "Still, Jews were not thought to endanger society by their supposed homosexuality but rather by their evil heterosexual drives. [...] But while family life was intact among the Jews themselves, it
was, so racists asserted, directed against the family life of others." (Mosse 1985:
142) As Susannah Heschel has emphasized, it was precisely the fluctuation in
antisemitic discourse that made the Jewish man appear "both as a man in the
most extreme sense, a sex-obsessed predator [...], as well as an abnormal man,
one who is effeminate and even menstruates." (1998a: 86) Without referring to
early discussions in Wilhelmine sexology, namely to Magnus Hirschfeld and
Karl Heinrich Ulrichs, Sander Gilman speaks of a "third sex" (1995: 156-157)
with respect to the Jewish man. All of these authors, even when they theoret-

ically draw totally different conclusions from this, nevertheless underline the effeminization of Jewish men derived from circumcision as a central aspect of the discourse. Thus, Gilman summarizes his comprehensive medical history studies on the syndrome of circumcision in the cultural discourse of the nineteenth century as follows: "The circumcised Jew became the representative of the anxiety-provoking masculine. [...] The very body of the (male) Jew became the image of the anxiety generated by the potential sense of the loss of control." (1993a: 9) This loss of control was also understood in sexual terms and in older colonial discourses and it had already been projected upon colonized groups such as the autochthonous populations of India, Africa, or the Americas. (cf. Lewis 1996; Mc Clintock 1995; Schülting 1997) The masculinist imaginary was a target of Daniel Boyarin's 2003 essay, "Homophobia and the Postcoloniality of the 'Jewish Science.'" He compares constructions of "blackness" and Jewishness and brings together two postcolonial subjects, Freud and Fanon. Jan Nederveen Pieterse had already indicated that the processes of "othering" did not advance in only one direction, but were instead, in the sense of an entangled history, an interplay of overseas and inner-European colonial discourses:

> While "others" mirror Europe's negative self or split-off shadows, European hierarchies re-emerge with the internal "others" reconstructed in the image of the overseas shadow. [...] Indeed, virtually all the images and stereotypes projected outside Europe in the age of empire had been used first within Europe. (1992: 212, 215)

Particularly in view of the long history of Christian anti-Judaism, whose legacy was taken up by antisemitism, the historical chronology of internal and external boundaries must also be read in a reversal of the chronological course of events, as Tudor Parfitt has stated: "From the very beginning of European expansion Judaism was employed in the decipherment of religions, and Jewish ancestry was used as likely explanations for the people Europeans encountered." (Parfitt 2005: 53) Susanne Zantop (1997), Susannah Heschel (1999), Jonathan Hess (2012), and Achim Rohde (2005)—to name only a few scholars—reconstruct the discourse and the "colonial fantasies" around the "Jewish Question" in Germany within a postcolonial theoretical frame. Aamir R. Mufti (2007) opens up a European and global perspective. By 1900, at a time of highly sexualized antisemitism, the cultural practice of circumcision brought the Jewish population (once again) within proximity of the "primitive" peoples overseas. This was due especially to the new, comparative studies in the fields of ethnography and the sexual sciences, such as those of Wilhelm Wundt and Paolo Mantegazza, who were referred to also by Sigmund Freud. Circumcision, that "uncanny" sign on the male genitalia (Geller 1993), became the medium of othering; "it suggested something perverse" (Geller 2007). In his later studies on circumcision Geller viewed it as an apparatus (Foucault: *le dispositif*) that determined discourses and practices in European identity- and alterity-formation:

> 'Circumcision' became both an apotropaic monument and a floating signi-fier that functioned as a dispositive, an apparatus that connected biblical citations, stories, images, phantasies, laws, kosher slaughterers [...], ethno-graphic studies, medical diagnoses, and ritual practices [...] in order to pro-duce knowledge about and authorize the identity of *Judentum* – and of the uncircumcised. (2007: 26)

Precisely the relative, at least publicly, invisibility of circumcision certainly also generated an antisemitic politics of visibility that focused on the body—especially the nose—of the male Jew:

> By the end of the nineteenth century the body of the Jew came to be the body of the male Jew, and it was the immutability of this sign of masculine difference that was inscribed on the psyche of the Jew. The fantasy of the dif-ference of the male genitalia was displaced upward – onto the visible parts of the body, onto the face and the hands where it marked the skin with its blackness. (Geller 2007: 21)

Along with the aspect of cultural masculinity, the sociability of the (male) Jew also became a problem. As analogous to the female, as Gilman stresses, or coded as "queer," as stated by Boyarin (1997) and Geller (2007), the Jewish man moved culturally into the realm of the homosexual, who was defined as deviant. (Mosse 1985) As an ultimately indefinable gender that oscillated between an abject, male, or oversexed femininity and a homosexualized or "less-than-virile" (ibid: 8) masculinity, Jews challenged the bourgeois gender order as a whole. In contrast to this antisemitic effemminization of the Jew-ish man, Talmud expert Daniel Boyarin claims and reconstructs a centuries-old "positive sense of self-femminization within [mostly premodern Eastern] rabbinic representations" (1997: 143). Boyarin's idiosyncratic spelling (double m) of "effemminization" is significant. He does not intend to ascribe "some form of actual or essential femininity to certain behaviors or practices [... nor] to reify or celebrate the 'feminine' but to dislodge the term." (ibid: 4)

He concentrates his argumentation on the analysis of the gender/sex system of traditional Ashkenazic culture of premodern Eastern Europe. Thus, he sees two different models of masculinity that have opposed each other in European civilization since the Roman Empire and the Jewish Diaspora: on the one hand, the Roman-coded "heroic" model with its emphasis on "male" values, such as honor, valor, a readiness for war, and physical fitness; and, on the other hand, the traditionally "unheroic" "Ashkenazic model of a gentle, nurturing masculinity, exemplified in the eroticized figuration of the Yeshiva-Bokhur, the pale and meek student of the Talmud." (Bunzl 2000: 328) This Jewish-feminine model of masculinity, in Boyarin's view, was conceivable in the Christian-influenced culture only for the career of a monk, but not that of a sexually active family, as it is in Judaism. However, with the parallel development of the modern, antisemitic stereotype of the "female Jew" and that of the "homosexual" as "deviant" and "degenerate," these discourses ultimately merged at the fin de siècle and produced, according to Boyarin's radical thesis, "a perfect and synergistic match between homophobia and antisemitism." (1997: 209 Based on this cultural analysis, Daniel and Jonathan Boyarin (1997) proposed in the introduction to *Jews and Other Differences* a methodological renewal of Jewish cultural studies by appropriating methods and questions of gender, queer, and postcolonial studies. In this they ascribe key significance to the history of sexuality, in particular the scientific "invention" of homosexuality in the late nineteenth century:

> Basic theoretical questions about the history of sexuality will be central to any endeavor in Jewish cultural history. A question as central to contemporary cultural studies most broadly conceived as whether "homosexuality" has always existed or is a specific historical cultural phenomenon will take its place as a central issue for Jewish cultural studies as well. (1997: x)

As Geller (2007), Boyarin (1997), Gilman (1993), and Pellegrini (1997a) have demonstrated in their works in very different ways, in the history of antisemitism, racial difference has always been entangled with sexual difference. "For Jewish male bodies, marked for an anti-Semitic imaginary by overlapping layers of blackness, effeminacy, and queerness, the sexualization of 'race' and the racialization of 'sex' are constitutive features." (Pellegrini 1997a: 108; see also Pellegrini 1997b: 17) As Matti Bunzl has emphasized, these early studies "have a significant blind spot, which suggests the need for further work at the intersection of Jewish and queer studies. [...] While the interpretive move uncovers the queer valence of modern Jewish identities

[...] Boyarin never addresses possible Jewish inflections in the constitution of homosexuality." (2000: 337) In the 2003 anthology *Queer Theory and the Jewish Question*, Daniel Boyarin, Pellegrini, and Daniel Itzkovitz react to Bunzl's intervention and exemplify the queer studies and postcolonial approach to Jewish studies through historical case studies that follow the queer-Jew connections in literary examples, in the history of homosexuality, and in new readings of Freud's theory of sexuality. The both antisemitic and homophobic ascriptions, however, were also internalized by Jewish authors and sometimes, as often demonstrated (cf. Arens 1995) by Otto Weininger, for example, even intensified. (cf. Boyarin 1997; Gilman 1993a) In his 1903 study *Sex and Character*, which rapidly became a popular science best-seller, the homophobic, antisemitic, and misogynous trends in Vienna's fin de siècle were linked in a symptomatic as well as diagnostic way. For Weininger, a Jew who converted to Protestantism, it was certainly threatening that "Man has everything within him. [...] He can reach the greatest heights or degenerate most profoundly, he can become an animal, a plant, he can even become a woman, and that is why there are female, effeminate men." (2005 [1903]: 162) He saw the same possibility of adaptation with regard to being Jewish. Judaism, for him, was neither a "race" nor a "people," but a psychological opportunity for every individual: *"Judaism must be regarded as a cast of mind, a psychic constitution which is a* **possibility** *for* **all** *human beings, and which has only found its most magnificent* **realization** *in historical Judaism* [here and in the following, emphasis in original]." (ibid: 274) Just as the virile man stands opposite the effeminate one, the modern Aryan man opposes the Jew, according to Weininger, as a psychological possibility of his self. The *tertium comparationis* of the Jew and the homosexual, however, is their "femininity." In the introduction to chapter 13, "Judaism," Weininger ties the Jews even more to "femininity":

> If one thinks about the woman and the Jew, one will always be surprised to realize the extent to which Judaism in particular seems to be steeped in femininity, the nature of which I have so far only tried to explore in contrast to masculinity *as a whole without regard to any differences* within it. (ibid: 276)

At the end of his book, Weininger views the woman and the Jew, both of which he says have "no personality" or "intelligible self" (ibid: 278) as coming together in secular, liberal modernity: "The *spirit of modernity* is Jewish. [...] Our age is not only the most Jewish, but also the most effeminate of all ages." (ibid: 299) It is not so much Weininger's mental disposition—he committed suicide shortly after his book was published—that makes his work so fascinating, but the fact that *Sex and Character* became so popular and consolidated the "spirit" of his times. This overdetermined mixture of homophobia, antisemitism, and misogyny was a distilled concentration of "the ordinary thought of his time and place." (Boyarin 1997: 237)

Between the Poles of Oriental Femininity and Jewishness: the *Beautiful Jewess*

In view of the crucial role played by the effeminization of the Jewish man in antisemitic discourse, according to Ann Pellegrini, the difference of the Jewish woman also consists of external ascriptions in which gender, sexualization, religion, and race played a role. Yet, as Barbara Hahn has argued on the basis of Bernard Picart's *Céremonies et costumes religieuses* (1727–1743), Jewish women were seldom as clearly marked as Jewish men were. (Hahn 2005: 33) Along with the emancipation of the Jews—during the early nineteenth century at the latest—however, the Jewish woman, as the "Beautiful Jewess", became a literary, artistic, and theatrical figure in Europe: "This figure, which was born in the [19th] century, forcefully expanded into the European imaginaries [Castordiadis]," (Fournier 2011 : 7) wrote Éric Fournier, also explaining the seismographic role of this cultural invention:

> More than other representations of the Jewish world, this ambivalent figure of the Other did in fact appear with an intensified plasticity, which was capable of expressing, in a frenetic manner, the entire range of judgments and opinions about Judaism, from philo-Semitism to anti-Semitism. (ibid: 9)

As Florian Krobb (1993) has shown, in the first and thus far only German-language book on the "Beautiful Jewess", the Jewish woman in (German-language) literature before the fin de siècle embodied not so much a negative difference but functioned instead as an ambivalent mediating figure. (See also Frübis 1997; Ludewig 2008) In the stereotypical, repeated master narrative of the "Beautiful Jewess", as the daughter of an often antisemitically exaggerated father (a mother is rarely present), she stood between the Jewish and Christian worlds. As an object of Christian male desire, as a lover, or even as a later wife of a Christian man, the completely assimilated Jewish woman ultimately also converts to Christianity.[3] This acid test between the cultures and religions, however, often ended for the "Beautiful Jewess" with her sacrificing her own identity, self-denial, or even with her death. This has been presented in different ways, but always associated with serious consequences, by, for instance, Sir Walter Scott in *Ivanhoe* in 1820, Eugène Scribe in his libretto to Fromental Halévy's opera *La Juive* (The Jewess) in 1835, and Franz Grillparzer in his play *Die Jüdin von Toledo* (*The Jewess of Toledo*) of 1872. Florian Krobb considers the literary motif of the "Beautiful Jewess" to be a "pan-European phenomenon," in which the characterization does not always have clear-cut distinctions between "the Jewish and the feminine." (1993: 192) Some French painters like Eugène Delacroix and Charles Landelle created iconic portraits of "belles juives," in which the motifs of the Jewess as oriental and the oriental Jewesses that they actually saw during their Middle Eastern travels merged. One of the most iconic of these "Beautiful Jewesses" is Landelle's idealized yet alien *Jewess from Tangier* from 1908. Her noble, spiritualized beauty and heightened femininity is paired with long, sensual black hair and a very thin and diaphanous Orientalized dress. In her idealized white-skinned femininity, she shows no obvious negative markers of Jewishness.

At the same time the fascinating ambivalence of the figure raises the question as to precisely how her Jewishness and her femininity work together in each case. Even for Otto Weininger, the Jewish woman personified the essence of "femininity" or the "eternally female." In *Sex and Character* he wrote that "No woman in the world represents the *idea* of Woman as perfectly as the Jewess [...]. But the Jewess can seem to represent more fully both poles of femininity, as a housemother with many children and as a lustful odalisque, as Cypris and as Cybele." (2005: 289) To describe the double difference of the imaginary Jewess, a *tertium comparationis* of her femininity and her Jewishness has to be found. Her orientalization served this purpose. (Fournier 2011: 27-29) The physical beauty and sensuality of the Jewish woman, her dark hair, her "Eyebrows á L'orientale" (Ockman 1991: title) and sometimes even her clothing, were almost always described using orientalizing tropes and characteristics.

---

3   This master narrative of the "Beautiful Jewess", which is reproduced today with regard to Muslim women, depicts some similarities to the oft-cited sentence by Gayatri Chakravorty Spivak concerning the imperial narrative of salvation (in Spivak with reference to the Hindu practice of suttee): "White men are saving brown women from brown men." (Spivak 1988: 297)

Fig. 1: Charles Landelle: Jewess from Tanger (1908), Museum of Fine Arts, Reims.

Public Domain, Wikimedia Commons.

Fournier reconstructed this process as it pertains to France:

> The "Beautiful Jewess" inscribes herself forcefully into the invention of the Orient by the fascinated scholars, both as a discursive matrix and through a feeling of foreignness. [...] In the middle of this long list of exotic beauties—the Turkish, Egyptian, Greek, Moorish, Armenian, Abyssinian, Coptic—the Jewess appears as the most troubling of them all. (ibid: 27)

As Andrea Polaschegg demonstrated in her comprehensive, pioneering work on German Orientalism, which offers a critique of Edward Said and at the same time exceeds Said's scope, also in German Oriental studies and aesthetics of the Orient this cultural field had already been tapped starting in the late eighteenth century as a referential reservoir for representations of Biblical and contemporary Judaism. The appropriation of orientalizing traits followed traditional images and narratives, but the process developed a complex dynamic of its own, "as these [...] acts of reference always produce a surplus of meaning." (2005: 284) In view of the fact that, in the eighteenth century, the Hebrew Bible was already recognized as a literary text and had thus undergone a "poetic, historical, and oriental [...] transformation," it is not surprising that it was biblical figures of women and girls that inspired the imaginations of modern authors. Although Krobb does not go into the intertextual and historical phenomenon of the orientalized "Beautiful Jewess", he often cites precisely from relevant passages in novels in which the Jewish woman is introduced via orientalized biblical figures: for example, from a short passage from Countess Ida von Hahn-Hahn's story *Maria Regina* of 1850, which lacks any explicit mention of the name Judith: "She had that special something, as if she could cut off the head of a Holofernes if need be." (cit. in Krobb 1993: 188) In another example, the novel *Esthers Ehe* (Esther's Marriage, 1886) by Hermann Heiberg, a number of orientalizations are combined with antisemitic tropes of the "salon Jewess." When Baroness Christine's son presents the young Jewish woman Esther as her future daughter-in-law, the Christian mother of noble pride contradicts him with the words: "A Jewess? Her? Oh! [...] The black Oriental whose great grandfather [...] lent gold for a usurer's interest. [...] And the future association with [...] smart and hot-blooded women with low décolletés and with all the darkly colored young male disciples of gold [...]!" (cit. in Krobb 1993: 189; ellipses in original) This even carried over to the likable figure of Lenore in Eugenie Marlitt's novel *Das Heideprinzesschen* (*The Little Moorland Princess*). The story, "with its Jewish title character, with which the best-selling author attempted in *Die Gartenlaube* (The Garden Arbor) magazine in the jubilee volume of 1871 to offer a liberal appeal for tolerance against the emerging chauvinism" (Krobb 1993: 192-193), also makes reference to the figure of Salome of all things when describing the young Jewish woman: "Now I know where my little favourite got her Oriental face. Yes, yes, it must have been just such a black-haired girl, with feet of quicksilver, who beguiled Herod to give her the head of John the Baptist!" (Marlitt cit. in Krobb 1993: 186) In contrast to Judith, whose murder of the tyrant Holofernes was long passed down—after it appeared in the Septuagint and the Protestant Apocrypha—as a heroic, patriotic act of assertiveness and as "a paragon of self-sacrificial martyrdom for a noble cause" (Dijkstra 1986: 377), Salome was regarded very early on as a canonical figure of anti-Judaism. It is known that she was not only a beautiful Jewish princess who was connected to the beheading of John the Baptist, but already as a biblical figure she performed a seductive dance that Oscar Wilde was later to call the "Dance of the Seven Veils." All in all, modern "Beautiful Jewesses" appeared often enough in European literature as singers, actresses, dancers, or even as prostitutes and courtesans, as in Balzac's novels, or were associated with masquerade balls, parties, or dance events. (Fournier 2011: 33-35) The imaginary proximity to seduction, sexuality, theater, and dance, as well as to masquerade and costumes, certainly had just as much to do with their femininity—situated outside of bourgeois gender roles—as with their Jewishness. At the same time, Polaschegg infers from the increased presence of these characters on the stages of European theaters and opera houses that "the prominence of said Oriental figure device on the opera stages does in fact suggest a specific affinity of this west-eastern subject for dramatic or even music-theatrical art forms and aesthetics." (2005: 173)

However, in the nineteenth century Jewish women played a pan-European role not only as fictive actresses, dancers, and singers, but also as real ones. With reference to highly visible Jewish actresses such as Rachel and Sarah Bernhardt, Ann Pellegrini reiterates her question about the cultural space occupied by Jewish women in the nineteenth century: "The French stage was dominated and dazzled by Rachel in the first half of the nineteenth century and then, in the latter half [...] by Sarah Bernhardt.[...] Jewishness—as performatively constituted and publicly performed—clearly needs to be thought through the female Jewish body, no less than through the male." (1997a: 110; 1997b: 19) Like no other actress of her time, Sarah Bernhardt, who had in fact been baptized and was raised in a convent, was made into the epitome of the "Beautiful Jewess", and the embodiment of a modern Salome. The fantasized links between Sarah Bernhardt and Salome were so great that "Oscar Wilde wrote his Salome for her." (Fournier 2011: 249)

In his 1993 essay, "Salome, Syphilis, Sarah Bernhardt, and the 'Modern Jewess,'" which Ann Pellegrini also refers to, Sander Gilman examines the discursive production of the Jewish woman around 1900, asking "under what circumstances does her 'Jewishness' and under what circumstances does her 'femininity' become her defining moment?" (1993b: 197) However, because in the antisemitic discourse of the time the Jewish man is coded as "female," Gilman begins his study with a vexatious paradox:

> When Jewish women are represented in the culture of the turn of the cen-
> tury, the qualities ascribed to the Jew and to the woman seem to exist simul-
> taneously and yet seem mutually exclusive.[...] When we focus on the one,
> the other seems to vanish. (ibid: 195)

In order to grasp this simultaneous appearing and vanishing of gender and
race regarding the Jewish woman, Gilman broadens the thesis of the deceptive
correlation between antisemitic and sexualizing tropes to include the construction of the Jewish woman. According to Gilman it is also true for the
Jewish woman that, to a certain extent, she becomes a vessel for transgressive images of ("female") sexuality/identity or those repressed by and which
threaten the normative ideal: "Central to the arbitrary but powerful differentiation between the stereotype of the Jewish man and that of the Jewish
woman is the different meaning of male and female sexuality at the fin de
siècle." (ibid) Just as the Jewish man is seen as effeminized and thus the negative Other of the strictly heterosexual-male Gentile, Gilman says, the Jewish
woman, too, is constructed as the "exclusionary feminine" (ibid: 197) or the
countertype to the normative ideal of the passive and passionless housewife,
as was still defended by the Moral Purity Movement around 1900.[4] On the
other hand, ascriptions of femininity, especially if they are accompanied by
transgressions or confounding of the gender order like in the figure of the
deadly *femme fatale*, acquire a negative, sometimes even a stigmatizing, pejorative character. The "Beautiful Jewess" Ann Pellegrini notes was sometimes
a "deceptively feminine figure, 'deceptive' because her beauty concealed her
powers of destruction" (Pellegrini 1997: 129). Challenging the order of binary
thinking, putting into question the categories of "female" and "male", liminal
figures of a "third sex" or "third term" (Garber 1992: 11), have furthermore often
been connected to a monstrous, multiform "abject femininity".

The "femininity puzzle" of the Jewess contains all figures of female otherness, from the sexually active "phallic" woman and the courtesan to the "intellectual woman" to the bluestocking. (Gilman 1993b: 355) Sometimes the "Beautiful Jewess" disappears entirely behind and in the stereotype of the *femme
fatale*, and sometimes her Jewishness is emphasized as a source of seductive
and destructive energy. It is no coincidence that Gilman chooses the figure

---

4   John Fout (1992) has shown how around 1900 the Christian Values or Moral Purity
     Movement fought to defend this bourgeois gender order.

of Salome, "one of the master narratives of this stereotype at the fin de siècle" (ibid), as the object of his study. Admittedly, he studies Salome as she is
presented by non-Jewish, European – especially German – authors as "the essential 'woman'," whose femininity is used to "simultaneously evoke [...] the
essential 'Jew.'" (ibid) Even today, as Shelley Salamensky states, a "near complete absence of scholarship on Wilde vis-à-vis the Jew" creates difficulties,
because "Wilde's conflicted uses of the figure of the Jew are key to understanding central issues not only in *Salomé*." (2012: 215) What Gilman does not
examine, however, is the complex task that the wide spectrum of the orientalizations of Salome, as shown in chapters six and seven, assumed in the late
nineteenth century in this game of deception between "femininity" and Jewishness. Decisive configurations of the Salome story before and around 1900,
which would later influence Oscar Wilde, were linked in France to names such
as Gustave Flaubert, Gustave Moreau, and Joris-Karl Huysmans. Starting with
Flaubert's story *Herodias* (1877), continued in Moreau's paintings *Salomé* (1871)
and *L'Apparition* (1876), and culminating in Huysmans's 1884 novel *À Rebours*
(*Against Nature*), Salome is entirely separated from her (historical) Jewishness.
As a dancer, who was both erotic and deadly, she is instead transformed into
the epitome of the "femme fatale Orientale" (Fournier 2011: 197). What began
as Flaubert's attempt to create a Salome, who "is nothing more than a paradox of an eternal femininity" (ibid: 199), culminated in Huysmans's fiction of
a "superhuman, strange Salome" (1998: 46, cit. in Fournier 2011: 200) that no
longer had any trace of a "Beautiful Jewess", but all the markings of a fascinating, artificially created *female evil*, as was widespread in the imagery at the fin
de siècle. (Praz 1970) To be sure, it was Oscar Wilde who first created Salome's
gruesomeness in literature; Flaubert had still portrayed her as simply a tool
of her mother Herodias.

Oscar Wilde and his Salomé as a *Figure of the Third*[5]

It all began in 1891 with the play published in French by Oscar Wilde, in which a new figure of Salome took the stage. The author presented her for the first time as a desiring woman and as the independent choreographer of her legendary "dance." When the rehearsals for the play were already well underway in 1892 with Sarah Bernhardt—Wilde's favorite Salome—it was banned for all British stages by The Lord Chamberlain, the chief censor, with the justification that, in it, biblical characters were acting within a "secular" scene. Four years later the play celebrated its premiere in Paris. Oscar Wilde was unfortunately unable to attend the performance, as he was at the time serving a two-year prison sentence for his homosexuality. In 1901, a year after Wilde's death, the play premiered in Berlin. Nevertheless it was not until Richard Strauss's operatic version of the material and the premier of his *Salome* in Dresden in 1905 that Salome began her triumphal march, continuing to the present day, on opera stages around the world. Even before Salome's dance was presented as a dance on opera stages, the "Dance of the Seven Veils" had developed a life of its own. As demonstrated in chapter eight, since 1907 the Canadian "barefoot" dancer Maud Allan had been performing her own *Salome* choreography with growing success in London music halls, bringing the Salomania of the times to a pinnacle. By combining Oriental fantasies and Greek ritual figures with gymnastic and dance elements from the Life Reform Movement, the dancer opened up for many women "a set of codes for female bodily expression that disrupted the Victorian conventional dichotomies of female virtue and female vice and pushed beyond such dualisms. Allan used the 'Orient' as a register for female sensual expression." (Walkowitz 2003: 6) This controversial dance performance was scandalous not only because a "white" woman was adopting supposedly oriental forms of bodily expression, but in particular because Allan's Salome did not simply dance *around* the head of John the Baptist as her "reward," but *with* the severed head of the saint.

Shortly after Allan had taken on the role of Salome in 1916 in a private staging of Wilde's banned play, Noel Pemberton Billing, an advocate of the

---

5   The *figure of the Third* refers historically to the concept of the "third sex," as used in German-language sexology and by sexual activists such as Karl Heinrich Ulrichs and Magnus Hirschfeld. However, it also refers to the generally queer and transgressive potential of the figure of the "Jew" in Antisemitic discourse (see Holz 2004) and Salome around 1900. (Garber 1992)

right-wing Movement for Purity in Public Life, accused her in his paper *The Vigilante*, under the headline "The Cult of the Clitoris," of "illicit sex" and "political intrigue" (cit. in Cherniavsky 1991: 16). Allan filed libel charges against Pemberton-Billing. In the end, she nevertheless became both the 'perpetrator' and the 'accused' within the trial, which destroyed her career and her life.

The figure of Salome, however, was also connected with homosexuality, especially as a result of the humiliating trial against Oscar Wilde in 1895. One can only speculate how long this scandal, which long made homosexuality an object of public debate, also shook both the heteronormative façade and the tabooed homophile undercurrent of the colonial empire. (Aldrich 2003: 6) Authors who saw Wilde's Salome as his alter ego and regarded her rejection by the morally pure prophet John the Baptist as Victorian resistance to homosexual desire tended to interpret the material as border-crossing. Thus, Elaine Showalter poses the question, "Is the woman behind Salome's veils the innermost being of the male artist? Is Salome's love for Jokanaan a veiled homosexual desire for the male body?" (1990: 151) Katherine Worth, who has examined the motif of veiling and unveiling in Wilde's works, concludes that "unveiling was an appropriate image for the activity which Wilde regarded as the artist's prime duty: self-expression and self-revelation." (1983: 66-67) Other authors, such as Marjorie Garber, view Salome's gender-border-crossing, queer dance as the actual taboo breach. Not the intensified sensuality, but the "paradox of gender identification, the disruptive element that intervenes, transvestism as a space of possibility structuring and confounding culture. *That* is the taboo against which Occidental eyes are veiled." (Garber 1992: 342) Still, the 1923 American film *Salomé*, which was co-directed by and starred the bisexual Jewish actress Alla Nazimova, was rumored to have featured an all-gay cast.

For Wilde, a former Oxford student of ancient philology, who was greatly influenced by Walter Pater, the influential art critic and a source of inspiration for aestheticism, the play was a tragedy and Salome a heroine to be taken seriously, with whom he sympathized. The claim that he himself once donned the costume of Salome, however, as Garber also supported based on a photograph published in Richard Ellmann's 1987 biography of Wilde, has meanwhile been refuted. As can only be sketched here briefly, the discursive nodal points surrounding Oscar Wilde's Salome and Maud Allan's performance around 1900 include many themes that also belonged to cultural antisemitism, but there were no direct links between them. A lone exception to this was a diatribe at the end of Allan's trial: A particularly phobic line of argumentation by Pemberton-Billing culminated in his blatantly antisemitic description of Maud Allan as a spy aligned with "'German-Jewish' interests [and] who promoted Salome productions and who was protected by the present government." (cit. in Walkowitz 2003: 35; see also Walkowitz 2012: 89)

As Bram Dijkstra emphasized in *Idols of Perversity: Fantasies of Feminine Evil in Fin-de-Siècle Culture,* his comprehensive, comparative study of literary and visual interpretations, the Salome figure underwent a transformation around 1900. Her murderous fascination was increasingly tied to her virginity. At the same time, the "virgin dancer," according to Dijkstra, increasingly epitomized the "perversity of women: their eternal circularity and their ability to destroy the male's soul even while they remained nominally chaste in body." (1986: 384) In Stéphane Mallarmé's 1864 poem "Hérodiade," Salome "murmurs contentedly as she gazes fixedly at herself in the mirror: 'The horror of my virginity/Delights me [...].'" (ibid: 385) Dijkstra also mentions examples of French portrayals of Salome as a Jewish woman, although verification of this in the sources is relatively meager. Except for an unknown author named Charles Besnard, who published a poem "The Jewess Salome" in a Parisian magazine in 1897, Dijkstra refers only to an anonymously written 1917 work entitled *Famous Pictures Reproduced from Renowned Paintings by the World's Greatest Artists.* Therein, according to Dijkstra, the author emphasized while commenting on a Salome painting by Jules Lefebvres, "that the master had succeeded in portraying in his painting of the daughter of Herodias, 'an essentially Semitic type of the antique period, with the sensuous and soulless beauty of the tigress rather than the woman.'" (ibid: 387) As evidence of pronounced antisemitic depictions of Salome, he offers only Max Slevogt's 1895 painting "Salome's Dance." (see ibid: 386-388) However, in the painting it is not Salome but only the men gazing at her dancing who are portrayed in a racist manner as Jewish.

Regarding the French reception of the subject matter in the early twentieth century, Éric Fournier made a significant observation. He wrote that, at the time, the figure of Judith, who beheads Holofernes, and that of Salome, who demands the head of John the Baptist as a reward for her dance, merge into a single monstrous figure: that of an actively murderous seductress. According to Fournier her Jewishness is "so evident that there is no need to mention it explicitly." (2011: 210) Precisely because their Jewishness is integrated into the dangerous, transgressive, virginally "phallic femininity" of Judith and Salome to such a degree that it is (un)recognizable, Fournier asserts, they are "the most horrifying '"Beautiful Jewesses' possible." (ibid) Analyzing the German commentaries to Strauss's opera *Salome*, Gilman comes to similar conclusions to those of Fournier (1993b: 210). Even in extremely antisemitic interpretations, such as the one by Hans F. K. Günther (1930) in *Rassenkunde des jüdischen Volkes*, in which the Jewish manner of speaking ("mauscheln," that is, Yiddish, or German with Yiddish intonation and vocabulary) is described based on the five Jews who appear in the opera as the "special nature of the Jew's body," Gilman says that "only the males, the five argumentative Jews and King Herod, [are] seen to be the racial representatives of the world of the Jews in Richard Strauss's opera." (ibid: 198) There must be something very special about their sexuality that lets the Jewishness of Salome and Judith disappear behind their "femininity."

The Psychoanalytical Theory of Femininity as "Dark Continent"

According to Karin Hausen's "Family and Role-Division. The Polarization of Sexual Stereotypes in the Nineteenth Century. An Aspect of the Dissociation of Work and Family Life" (1981), an article that has become a classic, the bourgeois gender code divided social relationship between men and women into two mirroring spheres of labor. This bourgeois gender order, in which women function as "gender characters," was presented ideologically as "reciprocal." Within this bipolar matrix, the social division of labor unfolds in the relationship between *society* on the one hand – professional and work world, the public – and *community* on the other – home, family, intimacy. Although modern, differentiated society is defined as "gender-neutral," it is naturalized in the 19th century, at least for the hegemonic bourgeoisie, in which women functioned as housewives, and reshaped by the hypostasized "reciprocity of gender characters" (Hausen 1976). Especially against this background of a normalized gender order the figure of the "Beautiful Jewess" became an embodiment of multiform, sometimes idealized but also demonized femininity.

Against this background, the "femininity puzzle" is linked to the attempts to throw light on, to use Freud's colonial image, the "dark continent" of female sexuality. Freud notoriously referred to female sexuality as an unknown, unexplored country. In "The Question of Lay Analysis" (Freud (1925-26/1948): SE 20: 212), he writes: "We know less about the sexual life of little girls than of boys. But we need not feel ashamed of this distinction; after all, the sexual life of adult women is a 'dark continent' for psychology." Here Freud constructs girls and women in general as the mysterious Other of European man. "Perhaps fearing her difference, he makes her other, obliterating the specificity and difference of her body by turning it into a fetishized metaphor of the unknown: 'dark continent,' and it is defined as lack.[...] Leaving the metaphor of the 'dark continent' in its original English, Freud grants it a further aura: of colonialism and its projection of a mysterious Africa." (Khanna 2003: 49) The metaphor of the "dark continent" was indeed first used by H. M. Stanley in his explorer narrative of Africa: *Through the Dark Continent* in 1878 (see Khanna 2003: 49-50). In colonial discourse the connection of "unknown counties" and "racialized difference" to femininity refers to a then widespread imaginative intersection of colonial Otherness and mythical feminization.

> In the discourse of race, darker peoples were thought of as "female." [...] This means that there was a recurrent cross-referencing of hierarchies encoded in metaphors: first, "others" were seen in the image of "females" [...]; then, by way of feedback, females were re-coded in the image of the "others". [...] The "femininity" or "passivity" attributed to the "darker races" has often been mentioned. (Nederveen Pieterse 1992: 220-221)

According to Gilman (1993b: 37) the pejorative tone of the description of female sexuality as "dark continent" and impenetrable obscure further "parallels the anti-Semitic rhetoric of the hidden nature of the Jew and the Jew's mentality widely circulated, even in medical literature, at the turn of the century." However, in his scientific writing Freud transferred the discourse of race to that of gender. This chapter pays particular attention to transgressive and liminal forms of femininity such as those attributed to Jewish women. As Pellegrini (1997: 129) argues about the orientalized stereotype of the "Beautiful Jewess": "Her dark hair and black eyes not only recall the 'darkness' of the Jew but also anticipate Freud's description of femininity *tout court* as the 'dark continent'. The hyperbolic femininity of the *belle juive* [sometimes even, U.B.] conceals her perverse masculinity."

In the concluding sections we first return to the great significance of Freud's psychoanalysis for the early gender/sexuality discussion in Jewish studies. Geller, Boyarin, and Gilman examine Sigmund Freud's theory of sexuality, also as an expression of "Freud's Jewish Question" (Geller 2007: 17). This chapter aims to explore the theoretical absence of the "Jewish female" in these approaches by referring to the traces of repression of the Jewish woman in Sigmund Freud's theory of femininity. As Ann Pellegrini states: "In the collapse of Jewish masculinity into an abject femininity, the Jewish female seems to disappear." (1997a: 109; 1997b: 18) Pellegrini directs this question clearly to her male colleagues, who largely focused on the "Jewish man" when speaking of the cultural production of Jewishness.[6] In very different ways, Daniel Boyarin, Geller, and Gilman analyze Freud's theory of "normal," i.e., "heterosexual," masculinity as the main example of the effect of antisemitic effeminization at the fin de siècle. Whereas Gilman interprets Freud's concept of masculinity as the product of a universalizing shift, and Boyarin sees it as a homophobic reaction, Geller makes out a defensive and exaggerated action in Freud's "ideal of the fighting Jew – of masculine Judaism." (2008: 159) For all three, his psychoanalysis is also the struggle of an assimilated Jew for "heroic" or gentile masculinity. Placing psychoanalysis historically within the context of the antisemitism, homophobia, and misogyny that prevailed at the time does not amount for these authors to a biographical reduction; instead, to use Daniel Boyarin's words, this is a matter of putting "psychoanalysis itself on ... a Foucauldian couch of cultural poetics and critique." (1995: 137) Gilman reconstructs how, in Freud's theory of sexuality, the antisemitic stereotype that marks the Jewish man as "castrated" and thus "feminine" is transmuted into the characterization of the woman in general. It is no longer the Jewish man, who in the psychoanalytical gender theory thus runs the risk due to his "flawed" genitals of being considered an "effeminate Jewish male" (1997: 27), as hysterical, or even as "castrated"; instead, now all women are "castrated," tend toward hysteria, and suffer from penis envy. Gilman explains: "In Freud's scientific writing this set of images was transferred exclusively to the image of women." (1993a: 37) In this way, the threatening "racial-physical" difference between the Jewish and the Gentile man is excised and at the same time shifted, according to Gilman. As a gender difference it returned in the body of the woman. Geller is correct in rejecting this reading of Freud's gender theory, as Gilman "has let the indigenous misogynist discourses of Europe off the hook by 'explaining' Freud's often stereotypical and misogynist discourse on women as his defensive displacement of the discourses of racial antisemitism." (2007: 19) Geller and Boyarin also assume Freud's "fight" for "heroic" masculinity; Boyarin says "Freud accepts the characterization of Jews as differently gendered, as indeed female, and tries to overcome this difference." (1997: 239) Thus, Freud's theory of the Oedipus complex can be

---

6   Jay Geller was self-critical in referring to this gender blindness within Jewish cultural studies when he confirmed that virtually all studies "examining the role of gendered representation and self-representation in German-Jewish cultural history ... focused almost exclusively on men." (2011: 359-360)

reinterpreted, in particular the assumptions based on it, in such a way that castration anxiety is the lynchpin of universal "masculine" subjectification and that the woman in her constitution is a deficient being. (Schnurbein 2005) However, when Gilman claims that Freud's theory of femininity is just a reflection of his defense against the antisemitic stereotype of an effeminate, "castrated" male Jew, that is, a transformation of the difference of race between the Jewish and the Gentile man into a generalized difference of sex, between all men and all women, then he is at the same time implying, according to Pellegrini, that "masculinity has no gender and femininity, no race, [and] he treats race and gender as discrete, rather than mutually informing, structures." (1997a: 118; see also 1997b: 28) With that, in addition to his denial of the real (also for Freud), effective misogyny around 1900, this reveals another blind spot in Gilman's analysis, so that I would like to cite Pellegrini in asserting that "the Jewish woman cannot appear in Gilman's analysis except in drag: as a Jewish man or as a 'whitened' and presumptively Gentile woman: *All Jews are womanly, but no women are Jews.*" (ibid)

The Trace of Repression of the Jewish Woman in Freud's Psychoanalysis

My point of departure in the following is the hypothesis that, in the development of psychoanalysis, the repressed or concealed "Jewish woman" – that is, most of Freud's female patients and the women in his Eastern European family of origin – can be discovered at the margins of the psychoanalytical theory of femininity itself. According to Freud, in order for the girl to materialize into the "normal" specimen of "properly passive femininity" (Pellegrini 1997a: 119; Pellegrini 1997b: 29) with a basically desexualized vaginal female sexuality (Schlesier 1981: 149), she has to go through a number of painful processes. "Freud allows no doubt that the main feature of female Oedipus Complex — in contrast to that of the male — is its desexualization. Clitoral sexuality disappears through repression, and under the condition of the Oedipus Complex the vagina could not yet be discovered." (Schlesier 1981: 149) His theory that the (juvenile) vagina as an erogenous zone remains undiscovered in the so-called phallic stage of infantile sexuality can be considered a cornerstone of the Freudian castration model of "femininity." "Normal" adult femininity, however, Freud emphasizes even more, is based on a radical repression, a repression of clitoral sexuality: The pre-Oedipal sexuality of the girl, he moreover asserts, "is of a wholly masculine character" (1953 [1905]: 219). A girl, fantasizing and experimenting in a polymorphous perverse manner just as actively as a young boy, must renounce her masculinity, as (according to Freud) associated with the clitoris, in order to achieve "adult femininity": "Women change their leading erotogenic zone [...] together with the wave of repression at puberty, which, as it were, puts aside their childish masculinity." (ibid: 221) In a text on hysterical attacks, the psychoanalyst even spoke of "the typical wave of repression, which by doing away with her masculine sexuality, allows the woman to emerge." (1955 [1909]a: 234) Freud's theory of femininity is thus based not only on the theory of the infantile non-discovery of the "vagina as a woman's erogenous zone" (Schlesier 1981: 159); it also assumes that the "coexistence or even coincidence of clitoral and vaginal sexuality" (ibid: 158) is impossible. According to Sander Gilman, Freud's definition of the clitoris as a "truncated" penis, and thus as almost "male," was in keeping with a "popular fin de siècle [...] view of the relationship between the body of the male Jew and the body of the woman." (1993a: 39) They resemble each other through the "truncated" penis. In addition, Gilman continues, Freud must have also known that "the clitoris was known in the Viennese slang of the time simply as the 'Jew' (Jud)." (ibid) If for a moment we pursue this thesis, which is disputed in current scholarship, the "flawed" body of the (circumcised) Jewish male thus reappears in the body of the woman.

But the Jewish women and patients in Freud's life are more than merely the reflection or mirror, before and in which the drama of masculinities takes places. The generalized "neutral" ideal of the domestic, passive, and ultimately desexualized woman that Freud establishes in his theory is also a product of assimilation. It is "white, Christian, reproductive and hidden from view." (Pellegrini 1997a: 121; Pellegrini 1997b: 31) Normal, i.e., Western bourgeois "femininity," is for Freud the product of a painful performance, an achievement of repression that can also be read geographically and culturally. Precisely the requirement to repress early childhood clitoral "masculinity," which is at the core of the performative theory of femininity, reveals traces "of Jewish female difference," (ibid) according to Pellegrini. Jay Geller, too, says that it was in particular Jewish women who were characterized as phallic or masculine. As evidence Geller cites an antisemitic text, the *Handbuch der Judenfrage* (Handbook of the Jewish Question, 1936) by Theodor Fritsch: "One finds among the Jews a great number of feminine men and masculine women. This goes for both body and soul." (2011: 31) Daniel Boyarin also emphasizes that "there is strong evidence, however, that just as Jewish men were perceived as feminized—and queer—by European gentile culture, Jewish women were perceived as virilized, indeed as viragos." (1997: 354) Moreover, according to Pellegrini (1997a) and Boyarin (1997), in Eastern European Jewish family structures, which of course also influenced Freud, the mother played a far more dominant role than in bourgeois Viennese society. The American Jewish studies scholar Susannah Heschel has drawn attention within this context to another aspect of Jewish tradition. With respect to the *niddah* laws and the purity of the vagina as treated therein, Heschel claims that the vagina is the human body part "discussed most in classical Jewish literature." (1998a: 95)[7] In order to assimilate to the bourgeois gender order, the Eastern European Jewish family structure, with its dominant mothers, had to be forgotten and "civilized." Pellegrini and Boyarin now read the Freudian myth of the repression of male sexuality in girls (albeit not his theory of the infantile non-discovery of the vagina) as yet another allegory in an effort to "escape from *Ostjüdische* gender-trouble." (Boyarin 1997: 354n152)

> The girl's passage from active, preadolescent masculinity to passive, mature femininity ... also recalls the historical movement of Jews from Eastern Europe into the urban centers of Western Europe.... In Freud's subterranean geography of Jewishness, gender, and race, East is to West as phallic women are to angels in the house. (Pellegrini 1997a: 29; Pellegrini 1997b: 119-120)

Even in the inner-Jewish and Zionist discourse, as shown by Daniel Boyarin in "Homophobia and the Postcoloniality of the 'Jewish Science'" (2003: 178) and *Unheroic Conduct* (1997), Eastern European Jews, the so-called *Ostjuden*, and their "fundamental ways of the shtetl become conflated with those of the Orient" (Isenberg 2005: 101). They thus served, to the extent that they appeared to embody "Judaism's Oriental character and foreignness to Europe," as a negative model (Boyarin 1997: 280).[8] At this point the Oriental character of Jewish femininity is identical to a paradoxical image: the Jewish woman, on the one

---

7   Susannah Heschel (1998a) was prompted to ask, "Whose vagina is it? Or should the vagina be understood as a symbol, perhaps in parallel to the phallus, namely a symbol laden with the emotional significance that shapes gender identity? [...] The laws of niddah turn the vagina into a transcendental sign of gender identity and Jewish status." (p. 95) The implications of this remark unfortunately cannot be pursued in the present text.

8   Boyarin quotes Jacques Kronberg *Theodor Herzl*, 1993. 24. In other Zionist writings, the Eastern Jews could also be idealized and turned into a source of cultural revitalization. (Kalmar/Penslar 2005)

hand, as a strong mother, then as *femme fatale* and sexual predator; and, on the other hand, as a transgressive, "masculine" virago.

Judith or the *Taboo of Virginity*

In order to shed light on the "ambivalent position occupied by Jewish women" (Pellegrini 1997a: 119; Pellegrini 1997b: 29) in Freud's works, it is important to examine the fissures in the concept of the passive, non-threatening femininity. Wherever Freud's mythos of the castrated woman shows flaws, according to my hypothesis, and where he himself speaks of a femininity that is anxiety-inducing or even threatens castration, it is possible to observe a return of the repressed material. First and foremost is the obvious mythicization of the woman, which is reminiscent of colonial images, such as the overdetermined formula of femininity as the "dark continent," (Freud 1959 [1926]: 212) whose mystery cannot be understood. Aside from his posthumously published essay *Medusa's Head* (1922), Freud is concerned with a threatening femininity, especially in *The Taboo of Virginity* (1918). In this text, which seems like a belated afterthought to *Totem and Taboo* (1913), the psychoanalyst works with ethnographic reports on the wedding rituals and taboos of the "primitive peoples" in Africa and Australia, and with stories of "his" neurotic patients. However, he also makes references to modern literature. All of the texts revolve around the fear that emanates from the virgin and around the taboos connected with her. Freud very quickly broadens the scope of the fear of the virgin into the man's fear of female sexuality and women in general, when he writes: "The taboo of virginity is part of a large totality which embraces the whole of sexual life and at its core is a generalized dread of women. One might almost say that women are altogether taboo." (Freud 1957 [1910]: 198) Just as in *Totem and Taboo* Freud not only draws parallels between the imaginary and ritual world of the "primitive man" and that of modern anxiety neurotics; instead he stresses that nothing of the principal fear and dread of the woman is obsolete, but rather that it is "still alive among ourselves" (ibid: 199). Upon closer examination as to what makes up the fear and what "imaginary" dangers are connected with the woman, Freud asserts the following:

> This dread is based on the fact that woman is different from man, forever incomprehensible and mysterious, strange and therefore apparently hostile.

The man is afraid of being weakened by the woman, infected with her femininity and of then showing himself incapable. (ibid: 198–199)

In Freud's analysis, fear of the woman appears as a general male fear. It is not culturally or historically specific; it is expressed among the Australian Aborigines as well as modern neurotics. In fact, the fear comes closer, since "in all this there is nothing obsolete, nothing which is not still alive among ourselves." (ibid: 199) As Pellegrini correctly emphasizes, the specific masculinity, which according to the antisemitic stereotype is particularly threatened by an infectious femininity, was definitely culturally defined around 1900. This masculinity that feels threatened by femininity can only be a masculinity "in which male Jews, within Freud's own historical experience, were dangerously implicated" (Pellegrini 1997a: 122; Pellegrini 1997b: 33). As if to avoid this association, however, Freud quickly shifts to the "general" gender difference as the reason for men's narcissistic rejection of women:

Psychoanalysis believes that it has discovered a large part of what underlies the narcissistic rejection of women by men, which is so much mixed up with despising them, in drawing attention to the castration complex and its influence on the opinion in which women are held. (Freud 1957 [1910]: 199)

As we know from his famous sentence, for Freud "the castration complex is the deepest unconscious root of anti-Semitism." (1955 [1909]b: 36n1) His essay *The Taboo of Virginity* (Freud 1957 [1910]) does concentrate, however, on gender difference. It does not settle down with the reference to the castration complex as the reason for men's revulsion of women; instead, it goes so far as to claim that the danger emanating from the virgin is in fact real, though the only evidence provided for this "real" danger are fantasy images. As an example, Freud offers the dream of one of his patients, in which she wants to castrate her groom on their wedding night. Freud takes his second example from modern literature, here the tragedy *Judith* (1840) by Friedrich Hebbel, which tells the story of Judith and Holofernes. Freud wrote: "The taboo of virginity and something of its motivation has been depicted most powerfully of all in a well-*known* dramatic character, that of Judith in Hebbel's tragedy *Judith and Holofernes*." (Freud 1957 [1910]: 207) Clearly following Hebbel's sexualizing tendency, "Freud recasts the biblical heroine as a *femme fatale* who beheaded Holofernes not as an act of Jewish patriotism, but of sexual refusal." (Pellegrini 1997a: 129; Pellegrini 1997b: 33, 45) Quite a few painters have linked the two "Beautiful Jewesses": the actively killing Judith to the figure of Sa-

lome, especially when it comes to the presentation of the severed male head
– Holofernes' or John the Baptist's – on a tray or even a platter.

*Fig. 2: Domenico de Pace Beccafumi: Judith with the Head of Holofernes (ca. 1510),
Wallace Collection, London; Fig. 3: Antiveduto Grammatica: Judith with the Head of
Holofernes (1610), Nationalmuseum Stockholm; Fig. 4: Tizian: Salome with the Head
of John the Baptist (1570), Museo del Prado.*

Public Domain, Wikimedia Commons

Freud supports Hebbel's transformation of the heroic Jewish widow Judith, who kills the tyrant to save her people, into a fascinating, beautiful orientalized virgin who beheads the tyrant, whom she desires, in a mixture of
sexual paroxysm and revenge. He follows the sexualizing reinterpretation of
the story without hesitation, even viewing it as the reiteration of "an ancient
motive," elevating a Judith "purged" of all historical, biblical qualities to the
archetype of "dangerous femininity": "Beheading is well known to us as a symbolic substitute for castrating; Judith is accordingly the woman who castrates
the man who has deflowered her." (Freud 1957 [1910]: 207) Through his sexualization of Judith, Freud unwittingly reproduced the mainstream antisemitic
discourse, in which the mediating figure of the *belle juive*, which was clearly
still ambivalent around 1900, became a "fusion of the virgin and the whore"
that "is inflected by a racialized difference." (Pellegrini 1997b: 33) It is precisely
in Freud's sexual demonization of Judith that the repressed Jewish context,
albeit displaced and distorted, returns. Elements of the antisemitic discourse,
of misogyny and homophobia, were inherited from the mainstream culture.
The fear of de-masculinization, however, was genuine. In the light of a post-

colonial approach, Freud's essentializing of misogyny and castration anxiety "appear as an elaborate defense against the feminization of Jewish men." (Boyarin 2003: 186) At the same time, the abject femininity of these sexualized and orientalized Biblical figures, which goes beyond the dichotomous gender order, comes close to the monstrous.

Bibliography

Aldrich, Robert (2003): Colonialism and Homosexuality, London and New York: Routledge.

Arens, Katharine (1995): "Characterology." In: Nancy A. Harrowitz/Barbara Hyams (eds.), Jews and Gender: Responses to Otto Weininger, Philadelphia: Temple University Press, pp. 124–215.

Baader, Benjamin Maria/Gillerman, Sharon/Lerner, Paul (eds.) (2012): Jewish Masculinities: German Jews, Gender, and History, Bloomington Indianapolis: Indiana University Press.

Bauman, Zygmunt (1991): Modernity and Ambivalence. Ithaka: Connell University Press.

Boyarin, Daniel (1995): "Freud's Baby, Fliess's Maybe: Homophobia, Anti-Semitism, and the Invention of Oedipus." In: GLQ: A Journal of Lesbian and Gay Studies 2/1–2, pp. 115-147.

Boyarin, Daniel (1997): Unheroic Conduct: The Rise of Heterosexuality and the Invention of the Jewish Man, Berkeley: University of California Press.

Boyarin, Daniel (2003): "Homophobia and the Postcoloniality of the 'Jewish Science.'" In: Daniel Boyarin/ Daniel Itzkovitz/Ann Pellegrini (eds.), Queer Theory and the Jewish Question, New York: Columbia University Press, pp. 166–198.

Boyarin, Daniel/Boyarin, Jonathan (1997): "Introduction/So What's New?" In: Daniel Boyarin/Jonathan Boyarin (eds.), Jews and Other Differences: The New Jewish Cultural Studies, Minneapolis and London: University of Minnesota Press, pp. vii– xxii.

Boyarin, Daniel/Itzkovitz, Daniel/Pellegrini, Ann (eds.) (2003): Queer Theory and the Jewish Question, New York: Columbia University Press.

Brunotte, Ulrike (2004): Zwischen Eros und Krieg. Männerbund und Ritual in der Moderne, Berlin: Wagenbach Verlag.

Brunotte, Ulrike (2010): "Masculinities as Battleground of German Identity Politics: Colonial Transfers, Homophobia and Anti-Semitism around

1900." In: Waltraud Ernst (ed.), Grenzregime. Geschlechterkonstellationen zwischen Kulturen und Räumen der Globalisierung, Berlin: LIT Verlag, pp. 165–184.

Brunotte, Ulrike (2012): "Unveiling Salome 1900. Entschleierungen zwischen Sexualität, Pathosformel und Oriental Dance." In: Bettina Dennerlein/ Elke Frietsch/Therese Steffen (eds.), Verschleierter Orient, entschleierter Okzident. (Un-)Sichtbarkeiten in Politik, Recht, Kunst und Kultur, Munich: Fink Verlag, pp. 93–116.

Brunotte, Ulrike (2013): Dämonen des Wissens. Gender, Performativität und materielle Kultur im Werk Jane Ellen Harrisons, Würzburg: Ergon Verlag.

Bunzl, Matti (2000): "Jews, Queers, and Other Symptoms: Recent Work in Jewish Cultural Studies." In: GLQ: A Journal of Lesbian and Gay Studies 6/2, pp. 321–341.

Butler, Judith (2011 [1993]): Bodies that Matter: On the Discursive Limits of "Sex," New York: Routledge.

Cherniavsky, Felix (1991): The Salome Dancer, Toronto: McClelland & Stewart.

Davies, Helen (2011): "The Trouble with Gender in Salome." In: Michael Y. Bennett (ed.), Refiguring Oscar Wilde's Salome, Amsterdam and New York: Rodopi, pp. 55–70.

Dierkes-Thrun, Petra (2011): Salome's Modernity: Oscar Wilde and the Aesthetics of Transgression, Ann Arbor: University of Michigan Press.

Dijkstra, Bram (1986): Idols of Perversity: Fantasies of Feminine Evil in Fin-de-Siècle Culture, New York and Oxford: Oxford University Press.

Doane, Mary Ann (1991): "Dark Continents: Epistemologies of Racial and Sexual Difference in Psychoanalysis and the Cinema." In: Mary Ann Doane (ed.), Femmes Fatales: Feminism, Film Theory, Psychoanalysis, New York: Routledge, pp. 209–248.

Ellmann, Richard (1987): Oscar Wilde, London: Hamilton.

Eßlinger, Eva/Schlechtriemen, Tobias/Schweitzer, Doris/Zons, Alexander (eds.) (2010): Die Figur des Dritten. Ein kulturwissenschaftliches Paradigma. Frankfurt am Main: Suhrkamp.

Foucault, Michel (1978): The Will to Knowledge (History of Sexuality, vol. 1), trans. by Robert Hurley, London: Penguin.

Fournier, Éric (2011): La 'belle' Juive, Seyssel: Champ Vallon.

Fout, John C. (1992): "Sexual Politics in Wilhelmine Germany: The Male Gender Crisis, Moral Purity, and Homophobia." In: Journal of History of Sexuality 2/3, pp. 388–421.

Freud, Sigmund (1953 [1905]): "Three Essays on the Theory of Sexuality." In: James Strachey (ed.) (trans.), The Standard Edition of the Complete Psychological Works of Sigmund Freud, vol. 7, London: Hogarth Press, pp. 130–243.

Freud, Sigmund (1955 [1909]a): "Some general remarks on hysterical attacks." In: James Strachey (ed.) (trans.), The Standard Edition of the Complete Psychological Works of Sigmund Freud, vol. 10, London: Hogarth Press, pp. 229–234.

Freud, Sigmund (1955 [1909]b): "Analysis of a Phobia in a Five-Year-Old Boy." In: James Strachey (ed.) (trans.), The Standard Edition of the Complete Psychological Works of Sigmund Freud, vol. 10, London: Hogarth Press, pp. 1–147.

Freud, Sigmund (1957 [1910]): "The Taboo of Virginity." In: James Strachey (ed.) (trans.), The Standard Edition of the Complete Psychological Works of Sigmund Freud, vol. 11, London: Hogarth Press, pp. 193–208.

Freud, Sigmund (1959 [1926]): "The Question of Lay Analysis: Conversations with an Impartial Person." In: James Strachey (ed.) (trans.), The Standard Edition of the Complete Psychological Works of Sigmund Freud, vol. 20, London: Hogarth Press, pp. 212–222.

Fritsch, Theodor (1936): Handbuch der Judenfrage. Die wichtigsten Tatsachen zur Beurteilung des jüdischen Volkes, Leipzig: Hammer Verlag.

Frübis, Hildegard (1997): "Die schöne Jüdin. Bilder vom Eigenen und Fremden." In: Annegret Friedrich/Birgit Haehnel/Christina Threuter (eds.), Projektionen. Rassismus und Sexismus in der visuellen Kultur, Marburg: Jonas Verlag, pp. 112–130.

Garber, Marjorie (1992): Vested Interests: Cross-dressing and Cultural Anxiety, London: Routledge.

Geller, Jay (1992): "The Unmanning of the Wandering Jew." In: American Imago 49/2, pp. 227-262.

Geller, Jay (1993): "A Paleontological View of Freud's Study of Religion: Unearthing the 'Leitfossil' Circumcision." In: Modern Judaism 13/1: 49–70.

Geller, Jay (2007): On Freud's Jewish Body: Mitigating Circumcisions, New York: Fordham University Press.

Geller, Jay (2008): "The Queerest Cut of All: Freud, Beschneidung, Homosexualität und maskulines Judentum." In: Ulrike Brunotte/Rainer Herrn (eds.), Männlichkeiten und Moderne. Geschlecht in Wissenskulturen um 1900, Bielefeld: transcript, pp. 157–172.

Geller, Jay (2011): The Other Jewish Question: Identity, the Jew, and Making Sense of Modernity, New York: Fordham University Press.

Gilman, Sander (1991): The Jew's Body, London: Routledge.

Gilman, Sander (1993a): Freud, Race, and Gender, Princeton: Princeton University Press.

Gilman, Sander (1993b): "Salome, Syphilis, Sarah Bernhardt and the 'Modern Jewess.'" In: The German Quarterly 66/2, pp. 195–211.

Gilman, Sander (1995): Franz Kafka: The Jewish Patient, New York: Routledge.

Günther, Hans F. K. (1930): Rassenkunde des jüdischen Volkes, Munich: Lehmann.

Hahn, Barbara (2005): The Jewess Pallas Athena: This Too a Theory of Modernity, Princeton: Princeton University Press.

Hahn-Hahn, Ida (1865): Maria Regina. Eine Erzählung aus der Gegenwart, vol. 1: Vater und Töchter, Mainz: Franz Kirchheim.

Halperin, David M. (1986): "One Hundred Years of Homosexuality, review of *Die griechische Knabenliebe* by Harald Patzer." In: *Diacritics* 16/2, pp. 34–45.

Heschel, Susannah (1998a): "Sind Juden Männer? Können Frauen jüdisch sein? Die gesellschaftliche Definition des männlich/weiblichen Körpers." In: Sander Gilman/Robert Jütte/Gabriele Kohlbauer-Fritz (eds.), "Der schejne Jid": Das Bild des "jüdischen Körpers" in Mythos und Ritual, Vienna: Picus Verlag, pp. 86–96.

Heschel, Susannah (1998b): "Jewish Studies as Counterhistory." In: David Bial/Michael Galchinsky/Susannah Heschel (eds.), Insider/Outsider: American Jews and Multiculturalism, Berkeley: University of California Press, pp. 101–115.

Heschel, Susannah (1999b): "Revolt of the Colonized: Abraham Geiger's Wissenschaft des Judentums as a Challenge to Christian Hegemony in the Academy." In: *New German Critique* 77, pp. 61–85.

Hess, Jonathan (2012): German Jews and the Claim of Modernity, Yale: Yale University Press.

Hoare, Philip (1997): Wilde's Last Stand, London: Duckworth.

Hödl, Klaus (1997): Die Pathologisierung des jüdischen Körpers. Antisemitismus, Geschlecht und Medizin im Fin de Siècle, Vienna: Picus Verlag.

Huysmans, Joris-Karl (1998): Against nature, trans. By Margaret Mauldon, Oxford and New York: Oxford University Press.

Isenberg, Noah (2005): "To Pray Like a Dervish." In: Ivan Davidson Kalmar/ Derek J. Penslar (eds.), Orientalism and the Jews, Waltham: Brandeis University Press, pp. 94–108.

Kalmar, Ivan Davidson/Penslar, Derek J. (eds.) (2005): Orientalism and the Jews, Waltham: Brandeis University Press.

Kettle, Michael (1977): Salome's Last Veil: The Libel Case of the Century, London: Hart- Davis.

Kohlbauer-Fritz, Gabriele (1998): "'La belle juive' und die 'schöne Schickse.'" In: Sander Gilman/Robert Jütte/Gabriele Kohlbauer-Fritz (eds.), "Der schejne Jid": Das Bild des "jüdischen Körpers" in Mythos und Ritual, Vienna: Picus Verlag, pp. 109–121.

Krobb, Florian (1993): Die schöne Jüdin. Jüdische Frauengestalten in der deutschsprachigen Erzählliteratur vom 17. Jahrhundert bis zum Ersten Weltkrieg, Tübingen: Max Niemeyer Verlag.

Lewis, Reina (1996): Gendering Orientalism: Race, Femininity and Representation, London and New York: Routledge.

Ludewig, Anna-Dorothea (2008): "'Schönste Heidin, süßeste Jüdin!' Die 'Schöne Jüdin' in der europäischen Literatur zwischen dem 17. und 19. Jahrhundert – ein Querschnitt." In: Medaon. Magazin für Jüdisches Leben in Forschung und Bildung 3, pp. 1–15, September 5, 2013 (http://medaon.de/ar chiv-3-2008-artikel.html).

Marlitt, Eugenie (1889): The Little Moorland Princess, trans. by Annis Lee Wister, Philadelphia: J.B. Lippincott Co.

McClintock, Anne (1995): Imperial Leather: Race, Gender and Sexuality in the Colonial Contest, New York and London: Routledge.

Mosse, George (1985): Nationalism and Sexuality: Respectability and Abnormal Sexuality in Modern Europe, New York: Howard Fertig.

Mosse, George (1996): The Image of Man: The Creation of Modern Masculinity, New York: Oxford University Press.

Mufti, R. Aamir (2007): Enlightenment in the Colony: The Jewish Question and the Crisis of Postcolonial Culture, Princeton and Oxford: Princeton University Press.

Nederveen Pieterse, Jan (1992): White on Black: Images of Africa and Blacks in Western Popular Culture, New Haven and London: Yale University Press.

Nirenberg, David (2013): Anti-Judaism: The Western Tradition, New York: Norton.

Parfitt, Tudor (2005): "The Use of the Jews in Colonial Discourse." In: Ivan Davidson Kalmar/Derek J. Penslar (eds.), Orientalism and the Jews, Waltham: Brandeis University Press, pp. 51–67.

Pellegrini, Ann (1997a): "Whiteface Performances: 'Race,' Gender, and the Jewish Bodies." In: Daniel Boyarin/ Jonathan Boyarin (eds.), Jews and Other Differences: The New Jewish Cultural Studies, Minneapolis and London: University of Minnesota Press, pp. 108–149.

Pellegrini, Ann (1997b): Performance Anxieties: Staging Psychoanalysis, Staging Race, New York: Routledge.

Polaschegg, Andrea (2005): Der andere Orientalismus. Regeln deutsch-morgenländischer Imagination im 19. Jahrhundert, Berlin and New York: De Gruyter.

Praz, Mario (1970 [1930]): Liebe, Tod und Teufel. Die schwarze Romantik, vol. 2, Munich: dtv.

Rohde, Achim (2005): "Der innere Orient. Orientalismus, Antisemitismus und Geschlecht im Deutschland des 18. bis 20. Jahrhunderts. " In: Die Welt des Islams 45/3, pp. 370–411

Rohde, Thomas (ed.) (2000): Mythos Salome, Leipzig: Reclam.

Salamensky, Shelley I. (2012): "Oscar Wilde's 'Jewish Problem': Salomé, the Ancient Hebrew and the Modern Jewess." In: Modern Drama 55/2, pp. 197–215.

Sanyal, Mithu M. (2009): Vulva. Die Enthüllung des unsichtbaren Geschlechts, Berlin: Wagenbach.

Schlesier, Renate (1981): Konstruktionen der Weiblichkeit bei Sigmund Freud, Frankfurt am Main: Europäische Verlagsanstalt.

Schmale, Wolfgang (2003): Geschichte der Männlichkeit in Europa (1450–2000), Vienna and Cologne: Böhlau.

Schülting, Sabine (1997): Wilde Frauen, FremdeWelten. Kolonisierungsgeschichten aus Amerika, Reinbek bei Hamburg: Rowohlt.

Scott, Joan (1986): "Gender: A Useful Category of Historical Analysis." In: The American Historical Review 91/5, pp. 1053–1075.

Sedgwick, Eve Kosofsky (1985): Between Men: English Literature and Male Homosocial Desire, New York: Columbia University Press.

Showalter, Elaine (1990): Sexual Anarchy: Gender and Culture at the Fin de Siècle, New York: Viking.

Spivak, Gayatri Chakravorty (1988): "Can the Subaltern speak?" In: Cary Nelson/Lawrence Grossberg (eds.), Marxism and the Interpretation of Culture, Urbana: University of Illinois Press, pp. 271–313.

von Schnurbein, Stefanie (2005): "Sander L. Gilman: Freud, Identität und Geschlecht." In: Martina Löw/Bettina Mathes (eds.), Schlüsselwerke der Geschlechterforschung, Siegen: Verlag der Sozialwissenschaften, pp. 283–295.

Walkowitz, Judith R. (2003): "The 'Vision of Salome': Cosmopolitanism and Erotic Dancing in Central London, 1908–1918." In: The American Historical Review 108/2, pp. 2–38.

Walkowitz, Judith R. (2012): Nights Out: Life in Cosmopolitan London, New Haven: Yale University Press.

Weininger, Otto (2005 [1903]): Sex and Character, ed. by Daniel Steuer/Laura Marcus, trans. by Ladislaus Löb, Bloomington and Indianapolis: Indiana University Press.

Worth, Katharine (1983): Oscar Wilde, New York: Macmillan.

Zantop, Susanne (1997): Colonial Fantasies: Conquest, Family, and Nation in Precolonial Germany, 1770–1870, Durham: Duke University Press.

2. Queering Judaism and Masculinist Inventions: German Homonationalism around 1900

As John C. Fout has emphasized, "a 'new', historically specific stage in the history of sexuality" (Fout 1992: 389) occurred around 1890. The time saw not only the founding of psychoanalysis and sexology but also the production of multiple "sexualities, including the 'homosexual,' the racialization/gendering of antisemitism, and the sharp increase in contemporary Christian homophobic discourse (the 'Christian Values' movement)" (Boyarin 1997: 208-209). This chapter argues that current (homo)nationalism, which has its focus on the "Muslim Other" (Puar 2007) must be placed in a historical genealogy. The case study focuses on the Second German Empire, wherein the discourse of political crisis was represented by a "male gender crisis," which revolved round the Kaiser and his alleged "homosexual" circle. Just as with debates within the incipient gay movement, the discourse focused on the dispositive of "normal masculinity" as representative of the nation/state. The chapter addresses a religious contour of, and possible Jewish inflection in, this discursive constitution of homosexuality. The sexualization of Jewish religion played a significant role in marking an internal differentiation between an "effeminate," "degenerate" Jewish homosexuality and an "ultra-virile," Aryan, and state-supportive "inversion" of the "masculinists" around Hans Blüher. They were the right-wing, antisemitic part of the early gay rights movement in Germany. Their key model of an ideal state became the homoerotic "Male Band" as a misogynist and antisemitic form of male society.

Genealogies of Contemporary Discursive Struggles

Since the early European headscarf debates and the diverse discourses of homonationalism (Puar 2007), not to forget the "muscular Islamophobia"

(Scheibelhofer 2013: 1) of "angry white men" (Kimmel 2013: 1), gender, religion, and sexuality have increasingly become sites of Western identity politics. They have operated as markers and media of "boundary debates between the religious and the non-religious" in Western "multiple secularities" (Kleine and Wohlrab-Sahr 2016: 2). Today it is mostly the Muslim Other, it's religion and culture, that is constructed as Europe's enemy. Especially here, but also in the US, the discursive tension between secularism –– as an enactment of political, mostly Western supremacy –– and (foreign) religion has influenced the ongoing public discourse on *Self* and *Other*. During the time of Enlightenment the "Jewish Question" that means the debate around the possible assimilation of the Jewish minority was the litmus test of political universalism. As Jonathan Hess argues, it was the question "of how participation in a modern, secular state could ever be compatible with the Jews' suborn adherence to an antiquated, Oriental religion. (Hess 2002: 4)." During the Hobsbawmian long 19th century European national discourse was connected to a heteronormative gender order and a heroic embodiment of masculine hegemony (Mosse 1985,1996; Brunotte 2015b). Today, however, as Paul Mepschen asserts "LGBTIQ rights and discourse are employed to frame Western Europe as the 'avatar of both freedom and modernity' but to depict its Muslim citizens, especially, as backwards and homophobic." (Mepschen 2019: 82; citing Butler 2008: 2).

In some Western European countries, especially in the Netherlands, homonationalism has been spread broadly over different political parties and has been connected to social-democratic as well as right-wing world views. An often orientalized, presumably homophobic Islam has played a significant discursive role as the "religious" antagonist of modern "secular nostalgia" (Bracke 2011: 32). Joan Scott coined the term "sexularism" to emphasize the metonymical relation between current ideologies of secularism and issues of sexuality (Scott 2009). My analysis takes a historical perspective on the discursive construction of the opposition between religious and secular cultures in Europe, unearthing an entanglement between historical antisemitism and *avant la letter* homonationalism. In a recent article Sarah Bracke and Luis Manuel Hernándes Aquilar (2021: 1-21) systematically use the concept of the "Muslim Question" to analyze contemporary European discourses and practices to produce the Muslim minority as an *"alien body"* (ibid. 1) to the nation (cf. Farris 2014: 296-297). They (ibid.: 5) claim:

While European nation states have been shaped by different kinds of questions [...], the "Jewish Question" is a paradigmatic instance of such contestations and definitions of national belonging and citizenship, and resonates significantly with the "Muslim Question" in terms of a deep-rooted conceptual entanglement of race and religion in the production of difference.

Following Sara Farris (2014) Bracke and Aquilar Hernández bring *the 'Jewish Question' and the 'Muslim Question'" to bear upon each other* (ibid.: 4). Based on a well-established (Brunotte et.al. 2015) historical approach like that of Gil Anidjar (2012, 2014) and Ivan Kalmar/Derek Penslar (2005), this chapter emphasizes that Europe had historically not only formulated "different Questions," (Anidjar 2012) but that also orientalism had a long pre-modern history in "the Christian West's attempts to understand and manage its relation with both of its monotheistic Others [Judaism and Islam, U.B.] the Western image of the Muslim Orient has been formed, and continues to be formed in inextricable conjunction with Western perceptions of the Jewish people." (ibid.)

Especially since the late 18th century Western orientalism has always included the Jews and has not only been focused on Muslims and Islam (cf. Kalmar Penslar 2005). Against this historical backdrop, the chapter concentrates on the sexualized version of the "Jewish Question" and the discursive intertwinement of Jewishness and homosexuality around 1900. It focuses on the intersection of religion, gender, and race within the early German homosexual emancipation movement in late imperial Germany (Somerville 2000; McCall 2005; Crenshaw 1991). The goal is to unearth a right-wing homonationalism *avant la lettre* in Germany.

Following Stoler's early criticism of Foucault, I will add a colonial-orientalist perspective to analyze the genealogy of sexuality (Stoler 1995: 5–6; Massad 2007; see also Brunotte et al. 2015; Rohde et al. 2018). In contrast to Europe's older colonial, homoerotic fantasies (Aldrich 2003; Massad 2007; Boone 2014), today's homonationalism often depicts male Muslims as patriarchic, backward, and homophobic (Mepschen and Duyvendak 2012). To be able to analyze the overall picture of the colonial dimensions within the history of sexuality, we have to include Europe's "inner Orient" (Rohde 2005: 1) and "internal outsiders": the Jews (Brunotte et al. 2017: 1). This perspective is especially relevant for the case study on Germany. The very nature of Germany's colonial exceptionalism –– that is, its late colonialism –– had a decisive impact on the perception of a racial Other *within* the contact zone of an internal colonial encounter. This inner colonialism articulated itself in German antisemitism.

The inclusion of antisemitism in the research field of orientalism offers exciting perspectives on the study of the intertwinement of colonialism, gender, religion, and sexuality. Furthermore, "the project of Jewish emancipation (in the late 18th century) provided the ultimate test, in practice, of the rational ideals of Enlightenment" (Hess 2002: 6) and of secular universalism.

In reference to Stefan Dudink's work on sexual nationalism (Dudink 2011; Dudink and Jaunait 2013), I support the hypothesis that current homonationalism does not represent a unique political development, nor is it completely new; rather, it can and must be placed in a complex historical genealogy.

> From such a perspective the current *configuration* of homosexuality and nation — from exclusion to inclusion, from margin to center, from other to self — is new. The *discursive materials*, however, out of which this configuration has been crafted are not necessarily new and may well be old. The move from old to new nationalism appears then as a move within the same discursive field. (Dudink 2011: 260)

The case study suggests analyzing the possible discursive intersection of Jewishness and homosexuality around 1900 in Germany. Also Matti Bunzl follows the antisemitic "racial contour of the modern discursive figure of the homosexual" back to its historical embeddings and differentiations in *fin-de-siècle* Germany (Bunzl 2000: 338). "German historiography has rarely explored the relationships between these discourses and their potentially reciprocal effects" (Bruns 2018: 90). In the Anglo-Saxon sphere, however, Jewish studies and queer studies were first brought together in the anthology *Jews and Other Differences: The New Jewish Cultural Studies* (Boyarin and Boyarin 1997) as well as in Daniel Boyarin's book *Unheroic Conduct: The Rise of Homosexuality and the Invention of the Jewish Man* (1997). The editors Daniel and Jonathan Boyarin postulate an entangled history of modern constructions of gender/sexuality and antisemitism. This chapter builds on their work.

The Male Gender Crisis and the Protestant Moral Purity Movement

As thorough historical analysis has shown, the state was not only an exclusively male domain of power in nineteenth-century nationalist discourse, but it also had a masculine connotation (Mosse 1985; Dudink 2011; Brunotte and Herrn 2008). Within the German Second Empire (1888–1918) the discourse of political crisis was intertwined with a discourse of "male gender crisis" (Fout

1992). The latter revolved around Kaiser Wilhelm II and his purportedly homosexual circle of aristocratic friends. Before the beginning of the Eulenburg-Moltke trial between 1906 and 1908, Prince zu Eulenburg-Hertefeld, a close friend of the emperor, was already accused of being a homosexual. The identity of the nation was, however, based on the codes of honorable, "masculine" behavior. Widely propagated by the daily press and parodied in caricatures through the figure of the aristocratic officer involved in homoerotic scenes, the German military was confronted with a scandal. The debate around the political quality of "normal masculinity" and the then recently coined term homosexuality spoke not only of violating the anti-sodomy paragraph 175 of the German *Strafgesetzbuch* (Criminal Code; henceforth, § 175 StGB) but also of a downright degeneration of the state. In this discourse, the figure of the (feminized) aristocrat and that of the homosexual became "the symbol of a threatening 'feminization' of the state and the German nation" (Bruns 2008b: 79; see also zur Nieden 2004: 329). Strengthened by leading sexologists such as Richard von Krafft-Ebing, the discourse on "moral decay," "sexual perversion," and "pathology" became interwoven with notions of degeneration (Krafft-Ebing 1886: 265). The most powerful opponent of sexual reform was, however, the Protestant moral purity movement and church-related organizations. In general, moral purity commentators agreed with Krafft-Ebing's findings about sexual behavior, "but his views on the decriminalization of sexual activities between consenting adults they saw as hateful" (Fout 1992: 393). The purity activists fought against "moral decline," women's emancipation, and homosexuality. The majority of the moral purity movement, all promoters of "Christian family values" and the patriarchal gender order, came from "elite male professions" (406). They founded numerous male associations, such as the Men's League for the Battle against Immorality *(Männerbund zur Bekämpfung der Unsittlichkeit)* or the German League for the Battle against Women's Emancipation *(Deutsche Bund zur Bekämpfung der Frauenemanzipation)*, to defend Christian norms and the degeneration of society and state. From a traditional Christian view, homosexuality was a sin, which would lead to a "decline in the family life of the nation" (414).

In connection with the Eulenburg trial and the public debate on homosexuality, "healthy" masculinity became a popular icon of national identity politics in Germany. A strong re-masculinization of the state was supposed to serve as the most effective remedy against the decadent circle around the emperor. However, contrary to the goals of the moral purity movement, the Eulenburg trial and the public debate on gender and sexualities also popularized the knowledge production on homosexuality. As Harry Oosterhuis (2000) claims, a multiplication of public discourses on sexuality also opened up new fields of gay self-invention. Yet, within national sexual politics in Wilhelmine Germany (Wilhelm II, 1888–1918), not only homosexuals were "internal Outsiders" (Brunotte et al. 2017: 1), but also Jews. Bunzl even postulates that the construction of the homosexual as the nation's "constitutive other" was intrinsically linked to the antisemitic figure of the effeminized and hypersexualized male Jew (Bunzl 2000: 339). The two groups, male Jews and homosexuals, were characterized through the same bodily and mental traits and merged into the embodiment of a dangerous conspiracy (Mosse 1985).

"Third Sex" versus Masculinism: The Inner Division in the Discourse on Homosexuality

Against the background of the intertwinement of state- and gender-crises discourses, and a general dialectic of discursive repression and creation of sexualities in *fin-de-siècle* Germany, it is not surprising that the first gay rights movement started in Berlin. In October 1928 Wystan Hugh Auden moved to Berlin; his friend Christopher Isherwood followed him a few months later. Especially important to the lasting connection between London intellectual circles and those of Berlin were also the writers associated with the Bloomsbury Group. "The Berlin-Bloomsbury connection started before the First World War [...] and was cemented by Alix Strachey's extended stay in 1924-25, when she was translating Freud and being analyzed at the Berlin Psychoanalytical Institute" (Evangelista/ Stedman 2021: 29). It is Christopher Isherwood of course who has been most closely associated with Berlin, but Virginia Woolf also visited the city in the late twenties. The core of the Berlin myth consisted in the city's reputation for sexual tolerance and gender emancipation. In contrast to the strict normative rules in Britain, which still lay in the long shadow of the Wilde trials of 1895 and the tragic case of Allan in 1918 that put an abrupt end to British *Salomania*, in Berlin male and female homosexuality were broadly discussed and tolerated. Here, activists and sexologists explored new emerging intermediate forms of desire and sexual identities. Eve Kosofsky Sedgwick illuminated how

> the newly crystallizing German State was itself more densely innervated than any other site with the newly insistent, internally incoherent but

increasingly foregrounded discourses of homosexual identity, recognition, prohibition, advocacy, demographic specification and political controversy. Virtually all of the competing, conflicting figures for understanding same-sex desires — archaic ones and modern ones, medicalized and politicized; those emphasizing pederastic relations, or gender inversion — were coined and circulated mainly in Germany in this period, and through German culture, medicine, and politics. (Sedgwick 1994: 66)

The intersection of politics, i.e., the state, and struggles about the definition of sexualities and gender is striking in Sedgwick's description. As Andrew Hewitt (1996) states, it was the moment of historical crisis of traditions in late imperial Germany, out of which new homosexual identities and, I would add, an early form of right-wing homonationalism emerged. Already in the late 1860s, the German lawyer Karl Heinrich Ulrichs started a redefinition process of sexuality and homosexuality in nineteenth-century Europe (Beachy 2015). Ulrichs fought against the criminalization of same-sex love by arguing for its "naturalness" (Herrn 2008: 175) as an inborn desire. His core thesis was that of a "female soul in a male body" (Ulrichs 1994: 47). One of Ulrichs's further contributions to the early gay rights movement was his influence on the Jewish social democrat, medical doctor, and sexologist Magnus Hirschfeld. In 1897, Hirschfeld founded the Scientific Humanitarian Committee and petitioned the *Reichstag* to reform § 175 StGB of the German penal code, which criminalized sexual acts between males. Inspired by Ulrichs, Hirschfeld considered homosexuality as an inborn condition and a "third sex," which includes a surplus of "female substance." Later, however, in his theory of sexual intermediates (*Zwischenstufentheorie*), he introduced the idea of a multitude of sexualities and genders (see Hirschfeld 1910; Herrn 2008). Magnus Hirschfeld's left wing of the homosexual rights movement represented a reasonable counterpart to the Protestant moral purity movement. Yet, the historical context of the discursive struggles around 1900 (see Brunotte 2004, 2010; Bruns 2008a) indicates that the debate on homosexuality additionally functioned as a political ventriloquist for a more general modern crisis: the crisis of the "masculine" state. In the heated debates, the contrast between a "threatening" feminization and a "healthy" re-masculinization of the nation became a discursive tool, and "normal" masculinity functioned as a central category of reference for strategies to foster the ideal of hegemonic masculinity.

Hence, within the homosexual rights movement a group of activists emerged who argued for a fundamental, "healthy" masculinity of male-

male Eros and male social associations. Oosterhuis characterizes them as a "homosocial resistance to Hirschfeld's homosexual putsch" of a "third sex" (Oosterhuis 1983: 305). Hewitt coined the term "masculinists" (Hewitt 1996: 80) to characterize this group, which was represented by Benedict Friedländer, Adolf Brand, and later Hans Blüher. They were a faction in the homosexual emancipation movement "that perceived male-male Eros as a distillation of fundamentally masculine social instinct, and that therefore resists any attempt to explain homosexuality as a form of effeminization" (Hewitt 1996: 81). The masculinists were connected to the German youth movement and the right-wing "conservative revolution" in Germany (Breuer 1995). Most of them were scholars and artists who constituted the "self-proclaimed elite of manly men who pursued *eros uranios* and formed the Greek-miming *Gemeinschaft der Eigenen* (Community of the Special Individuals)" (Geller 2003: 98; see also Oosterhuis and Kennedy 1992).

The newly emerging *Männerbund* model of homosocial associations was based on the male fantasies associated with the late German colonial adventures, as well as the experience of romanticized and later openly *völkisch* male associations and bands of comrades organized around charismatic leaders (Widdig 1992; Brunotte 2004). In this historical context the male band as the new basis of the political began to be discursively placed in contrast to the women- and Jewish-coded family. Jews and women were in turn "held responsible for both the bureaucratic anonymity of modern public life and the 'feminization' of social life" (Geller 2007: 165).

From 1912 onward, Hans Blüher, author, sexologist, and early chronicler of the *Wandervogel* movement, fought against § 175 StGB and campaigned for the decriminalization of homosexuality. In the third volume of his book on the German *Wandervogel*, he describes the youth movement as an "erotic phenomenon" (Blüher 1912: 1). As a young man he was fascinated by psychoanalysis and influenced by Sigmund Freud (Neubauer 1996; Brunotte 2004: 70–89; Brunotte et al. 2017: 195–221). In these early years, Blüher contributed to Hirschfeld's Scientific Humanitarian Committee and sometimes published in his *Yearbook for Sexual Intermediate Types*. He refused all negative sexologist and psychoanalytical definitions of homosexual desire that saw it as "deviant," "symptomatic," or "displaced." Rejecting "third sex" theory as well as the mainstream homophobic assertion of the effeminate homosexual, he claimed, "sexuality creates (indeed, must create) *two* fully developed, originary and indestructible types of man: òne desires men, the other women" (Blüher 1919b: 167). All theories that pathologize inversion, he stated, "only take account of singular cases of illness and ignore the *Typus inversus*. A sincere, complete and satisfying dedication to one's own sex is *never* a mere avoidance of incest" (Blüher 1919b: 163). As Jay Geller points out, Blüher's early cooperation with Hirschfeld and his cooperation with Freud

> led several reviewers in Austrian *Wandelvogel* journals to attack Blüher . . . questioning his German identity. Such remarks as "Hey, is Blüher a Jew?" and "Blüher's book is sick. There is something like a struggle between the German race and another!" were printed. (Schmidt in Geuter 1994: 95; English translation in Geller 2007: 172 and 280)

In response to this criticism Blüher radically differentiated himself and his theories of "normal," "healthy" inversion from any Jewish connotations and broke off his cooperation with Hirschfeld and Freud. To strengthen the model of the *super virile* men-loving man, the *Typus inversus*, and the elite of manly man at the core of the new state, Blüher defined a second type of homosexuality along the lines of gender and race differences: the feminized and "degenerated" Jewish homosexual. In a letter to Freud from July 13, 1912, he described three versions of "inversion," two of them marked as "pathological":

> the feminine one . . . is characterized through a specific somatic constitution and is based on Hirschfeld's theory of intermediate phases, the normal [inversion] in the ancient sense, which I have explained to you is [by contrast] thoroughly healthy. The other versions one can well define as pathologic. (Blüher cited in Neubauer 1996: 142)

In radical contrast to Hirschfeld's model of the homosexual as a "third sex," Gustave Friedländer — whose influence on Blüher cannot be overestimated (Bruns 2018: 91–93) —created the notion of the homosexual hero of man (*Männerheld*) as the charismatic center of male associations: "both Blüher and Friedländer were concerned with establishing a continuum from homosexual desire through to patriotism, a concern that will lead Blüher to foreground in his work the theory of the state" (Hewitt 1996: 103). With his central thesis, that all relations between men, from friendship up to the state, are libidinously charged and therefore "'Eros determines their relationships, wherever men communicate with one another,' Blüher 'has introduced a sexual dimension into the study of politics and the state'" (Schoeps 1988: 143; Sombart 1988: 159). He was the first theorist who developed a state theory based on male-male eroticism and an early form of right-wing homonationalism. Blüher systematically synthesized the antisemitic and homophobic tendencies of the public mainstream discourse on homosexualities in Wilhelmine society and radicalized a discursively constructed opposition between the "healthy" Germanic inversion and the "degenerate" homosexuality of "effeminate" Jews.

Excursus: Jews and Judaism as Models of the Other in Colonial Discourse

As announced at the beginning of the chapter, I add a colonial perspective to analyze the genealogy of sexuality. Particularly in view of the long history of Christian anti-Judaism, the historical chronology of internal and external boundaries must be read as a reversal of the chronological course of events. "From the very beginning of European expansion Judaism was employed in the decipherment of religions, and Jewish ancestry was used as likely explanation for the people Europeans encountered" (Parfitt 2005: 53). Certainly, anti-Jewish discourse in the early modern age was mostly based on religious and ethnic differences. Nevertheless, the modern intertwinement of religious, cultural, and sexual-physical differences had precursors in religious history. As James Thomas (2010: 1738–39) emphasizes, the "discourses of modern racism not only antedate the social taxonomies arising out of nineteenth-century scientific thought, but it was Christianity which provided the vocabularies of difference for the Western world." Similarly, the queer gendering of Jews and their modern "queer sexualization" (Boyarin et al. 2003: 7) have a long, premodern genealogy. This genealogy has been intertwined with the "representation of the Jews as a carnal people . . . extending back to Patristic ideas of the Jews as a people of the flesh" (Eilberg-Schwartz 1992: 5). The idea that Jewish men differ from non-Jewish men by being delicate, meek, or effeminate in body and character is also deeply rooted in European Christian history. Many myths have emerged around Jewish circumcision. In the thirteenth century, for example, historians reported that their contemporaries believed Jewish men suffered from monthly blood flux and were like women. In antisemitic discourse, the circumcised Jew was depicted as the horrifying representative of an unfit and "crippled" masculinity. Jay Geller views circumcision even as a dispositive that determined discourses and practices in the formation of European Christian identity and alterity from the very beginning:

> "Circumcision" became both an apotropaic monument and a floating signifier that functioned as a dispositive, an apparatus that connected biblical

citations, stories, images, phantasies, laws, kosher slaughterers, . . . ethnographic studies, medical diagnoses, and ritual practices . . . in order to produce knowledge about and authorize the identity of *Judentum* — and of the
uncircumcised. (Geller 2007: 11)

In 1985, George Mosse already demonstrated that the stereotype of the effeminate Jewish man had become a central target of antisemitic discourse only
around 1900. At this historical moment the link between Jews and women was
extended to include the imaginary connection between Jews and homosexuality (Boyarin 1997; Brunotte 2015a: 199–202). Antisemitic discourse both characterized Jewish men as feminine, nervous, and unfit for military service and
also classified European Jewry as a whole as a "southern people," "semi-Asian,"
or even as Europe's "internal Outsiders" (Brunotte et al. 2017: 1). In his ground-
breaking study *Unheroic Conduct: The Rise of Heterosexuality and the Invention of
the Jewish Man* (1997), Daniel Boyarin claims that the antisemitic stereotype
of the feminized Jewish male is also a product of the hegemonic concept of
Western European heterosexuality (see also Baader et al.2012). Yet, the Jewish
man was characterized by a somewhat paradoxical contrast: on the one hand
as "female" due to his circumcision *and* as fixated on family, on the other hand
as "female" *and* in proximity to a pathologized homosexuality. Susannah Heschel emphasizes that it was precisely the fluctuation in antisemitic discourse
that made the Jewish man appear "both as a man in the most extreme sense,
a sex-obsessed predator, . . . as well as an abnormal man, one who is effeminate and even menstruates" (Heschel 1998: 86). Heschel underlines that the
feminization of Jewish men derived from their religious, prescribed circumcision resulted in a central stigma of "queer foreignness" in Christian identity
discourse.

Hans Blüher: Male Band (Männerbund) versus "Jewish Decadence"

As the excursus demonstrates, the antisemitic attacks of the masculinists
around 1900 built on the long (Christian) history of "queering" Judaism. In
1913, Blüher started his discursive battle against the Jewish sexologist and gay
rights activist Magnus Hirschfeld and his theory of the "sexual intermediate
types." His attacks against Hirschfeld's (model of) homosexuality were fundamentally antisemitic in character. Blüher concentrated all the traditional,
anti-Judaic and antisemitic stereotypes of the degenerated, womanly Jew to

inflect a negative model of modern homosexuality "by images of racialized Jewish difference" (Bunzl 2000: 338). Within these discursive struggles the putative effeminate, Jewish homosexual became the embodiment of purportedly modern, urban degeneration. Blüher (1914) stated that Hirschfeld and his followers were "truly deformed men . . . whose racial degeneracy is marked by an excessive endowment of female substance" (13). In the conclusion of his essay *Three Fundamental Forms of Homosexuality* from 1913 he claimed, "[effeminacy] is a form of decadent homosexuality that grows out of racial mixing [*Rassenmischung*], inbreeding [*Inzucht*], and misery [*Verelendung*]" (Geller 2007: 169 and note 50). These characteristics of sexual life of a society in decline were qualified as Jewish. However, in his chronicle of the *German Youth Movement*, Blüher (1912) mobilized *völkisch* ideology and stated that the membership of these associations of comradeship was characterized by means of a "strongly emphasized German racial type" (161). For Blüher the *super virile* male band was at the core of the social and the state. It was based on the "love for the Hero of Men" (Blüher 1918: 35; Blüher 1912: 57). In his text *Secessio Judaica* (1922), wherein the author proclaimed the exclusion of the Jews from German society, Blüher connected gender and race to explicitly ascribe effeminacy to the Jews as a "race." He stated, "the correlation of masculine nature with German essence and a feminine and servile nature with the Jewish essence is an unmediated intuition of the German people, which from day to day becomes more certain" (Blüher 1922: 49; English translation in Geller 2007: 177). As is shown in this quote, his masculinist *male band* was also a political weapon against the modern dissolution of the two-sphere gender order. The male band was built as the counterpart to the woman- and Jewish-coded family and the democratic modernization of society. Women and Jews were held responsible for both the bureaucratic anonymity of modern public life and the "feminization" of social life (cf. Brunotte 2004: 84; Geuter 1994: 161).

Male Band as a Colonial Transfer

The concept of the male band was a traveling theory and the product of knowledge gained through the belated German colonial adventure in Africa (cf. Brunotte 2004). As a product of the "imagined ethnography" (Kramer 1977: 1), the term *Männerbund* was an invention of the German ethnographer Heinrich Schurtz in his book *Altersklassen und Männerbünde* (Age Classes and Male Bands) from 1902. Far more important than its academic reception was the immense cultural-political impact that the indigenous organizational model of the *Männerbund* had on German politics. The *male band* advanced not only to the matrix of the "conservative revolution" but, far more, it became "the key concept of the political culture in Germany" (Sombart 1988: 171; see Widdig 1992). *Männerbund* was the term Schurtz used to describe the coming together of boys of the same age during their *rites de passage*. Schurtz explained that in many indigenous societies strong secret communities and sacred warrior bands developed from these originally temporary institutions of male-only associations. In his defense of the male band, Schurtz took up the contemporary gender-political debates on women's emancipation and the threat of a "feminization of society." Against this cultural background, Schurtz's thesis received its cultural and political relevance. It is not the family, but "rather the free association of male bands that constitute the progressive and culture-forming foundations of society and are the vehicle of almost all higher cultural developments" (Schurtz 1902: 61). Schurtz's fantasies of primitive manliness and male associations provided role models for the emigration (*Auswanderung*) of the male *Wandervogel* youth from the Wilhelmine fatherland.

Eventually, it was Hans Blüher who connected Schurtz's theory of the male band with the debate on the masculinity of the state and with the discourse on homosexuality. He stated that Schurtz skirted the homoerotic basis of these male associations and cited Karsch-Haacks's 1911 study on *Das Leben der gleichgeschlechtlichen Naturvölker* (The Same-Sex Love Lives of Primitive Tribes) to prove the "strong inclination toward inversion" in indigenous societies (Blüher 1921a: 99).

Erotics of State and "Race"

Finally, I analyze three central passages from Blüher's work. In these passages, the intertwinement of misogyny and antisemitism explicitly connects to his state and male band theory. In his version of a homonationalism *avant la lettre*, and following the Platonic model, the state is based on male-male Eros (see Brunotte 2004, 80–103). For Blüher, Eros is no sexological or biological, but a (philosophical) concept, and also an affective as well as meaning-making cultural force. In *Die Rolle der Erotik in der männlichen Gesellschaft* (The Role of the Erotics in Male Society) he programmatically claims, "beyond the socializing principle of the family that feeds off the Eros of male and female, a second principle is at work in mankind and 'masculine society,' which owes

its existence to male-male Eros, and finds its expression in male bonding"
(Blüher 1919b: 7). Blüher continues to explain:

> In all species where the familial urge is the sole determinant . . . the construc-
> tion of a collective is impossible. The family can function as a constitutive
> element of the State, but not more. And *wherever nature has produced species*
> *capable of developing a viable state that has been made possible only by smashing*
> *the role of the family and the male-female sexual urges as sole social determinants.*
> (Blüher 1919b: 6–7, emphasis in original; English translation in Geller 2007:
> 176)

The antisemitic inflection of the hatred against effeminate homosexuals in
masculinist discourse is well documented (Hewitt 1996; Bruns 2008b). This
antisemitism was not only connected to the construction of the figure of the
Jew as the stereotypical effeminate homosexual and *vice versa*, but also clearly
linked to Blüher's theory of the ideal state. In the second volume of *Die Rolle*
der Erotik (1919b), in a footnote, he creates the Jewish anti-type to the male-
bonded society. This anti-type connects the feminization of the Jews with their
presumed "hypertrophy of the family," and defines Jewry in general as a "race":

> With the Jews it is as follows: they suffer at one and the same time from
> a weakness in male-bonding [*Männerbundschwäche*] and a *hypertrophy of the*
> *family.* They are submerged in the family and familial relations, but as to
> the relations among men, the old saying holds true: *Judaeus Judaeo lupus.*
> Loyalty, unity, and bonding are no concern of the Jew. Consequently, where
> other people profit from a fruitful interaction of the two forms of socializa-
> tion (i.e., the family and the *Männerbund*), with the Jews there is a sterile divi-
> sion. Nature has visited this fate upon them and thus they wander through
> history, cursed never to be a people [*Volk*], always to remain a mere race.
> They have lost their state. There are people who are simply exterminated as
> peoples and therefore disappear, but this cannot be the case with the Jews,
> for a secret process internal to their being as a people constantly displaces
> the energy typically directed toward male bonding onto the family . . . Con-
> sequently, the Jews maintain themselves as *race* through overemphasis of
> the family. (Blüher 1919b: 170, emphasis in original; English translation in
> Hewitt 1996: 123 and 125)

Blüher solves the mystery of the stateless survival of the Jews by feminizing
them. Accordingly, the Jews submit exclusively to the female private sphere
of the family and to the femininely connoted reproductive instinct. However,

especially since the modern claim of Jewish assimilation into the secularized majority culture was raised, the problem of Jewish difference has taken on an extra threatening aspect. Therefore, it was ultimately the gender difference of Jewish "effeminate" masculinity that threatened the hegemony of the German male band. What the masculinists wanted to avoid was to allow "the unmanned or unmanly into the public sphere" (Geller 2007: 6–7). Blüher could only explain the survival of the stateless Jewish community through their devotion to the (for him) "female" family and to the reproductive instinct. As a consequence of their devotion to the womanly private sphere they "suffer from a weakness in male-bonding" and cannot participate in the state. Finally, Blüher (1919b) defines the Jews as a "mere race" (123).

The Sacralization of the Male Society as Nucleus of a New Religion

In the previous quotes, Blüher does not mention the role of Judaism as a religion and the role of lived religiosity as a medium and means of their survival in Diaspora. He also does not recognize male-focused Jewish religious practices such as attending a synagogue for prayer and study as a possible form of male bonding. From the early 1920s onwards, however, religion and religiosity began to play a stronger role in his definition of the "Aryan male band." In *Die Rolle der Erotik* Blüher attempts to build Christian charity on the love for the hero of men (Blüher 1919b: 231–232). He regards the circle of disciples around Jesus as the first *Männerbund*, which revolved around the highest of "men's heroes" (247). Blüher further elaborates on this topic in *Die Aristie des Jesus von Nazareth* (The Aristeia of Jesus of Nazareth) from 1921 and *Der Menschensohn* (The Son of Men) from 1920, in which he claims that Jesus' Eros was of pagan quality. Eros refers particularly to Jesus' own sex/gender (Blüher cited in Brunotte 2004: 89 and 447). In the second volume of *Die Rolle der Erotik* Blüher stated, "the sacred in the *Männerbund* and the male-male eroticism always combines with an exuberance of the human. It is an intoxicating and solemn event. Something builds itself up in male societies that occurs nowhere else: the *covenant* arises in the hour of the highest charge" (Blüher 1919b: 217).

As a discursive result of this sacralization, the male-bonded state has acquired the traits of a soteriological model that is a model of a state that asks for sacrifices and offers transcendence. The new state "presupposes the potential insignificance of the individual, service to the whole, sacrifice to the transcendent collective" (Blüher 1919b: 4–5). As Klaus von See (1992) writes,

Blüher established the *Männerbund* in the 1920s "as the nucleus of a new religion, a new empire, or even a new humanity" (98). The tendency towards a sacralization of the male society, the state, and its homoerotic Eros on the one hand and its Christological interpretation on the other went hand in hand. He sought "to raise the state as high as possible . . . and to let the individual merely disappear in front of it." He called this view of the state "sacred" (Blüher 1919b: 2–3). At the end of *Die Rolle der Erotik* he even declares the new *covenant* to be a seal of the old covenant that was broken in its youth, a "sacrament" (221). In *Familie und Männerbund* (Family and Male Band) he speaks of *Männerbund Mysterien* (male band mysteries) and *heilige Päderastie* (holy pederasty) (1918: 36). Supposedly Christian morality and the camaraderie of men, the repeatedly emphasized "love of the hero" (Blüher 1919b: 247) should become the basis of the state. Similar to Nietzsche and his *Übermensch*, Blüher ultimately tried to reinstate the hero by connecting Germany with classical Greek and Germanic heroes, for, according to Blüher, "Herakles, Theseus, Siegfried . . . these sons of gods are men's favorites set in heaven" (Blüher 1921a: 246). At the beginning of Blüher's masculinist campaign against the § 175 StGB, however, the theory of male society based on the elite of homoerotic men also served as a discursive tool to defend his beloved Emperor Wilhelm II. Nicolaus Sombart analyzes this early political function of Blüher's theory as follows:

> If the central statement within the Eulenburg trial was "homosexual men are threatening the security of the state; homosexual men are not fit for the hard work of politics," then Blüher claimed, "the state is sustained by a male-masculine eroticism and politics is essentially and exclusively an affair of homoerotic men!" (Sombart 1988: 169)

Within the political power struggle in late imperial Germany and the Weimar republic, Blüher inscribed the masculinist version of homoerotism into the new right-wing models of hegemonic masculinity. (see Brunotte 2004 for the further reception history of the *Männerbund* in the Weimar Republic and under National Socialism)

Conclusion

The analysis of the discursive struggle concerning homosexuality around 1900 in Germany has shown that masculinity was a key reference within the debate. It further demonstrates that the figure of the homosexual was defined in terms of a racialized gender dichotomy. To participate in the normative model of hegemonic masculinity, the masculinists invented a new category of homosexuality. They constructed a contradiction between a Germanic, healthy, men-loving invert and the figure of a decadent, feminine, Jewish homosexual. Not homosexuality per se, but homosexuality already racialized as Jewish, became the key link between homophobia and racism.

This chapter has uncovered the existence of a racialized, right-wing *fin-de-siècle* homonationalism in Germany. After World War I, Blüher's theories participated in a mainstream tendency of "German nationalist discourse to renew the German nation's masculine nature and reinstate its male-defined political order" (Bruns 2018: 96). Concerning contemporary "sexularism" (Scott 2009), we have to be aware that not every homonationalism is a kind of "gay racism" (Puar 2013: 337). In the Netherlands, for example, homonationalist ideas have not only been connected to Pim Fortyun and Geert Wilders, but also to social-democratic and liberal national parties and cultural discourse (see Mepschen 2019). However, some of the general discursive strategies of homonationalism, as the feminization of homosexuals and the racialization as well as orientalization of religious and cultural difference in national political discourse, remain relevant in contemporary Europe especially with its "Muslim Question".

Bibliography

Aldrich, Robert (2003): Colonialism and Homosexuality, London/New York: Routledge.

Anidjar, Gil (2012): "On the European Question", Forum Bosnae 2, no. 3: 13-27.

Anidjar, Gil (2014): Blood. A Critique of Christianity, California: Columbia University Press.

Baader, Benjamin Maria/Gillerman, Sharon /Lerner, Paul (eds.) (2012): Jewish Masculinities: German Jews, Gender, and History, Bloomington: Indiana University Press.

Beachy, Robert (2015): Gay Berlin: Birthplace of a Modern Identity, New York: Alfred A. Knopf.

Blüher, Hans (1912): Die deutsche Wandervogelbewegung als erotisches Phänomen: ein Beitrag zur Erkenntnis der sexuellen Inversion. With a preface by Dr. Magnus Hirschfeld and an afterword by Hans Blüher, Berlin: Bernhard Weise Buchhandlung.

Blüher, Hans (1913): Drei Grundformen der Homosexualität: eine sexologische Studie, Leipzig: Max Spohr.

Blüher, Hans (1918): Familie und Männerbund, Leipzig: Der Neue Geist.

Blüher, Hans (1919a): Die Rolle der Erotik in der männlichen Gesellschaft: eine Theorie der menschlichen Staatenbildung nach Wesen und Wert, Bd. 1: Der Typus inversus, Jena: Diederichs.

Blüher, Hans (1919b): Die Rolle der Erotik in der männlichen Gesellschaft: eine Theorie der menschlichen Staatenbildung nach Wesen und Wert, Bd. 2: Familie und Männerbund, Jena: Diederichs.

Blüher, Hans (1920): Der Menschensohn, Blüher-Archiv Berlin: Staatsbibliothek, Box IV.

Blüher, Hans (1921a): Der Charakter der Jugendbewegung, Lauenburg: Adolf Saal.

Blüher, Hans (1921b): Die Aristie des Jesus von Nazareth: Philosophische Grundlegung der Lehre und der Erscheinung Christi, Prien: Kampmann & Schnabel.

Blüher, Hans (1922): Secessio Judaica: Philosophische Grundlegung der historischen Sicht des Judentums und der antisemitischen Bewegung, Berlin: Weiße Ritter.

Blüher, Hans (1965): Studien zur Inversion und Perversion: das uralte Phänomen der geschlechtlichen Inversion in natürlicher Sicht, Hans Joachim Schoeps (ed.), Schmiede/Stuttgart: Franz Decker.

Boone, Joseph A. (2014): The Homoerotics of Orientalism, New York: Columbia University Press.

Boyarin, Daniel (1997): Unheroic Conduct: The Rise of Heterosexuality and the Invention of the Jewish Man, Berkeley: University of California Press.

Boyarin, Daniel/Boyarin, Jonathan (1997): "Introduction /So What's New?" In: Daniel Boyarin/Jonathan Boyarin (eds.), Jews and Other Differences: The New Jewish Cultural Studies, Minneapolis: University of Minnesota Press, pp. vii–xxii.

Boyarin, Daniel/Itzkovitz, Daniel/Pellegrini, Ann (eds.) (2003): Queer Theory and the Jewish Question, New York: Columbia University Press.

Bracke, Sarah (2011): "Subjects of debate: Secular + sexual exceptionalism, and Muslim Women in the Netherlands." In: Feminist Review 98(1), pp. 28–46.

Bracke, Sarah/Hernández Aquilar, Luis Manuel (2021): "Thinking Europe's 'Muslim Question': On Trojan Horses and the Problematization of Muslims" Critical Research on Religion, pp 1-21.

Breuer, Stefan (1995): Anatomie der Konservativen Revolution, Darmstadt: Wissenschaftliche Buchgesellschaft.

Brunotte, Ulrike (2004): Zwischen Eros und Krieg: Männerbund und Ritual in der Moderne, Berlin: Wagenbach.

Brunotte, Ulrike (2010): "Masculinities as Battleground of German Identity Politics: Colonial Transfers, Homophobia and Anti-Semitism around 1900." In: Waltraud Ernst (ed.): Grenzregime: Geschlechterkonstellationen zwischen Kulturen und Räumen der Globalisierung, Berlin: LIT Verlag, pp. 165–84.

Brunotte, Ulrike (2015a): "'All Jews are womanly, but no women are Jews.' The 'Femininity' Game of Deception: *female Jew, femme fatale Orientale, and belle Juive*." In: Ulrike Brunotte/Anna-Dorothea Ludewig/Axel Stähler (eds.): Orientalism, Gender, and the Jews. Literary and Artistic Transformations of European National Discourses, Berlin: Walter de Gruyter, pp. 195–220.

Brunotte, Ulrike (2015b): Helden des Todes: Studien zur Religion, Ästhetik und Politik moderner Männlichkeit, Würzburg: Ergon.

Brunotte, Ulrike/Herrn, Rainer (2008): Männlichkeiten und Moderne: Geschlecht in den Wissenskulturen um 1900, Bielefeld: transcript Verlag.

Brunotte, Ulrike/Ludewig, Anna-Dorothea/Stähler, Axel (eds.) (2015): Orientalism, Gender, and the Jews: Literary and Artistic Transformations of European National Discourses, Berlin/Munich/Boston: Walter de Gruyter.

Brunotte, Ulrike/Mohn, Jürgen/Späti, Christina (eds.) (2017): Internal Outsiders—Imagined Orientals? Antisemitism, Colonialism and Modern Constructions of Jewish Identity. Diskurs Religion: Beiträge zur Religionsgeschichte und religiösen Zeitgeschichte 13, Würzburg: Ergon Verlag.

Bruns, Claudia (2008a): Politik des Eros: der Männerbund in Wissenschaft, Politik und Jugendkultur (1880-1934), Cologne: Böhlau.

Bruns, Claudia (2008b): "Männlichkeit, Politik und Nation—Der Eulenburgskandal im Spiegel europäischer Karikaturen." In: Ulrike Brunotte/Rainer Herrn (eds.): Männlichkeiten und Moderne: Geschlecht in den Wissenskulturen um 1900, Bielefeld: transcript Verlag, pp. 77–96.

Bruns, Claudia (2018): "How gay is Germany? Homosexuality, Politics, and Racism in Historical Perspective." In Achim Rohde/Christina von Braun/Stefanie Schüler-Springorum (eds.): National Politics and Sexuality in Transregional Perspective, London: Routledge, pp. 88–104.

Bunzl, Matti (2000): "Jews, Queers, and Other Symptoms: Recent Work in Jewish Cultural Studies." In: GLQ: A Journal of Lesbian and Gay Studies 6 (2), pp. 321–41.

Butler, Judith (2008): "Sexual Politics, Torture, and the Secular Time." In: British Journal of Sociology 59 (1), pp. 1–23.

Crenshaw, Kimberle W. (1991): "Mapping the Margins: Intersectionality, Identity Politics, and Violence against Women of Color." In: Stanford Law Review 43 (6), pp. 1241–99.

Dudink, Stefan (2011): "Homosexuality, Race, and the Rhetoric of Nationalism." In: History of the Present 1 (2), pp. 259–64.

Dudink, Stefan/Jaunait, Alexandre (2013): "Les Nationalismes Sexuels et l'Histoire Raciale de l'Homosexualité." In: Presses de Sciences Po. Raisons Politiques 49, pp. 43–54.

Eilberg-Schwartz, Howard (ed.) (1992). People of the Body: Jews and Judaism from an embodied Perspective, Albany: State University of New York Press.

Evangelista, Stefano/Stedman, Gesa (2021): "Happy in Berlin". In: Evangelista, Stefano/Stedman, Gesa (eds.): Happy in Berlin?. English Writers in the City. The 1920s and Beyond, Göttingen: Wallstein Verlag, pp. 15-52.

Farris, Sara R. (2014): "From the Jewish Question to the Muslim Question. Republican Rigorism, Culturalist Differentialism and Antinomies of Enforced Emancipation," Constellations 21, no. 2, pp. 296-307.

Fout, John C. (1992): "Sexual Politics in Wilhelmine Germany: The Male Gender Crisis, Moral Purity, and Homophobia." In: Journal of the History of Sexuality 2 (3), pp. 388–421.

Geller, Jay (2003): "Freud, Blüher, and the Secessio Inversa. Homosexuality and Freud's Theory of Cultural Foundation." In: Daniel Boyarin/Daniel Itzkovitz/Ann Pellegrini (eds.): Queer Theory and the Jewish Question, New York: Columbia University Press, pp. 90–120.

Geller, Jay (2007): On Freud's Jewish Body: Mitigating Circumcisions, New York: Fordham University Press.

Geuter, Ulfried (1994): Homosexualität in der deutschen Jugendbewegung: Jugendfreundschaften und Sexualität im Diskurs von Jugendbewegung, Psychoanalyse und Jugendpsychologie am Beginn des 20. Jahrhunderts, Frankfurt am Main: Suhrkamp.

Herrn, Rainer (2008): "Magnus Hirschfelds Geschlechterkosmos: Die Zwischenstufentheorie im Kontext hegemonialer Männlichkeit." In: Ulrike Brunotte/Rainer Herrn (eds.): Männlichkeiten und Moderne. Geschlecht in den Wissenskulturen um 1900, Bielefeld: transcript Verlag, pp. 173–96.

Heschel, Susannah (1998): "Sind Juden Männer? Können Frauen jüdisch sein? Die gesellschaftliche Definition des männlich/weiblichen Körpers." In:

Sander Gilman/Robert Jütte/Gabriele Kohlbauer-Fritz (eds.): "Der schejne Jid": Das Bild des "jüdischen Körpers" in Mythos und Ritual, Vienna: Picus Verlag, pp. 86-96.

Hess, Jonathan (2002): German Jews and the Claim of Modernity, Yale: Yale University Press.

Hewitt, Andrew (1996): Political Inversions: Homosexuality, Fascism, and the Modernist Imaginary, Stanford: Stanford University Press.

Hirschfeld, Magnus (1910): "Die Zwischenstufen-Theorie." In: Sexualprobleme 6, pp. 116-36.

Kalmar, Ivan D./Penslar, Derek J. (2005): "An Introduction." In: Ivan D. Kalmar/ Derek J. Penslar (eds.): Orientalism and the Jews, Waltham: Brandeis University Press, pp. xiii-xx.

Karsch-Haacks, Ferdinand (1911): Das Leben der gleichgeschlechtlichen Naturvölker, Munich: E. Reichardt.

Kimmel, Michael (2013): Angry White Men: American Masculinity at the End of an Era, New York: Nation Books.

Kleine, Christoph/Wohlrab-Sahr, Monika (2016): "Multiple Secularities—Beyond the West, Beyond Modernities." Research Programme of the HCAS, December 30, 2018. http://www.multiple-secularities.de.

Kramer, Fritz (1977): Verkehrte Welten: zur imaginären Ethnographie des 19. Jahrhunderts, Frankfurt am Main: Fischer Verlag.

Massad, Joseph (2007): Desiring Arabs, Chicago: University of Chicago Press.

McCall, Leslie (2005): "The Complexity of Intersectionality." In: Signs: Journal of Women in Culture and Society 30 (3), pp. 1771-1800.

Mepschen, Paul, and Jan Willem Duyvendak (2012): "European Sexual Nationalism: The Culturalization of Citizenship and the Sexual Politics of Belonging and Exclusion." In: Perspectives on Europe 42 (1), pp. 70-76.

Mepschen, Paul (2019): "A Postprogressive Nation: Homophobia, Islam, and the New Social Question in the Netherlands." In: Derks, Marco/ van den Berg, Marieke (eds.): Public Discourses About Homosexuality and Religion in Europe and Beyond, pp. 81-105.

Mosse, George L. (1985): Nationalism and Sexuality: Respectability and Abnormal Sexuality in Modern Europe, New York: Howard Fertig Pub.

Neubauer, John (1996): "Sigmund Freud und Hans Blüher in bisher unveröffentlichten Briefen." In: Psyche: Zeitschrift für Psychoanalyse und ihre Anwendungen 50, pp. 123-48.

Oosterhuis, Harry (1983): "Homosocial Resistance to Hirschfeld's homosexual putsch: 'the Gemeinschaft der Eigenen', 1899-1914." In: Mattias Duyves (ed.): Among Men, Among Women: Sociological and Historical Recognition of Homosocial Arrangements, Amsterdam: Amsterdam University Press, pp. 305–21

Oosterhuis, Harry (2000): Krafft-Ebing, Psychiatry and the Making of Sexual Identity, Chicago: Chicago University Press.

Oosterhuis, Harry/Kennedy, Hubert (1992): Homosexuality and Male Bonding in Pre-Nazi Germany: The Youth Movement, the Gay Movement and Male Bonding before Hitler's Rise: Original Transcripts from Der Eigene, the First Gay Journal in the World, London: The Haworth Press and Harrington Park Press.

Parfitt, Tudor (2005): "The Use of the Jews in Colonial Discourse." In: Ivan Davidson Kalmar/Derek J. Penslar (eds.): Orientalism and the Jews, Waltham: Brandeis University Press, pp. 51-67.

Puar, Jasbir K. (2007): Terrorist Assemblages: Homonationalism in Queer Times, Durham: Duke University Press.

Puar, Jasbir K. (2013): "Rethinking Homonationalism." In: International Journal of Middle East Studies 45 (2): pp. 336–39.

Rohde, Achim (2005): "Der innere Orient: Orientalismus, Antisemitismus und Geschlecht im Deutschland des 18. bis 20. Jahrhunderts." In: Die Welt des Islams 45 (3), pp. 370–411.

Rohde, Achim/von Braun, Christina/Schüler-Springorum, Stefanie (2018): National Politics and Sexuality in Transregional Perspective, London: Routledge.

Scheibelhofer, Paul (2013): "Muscular Islamophobia in Austria and beyond: Masculinism and contemporary anti-Muslim politics." Lecture presented at the conference Political Masculinities: Structures, Discourses and Spaces in Historical Perspective, University of Vienna, November 15–17, 2013.

Schoeps, H. Julius (1988): "Sexualität, Erotik und Männerbund. Hans Blüher und die deutsche Jugendbewegung." In: Joachim H. Knoll/Julius H. Schoeops (eds.): 'Typisch Deutsch': die Jugendbewegung: Beiträge zu einer Phänomenengeschichte, Opladen: Leske + Buderich, pp. 137–54.

Schurtz, Heinrich (1902): Altersklassen und Männerbünde: Darstellung der Grundformen der Gesellschaft, Berlin: Georg Reimer.

Scott, Joan (2009): "Sexularism: On Secularism and Gender Equality." RSCAS Distinguished Lectures. April 23, 2009. http://cadmus.eui.eu/bitstream/handle/1814/11553/RSCAS_DL_2009_01.pdf.

Sedgwick, Eve Kosofsky (1994): Tendencies, London: Routledge.

Sombart, Nicolaus (1988): "Männerbund und politische Kultur in Deutschland." In: Joachim H. Knoll/Julius H. Schoeops (eds.): 'Typisch Deutsch': die Jugendbewegung: Beiträge zu einer Phänomenengeschichte, Opladen: Leske + Buderich, pp. 155–76.

Somerville, Sibhan B. (2000): Queering the Color Line: Race and the Invention of Homosexuality in American Culture, Durham: Duke University Press.

Stoler, Ann Laura (1995): Race and the Education of Desire: Foucault's History of Sexuality and the Colonial Order of Things, Durham: Duke University Press.

Thomas, James M. (2010): "The racial formation of medieval Jews: a challenge to the field." In: Ethnic & Racial Studies 33 (10), pp. 1737–55.

Ulrichs, Karl Heinrich (1994): Forschungen über das Rätsel der mannmännlichen Liebe, Vols. 1–5, Hubert Kennedy (ed.), Berlin: Verlag Rosa Winkel.

von Krafft-Ebing, Richard (1886): Psychopathia sexualis: eine klinisch-forensische Studie, Stuttgart: Enke.

von See, Klaus (1992): "Politische Männerbund-Ideologie von der Wilhelminischen Zeit bis zum Nationalsozialismus." In: Gisela Völger/Karin von Welch (eds.): Männerbande/Männerbünde: zur Rolle des Mannes im Kulturvergleich, Vol. 2, Köln: Rautenstrauch-Joest Museum, pp. 93-102.

Widdig, Bernd (1992): Männerbünde und Massen: zur Krise männlicher Identität in der Literatur der Moderne, Opladen: Westdeutscher Verlag.

zur Nieden, Susanne (2004): "Die 'männerheldische heroische Freundesliebe' bleibt dem Judengeiste fremd. Antisemitismus und Maskulinismus." In Elke Vera Kotowsky/Julius H. Schoeps (eds.): Der Sexualreformer Magnus Hirschfeld (1868-1935): Ein Leben im Spannungsfeld von Wissenschaft, Politik und Geschichte, Berlin: Bebra Wissenschaft, pp. 329–42.

3. Modern Masculinity as Battleground of Identity Politics. Otto Weininger's *Sex and Character* (1903)

Following on from the previous analysis on Hans Blüher's "invention" of the *Männerbund* this chapter places a second influential response to the "masculinity-crisis-discourse" in the *fin de siècle* at its centre. Before discussing Otto Weininger's work in detail, the parallel development of the "masculine ideal" and the process of European nation-building is briefly sketched out.

At the time of the French Revolution and the Napoleonic Wars, the noble figures depicted by the French painter Jacques-Louis David and tempestuous, if dreamy, war heroes like the Kleistean *Prince of Homburg* embodied a new society, or at least a new, bourgeois ethos. Especially the German "wars of liberation" mark the beginning of the national myths of heroism and sacrifice. The volunteers of the Free Corps experienced a new model of equality and in giving their lives became patriots "who gladly laid down their lives on the altar of the fatherland" (Mosse 1977: 1). Poets and writers created a heroic national myth of masculinity, defined as the embodiment of the new ideals of law, virtue, morality and courage. At the same time, a cultural discourse contrary to this ethos grew up even then, and was intensified around 1900, among roving, nature-loving young people. This discourse found its first high point in Romanticism. In the unrequited lover *Werther*, and even more in the slacker good-for-nothing or the dreamer *Heinrich von Ofterdingen*, concepts of delicate, partly unsocialized and above all "feminine" masculinity appeared alongside the normative models of rationally controlled citizen and courageous warrior. This shaping of the artist as an "effeminate man" was not "about the re-evaluation of the feminine, but rather about the valorization of masculine femininity" (von Braun 1989: 57-58). "The word 'effeminate' [also] came into general usage during the 18th century, indicating an unmanly softness and delicacy" (Mosse 1995: 9). In spite of the revaluation that can be observed in romantic discourse, both the upheaval of the patriarchal order and the filial quest for identity continued into the middle of the 19th century, especially in the context of literary self-reflection (cf. Hohendahl 2002: 56-57). According to the American historian and specialist in masculinity studies, George Mosse (1995), this literary revaluation failed to call into question the normative national model of masculinity. Did that change with the German youth movement around 1900? In the turn-of-the-century *Wandervogel* not merely isolated, romantic (male) individuals but also a male collective (later called the male-band) and part of bourgeois youth acquired "female" and "erotic" qualities. As shown in chapter two Hans Blüher described the youth movement as an "erotic phenomenon" (Blüher 1912: 1). And we should also bear in mind that, with the slow detachment of sexuality from reproduction, with the women's movement, and also through the widespread awareness of male hysteria, nervousness and homoeroticism made increasingly evident by medicine, psychoanalysis and psychiatry, questions about male identity and sexuality pressed in a disturbing way into the discourses of cultural and political self-understanding.

As Uwe Hohendahl (2002) emphasized in a sketch of the problem in the "Crisis of Masculinity in the Late 18th Century," the *Storm and Stress* rebels who roved out from the shattered patriarchy and Enlightenment's cult of rationality could represent their bodies as the incarnation of both an aesthetic ideal and civic virtue. The second half of the 18th century also saw the birth of a stereotype of masculinity still effective today. Mosse dates the creation of a modern male ideal and a discourse of political masculinity to the same time as the rise of bourgeois society, that is, between the second half of the 18th century and beginning of the 19th. It was a slow process and many of the older, aristocratic norms and practices (such as duelling) took a long time to die, but eventually the bourgeois forms prevailed and the body itself (instead of its adornments) became the chief signifier of manliness. This image of man first appeared in France with the French Revolution and its ideal of the heroic fighter and martyr, embodied in ancient Greek figures such as Hercules and the Spartan king Leonidas. In the German-speaking countries, it was above all the aesthetic ideal of Laocoon and then models of bellicose heroism that developed around the so-called "Wars of Liberation" against Napoleon. In both societies, nationalism, a movement that emerged parallel to modern masculinity, played an important role because it adopted the masculine stereotype as a means of self-expression. Parallel to the establishment of a *religion civile* for the nation, the idealized male body and the hero who knows how to bridle his strength were held up by artists like David as symbols of moral beauty. Jacques-Louis David painted his heroic *Leonidas at the Thermopylae* from 1813-1814. He used the ancient costume of Sparta and the Greek struggle for democracy against the superior force of the Persians to represent the heroes of the French revolution. The Spartan King Leonidas is shown against the backdrop of the mountain pass at the moment before he sacrifices himself and his 300 soldiers to defend Greek democracy; the noble and statuesque male body emphasizes the classical allusions. In the context of European nation-building, this new (ancient) model of ideal masculinity represented heroic self-assertion over death and the triumph of national spirit and progress.

Fig. 5: Jacques-Louis David: Leonidas at Thermopylae (1813-1814), Louvre, Paris.

Public Domain, Wikimedia Commons

Mosse was one of the first to point out the complex relationship that has existed since the Enlightenment, and was particularly pronounced in the early 19th century, between the development of the bourgeois stereotype of masculinity, the formation of the bourgeois nation and state, and an expressly political aesthetic. The modern "aesthetics of masculinity" was based on the imitation of ancient body images and postures. The ideal of the masculine body in ancient sculptures, characterized by solid contours and clear lines, would come to represent the political ideal of the nation. According to Mosse, the most effective form of this development was indebted to classicism's discourse on ethical beauty. Across Europe, the noble hero who dominates his instincts would now splendidly reflect the civic virtues and health of the state on, as it were, the very marble of his skin. The noble proportions of this white male body displayed discipline, self-control, loyalty, courage, obedience and, last but not least, the readiness to die. In Germany, especially at the time of the Wars of Liberation in 1813, the ideal of masculinity as a symbol of individual and national renewal played a decisive role (cf. Mosse 1990, 1995).

A momentous difference between the German love of country and the French or English sentiment was, according to Klaus Heinrich (Rack/Heinrich 2006: 100), that in the German case "nationalism [...] was a substitute for a nation that was not there." Not least because of their compensatory role, both the imagined nation[1] and the stereotype of symbolic masculinity that stood for it underwent a phantasmatic exaggeration. This had already been expressed a few years before the Wars of Liberation in Fichte's *Addresses to the German Nation (Reden an die deutsche Nation)* of 1807/08 and their emphatic equation of the heavenly and earthly German nation. Promptly thereafter, the Romantic poets of the struggle against Napoleon would conjure up the imaginary fatherland in wildly bloodthirsty metaphors:

> The imaginary fatherland undergoes a sacralization, the heroes become martyrs of the holy German cause. Christian and national motives flow together no later than when the Germans want to seal their union with "unadulterated blood." Beginning in the second half of the 19th century, the theme of blood removes itself more and more from Christology and is transformed, via a naturalization of morality, into the "concern for the purity of the blood." (Brunotte 2015: 30; quotations within the quotation, Foucault 1978: 178)

---

1   Benedict Anderson's concept of "imagined communities" refers to the fact that modern nations are generally to be understood as "felt" and media-produced communities. (Anderson 2006 [1983]: Imagined Communities: Reflections on the Origin and Spread of Nationalism, London: Verso.)

In general it is no surprise that the "culture and ideology of hegemonic masculinity [also that of the martyr of the fatherland, U.B.] go hand in hand with the culture and ideology of hegemonic nationalism." (Nagel 2010: 249) Above all two scholars have decisively shaped the concept and theory of masculinity in gender studies and also as an independent field of research: one, the previously mentioned historian George Mosse, whose Jewish family was forced to flee Nazi-Germany to New York, and the other the Australian sociologist Raewyn Connell, whose name was Robert Connell before her sex change. Connell's book *Masculinities* (1995/2005) is still one of the most important approaches to masculinity studies. Building on Antonio Gramci's theory of hegemony as rule by agreement and consent, she coined the term "hegemonic masculinity." The special feature of her approach to gendered power dynamics is the integration of male-male relationality into the play of patriarchal power. For her the currently ruling configuration of hegemonic masculinity is defined not only in relation to subjugated women but also in relation to other forms of masculinity, or in her own words, "[h]egemonic masculinity is constructed in relation to subordinated masculinities" (Connell 2005: 77), such as homosexual men or men with a different skin color. Mosse created the term "countertypes" to define the constitutive Others of the above mentioned political-soteriological overloading of the white heterosexual masculine stereotype in nationalist discourse. (cf. Mosse 1995) They came increasingly into play at the end of the 19th century and may be seen as paranoid fission products representing the sick, ugly, impure and amoral. Before focussing on Otto Weininger's influential creation of a simultaneously misogynist, homophobe and antisemitic figure of the Other, this chapter will briefly sketch the outlines and central characteristics of the white, heterosexual and above all beautiful male norm. Mosse focuses his enquiry on the role and function of an ideal *Image of Man* (1995) within the process and representation of modern European nation-building. In this book he analyzes how the ennobled male body itself rather than its adornments became the chief signifier of ideal manliness. The beautiful masculine body, defined through allusions to ancient Greece and principles of harmony, proportion and (self) control, ensures both dynamic virility and social health and order. According to Mosse, every white heterosexual man could in theory ascend through processes of self-mastery and drill to the elevated domain of ideal political masculinity, which transcends the limitations of a particular gender:

At the time when political imagery like the national flag or the Jacobin's *cocarde* became potent symbols, the human body itself took on symbolic meaning. Modern masculinity was to define itself through an ideal of manly beauty that symbolized virtue. [...]. The masculine stereotype was strengthened, however, by the existence of a negative stereotype of men who not only failed to measure up to the ideal but who in body and soul were its foil, projecting the exact opposite of true masculinity. (ibid: 6)

This hegemonic model of middle-class masculinity was invoked not only as a symbol of personal and national regeneration, but also as basic to the self-definition of modern society. The "quiet grandeur" of the modernized ancient stereotype would henceforth reflect the bourgeois virtues and health of the state. The female national allegorical figures of *Germania*, *Britannia* and even *Marianne*, on the other hand, served in their statuesque chastity and respectability as guardians of tradition. They remained, according to Mosse, excluded from the politicized model of beauty represented by ideal form and hardened muscle. The connection between physical and moral constitution established by the anthropology of the Enlightenment was to be further developed scientifically in the course of the 18th and 19th centuries, particularly in Lavater's theory of physiognomy (cf. Mosse 1995: 26).

The true founder of this modern classicist "aesthetic of masculinity", however, is held to be the German art historian and archaeologist Johann Joachim Winckelmann (1717-1768). Winckelmann was born in Stendhal in the Altmark region in 1717 and came from a lower middle-class background. In 1755 [English 1765] he published his book *Reflections on the Painting and Sculpture of the Greeks* (*Gedanken über die Nachahmung der griechischen Werke in der Malerei und Bildhauerkunst*), which made him immediately famous. In the same year he travelled to Rome, where he was to live and work until his death. For Winckelmann, the study of the ancient Greeks, to which he devoted himself personally and professionally, meant much more than an aesthetic undertaking. The Winckelmann hero also represented an ethical ideal in the general classicist program of "noble simplicity and quiet grandeur," (Winckelmann, transl. Fuesli 1765: 30/31). In his classicistic striving for purity, Winckelmann stood against not only his Roman contemporary Piranesi and his somber visions of an underworld-like city, but also the baroque figures of Giovanni Bernini, which populated many Roman squares and displayed all the gestures of desire, violence and impermanence. Winckelmann's Greek ideal, on the contrary, was statuesque, purely masculine and noble in its proportions, without a gram of excess fat and expressive of sublime self-control. Correct observation and, above all, imitation of ancient sculptures should, according to Winckelmann, lead not only to a new art but also "make life whole." Not only the German *Gymnasium* and German art history were encouraged to learn from the Greeks; every citizen could learn from them formative "discipline" and proper "bearing." Thus Winckelmann's work already contained the life-reforming impulse that became so effective in the physical exercise and gymnastics movement in the wake of the 19th century. The idealization of the healthy and hardened naked male body in Greek sculpture signified at once two things: its purification of all sensuality and its neutralization. In Winckelmann's interpretation, the *Apollo Belvedere* is as aloof from the shallows of individual peculiarities as it is from manifestly erotic carnality. In this emphasis on the ideal purity and divine beauty of the sculptured male body, we cannot overlook, as Heinrich Detering (1995) has noted, a homoerotic undertone. There is no lack of ironic tragedy in the fact that precisely this male ideal, arising as it did in a homoerotic context, was to become in the course of the 19th century the hegemonic model of masculinity in whose name homosexuals were excluded, pathologized and persecuted. (see Brunotte 2013: 80)

At the core of Winckelmann's still abstract anthropological ideal is the demand for harmony between dynamics and order. Mosse particularly emphasizes the role of Winckelmann's well-known interpretation of Laocoon in the construction of the modern stereotype of masculinity, which conforms to the triad of balance, proportion and moderation. According to Winckelmann, Laocoon shows no "anger" or any other affect even in the desperate death-struggle with the serpents, but is rather full of self-control. The pain of the body and the greatness of soul are set against one another in such a way that they hold the entire body in balanced tension. Emulating this great paragon, the ideal man should have his inner "rage" and desires under control through discipline. According to Simon Richter, "these two forces, pain and soul, are held in a permanent synchronic tension. Indeed this tension produces the single expressive contour that figures Laocoon's body" (Richter 1992: 45). As we can read in the following quotation (in the translation by Fuesli) from his famous book, Winckelmann describes the model of an ideal *habitus* vis-à-vis the pain and expectation of death as a "semiotic system of representation" (ibid: 44):

Fig. 6: Laocoon, Vatican Museum.

Public Domain, Wikimedia Commons

The last and most eminent characteristic of the Greek works is a noble simplicity and sedate [quiet] grandeur in Gesture and Expression. [...] thus in the face of Laocoon this soul shines with full lustre, not confined to the face, amidst the most violent sufferings. Pangs piercing every muscle, every labouring nerve; pangs which we almost feel ourselves, while we consider – not the face, nor the most expressive parts – only the belly contracted by excruciating pains: these, however, I say, exert not themselves with violence, either in the face or gesture. [...] the struggling body and the supporting mind exert themselves with equal strength, may balance all the frame. [...] The expression of so great a soul is beyond the force of nature. (Winckelmann 1765: 30/31)

Henceforth a well-trained and as it were asexual, abstract male body was to be staged as a national symbol in the bourgeois societies of Europe (and later the

USA). This pure male body and its noble proportions display the core bourgeois virtues: discipline, self-control, loyalty, courage, obedience and readiness to die. The "massive popularization of the idealized male body on the 'purified' Winckelmannian basis of, above all, Greek sculpture, can hardly be underestimated" (Schmale 2003: 170). Winckelmann's body-soul model gained currency with classicistic elites and their artists "through the mass of copyists and media duplication, spreading into the gymnastic ideals of a Jahn and volunteer armies, and ultimately permeating the entire imaginary world of the nation with the abstract ideal of the male body" (ibid: 171). The social and cultural production of the modern male *habitus* as a biopolitical model, through drill, sports and paramilitary training, reflects the double aspect of gender-enactment and gender-embodiment.

With the help of the new masculine ideal, the rebelling sons were able to break free of their empirical existence around 1800 in the form of revolutionaries or gymnasts and volunteer soldiers, and set themselves up as symbols of the new patriotic universal. Like the patriarchal two sphere gender order, this split between politicized "neutral" virility and empirical sexuality was then called into question in fin-de- siècle "crisis of masculinity" discourse. This was owing not least to the accelerated historical dynamic brought about by the suffrage movement and the rising public visibility of those oppressed by the bourgeois class and gender order. Together with a gradual loosening of bourgeois morality and the waxing discourse on male hysteria and homosexuality in science and society, the bourgeois patriarchal construct of hegemonic masculinity as a neutral ideal of the universal began to suffer fundamental cracks. More and more it came into direct tension with sensuality, nervousness and ambiguous sexuality, and thus in a frighteningly different way with the concepts of the *terra incognita* of imagined femininity. Exactly this fact, however, "this permeation by the sexual, expresses itself at the end of the 19th century as the phantasm of a feminization of man [and yes, finally as a fearful vision, UB], of a feminization of culture" (Bublitz 1998: 39). Now beginning to act as Oedipus or Adonis, the subject of the Enlightenment as representative of the universal, which was encoded masculinely but was obliged to be as neutral as Odysseus tethered to the ship mast, ends up roaming the uncertain terrain of gender tension – a tension which, as a dynamic of knowing, as the story of Paradise and the Hebrew verb *jadà*[2] teach, is not snared in the limits of sex-

---

2   The Hebrew verb *jadà* means both sexual and spiritual "knowing." It linguistically sums up the gist of the Paradise story with its protagonists of Serpent, Eve and Apple on one

uality. It affects all processes of knowing, just as it by no means stops at the borders of "biological" sex drawn as bulwarks against comingling. On the contrary, according to Klaus Heinrich, "gender tension (Geschlechterspannung) also exists in each individual" (Heinrich 1995: 206). If now the male subject, which as rational subject detached from its sensual concreteness must embody the whole of the nation and the state, becomes sexual and nervous, then within the framework of the bourgeois gender polarity, as reconstructed by Karin Hausen (1978), this means it becomes feminine.

The discovery of bisexuality by Fliess and Freud and Magnus Hirschfeld's theory of intermediate sexual types is only a further milestone in a general process of awareness in which male desire gains in terrifying ambiguity. In this context, Freud's theorem of a purely male libido too turns out to be a defense thrown up against the dissolution of difference and identity. Sexuality, however, also figures as the ventriloquist of the more extensive shocks delivered to form and difference by the process of modernization in the upheavals around 1900. If, as Albrecht Koschorke (2000: 152) emphasizes, confusing body states of all kinds "present themselves in contemporary semantics as an intrusion into the male constitution of the body, it is because categories such as clarity, demarcation, distinction are given the predicate 'male,' while those such as comingling, dissolution and formlessness are given the predicate 'feminine.'" No wonder then that in the fierce cultural crisis debates of the time, both in Vienna and in Berlin, the supposedly moral "degeneration" of society was always described "as a crisis of male identity, [...] at whose center a nightmarish feminization of culture flashes up" (Bublitz 1998: 19). In general, a now predominantly defensive, dualistic and naturalistic gender struggle discourse conveys far more than the real gender struggles, because "the gender difference [now] becomes a suitable *metaphor* for other, more abstract crises of differentiation" (Koschorke 2000: 152-153) and thus a salient medium of modern reflection itself.

Michel Foucault, in the first volume of *History of Sexuality* (1978/1979), delineates the 19th century cultural process of the construction of homosexuality as a gender identity. He addresses the knowledge production initiated by sexualities in close relation to the evolving new power structures of modern society. Formerly in civil law, "sodomy" was a crime whose perpetrator was condemned only as a legal subject. Then, around 1900, homosexuality became

---

side and Adam on the other. Knowledge of wisdom is not possible without eros; it can be achieved only within the gender tension.

a sickness, relabeled and "medicalized." (Foucault 1978/1979) The new "science of sexuality" fostered increased attention on and the discursive production of so-called "perversions." At the same time, supported by European urbanization, an early homosexual rights movement was inaugurated in Berlin, whose first representative was the Jewish physician and Social Democrat Magnus Hirschfeld (cf. Beachy 2015: 85-101).

Antisemitism and Misogyny: The Case of Otto Weininger

As Jacques Le Rider and others have noted, in both Berlin and Vienna the "crisis of modernity-" (Le Rider 1993: 17) discourse condensed the political-cultural crisis into a perceived "crisis of masculinity." No other work of the turn of the century better gathers together, at once pathographically and seismographically, all the insights, fears and defense mechanisms of the polyphonic, simultaneously misogynous and antisemitic gender struggle discourse than Otto Weininger's bestseller *Sex and Character* (*Geschlecht und Charakter*) of 1903. According to Christine Achinger (2013: 122), "Weininger was not (only) defending the 'male' rational, bounded subject against the threat arising from sexual urges associated with 'woman,' but also against a threat to the autonomous subject emanating from modern society itself, associated in Weininger's work particularly clearly with the 'Jewish mind'." Jacques Le Rider (1993) and Sander Gilman (1995) have already pointed out the intersection of the figure of the "effeminate Jew" and the "modern woman" in *Sex and Character*. The first part of the work, which is more positivistic and medical, was submitted as a dissertation to the Philosophical Faculty of the University of Vienna. A year later, the 23-year-old Jewish doctoral student who had converted to Christianity published the work as a monograph, now supplemented by a second, more psychological-speculative part. "The book stuck the 'nerve of the times;' it belonged to a kind of 'philosophical journalism' that provided the bourgeoisie with a *Weltanschauung* until World War II" (Brude-Firnau 1995: 172). Shortly thereafter, the author committed suicide. For Gilman, the misogynous and antisemitic work, which immediately became a bestseller and decisively influenced both fin-de-siècle popular and scholarly discourse on women and Jews, is an expression of "intense, undisguised self-hatred" (Gilman 1995: 103).

The book is a response to both the often imputed "crisis of masculinity" and the increasing role of the women's movement in turn of the century Vienna. At the center of its radically modernity-critical remarks is the danger that emanates from a "feminization" of culture. Since for Weininger women primarily embody sexuality, the question he poses from the start is "What is woman?" (Gilman 1995: 173), and the question is animated by the deeply ethical concern to protect culture against the threat of female domination. Although proceeding from the thesis of a general bisexuality (cit. Le Rider 1990: 140), which had just emerged at the time, he develops the comparison of M (ideal man) and W (ideal woman) for heuristic purposes. It is no accident that W is defined by solely negative qualitative characteristics. The sub-title of Weininger's work is "an investigation of principles" and "it is indeed a grandiose attempt to trace every aspect of human life back to ontological dualism – chiefly to the polarity of male and female principles and toward the end of the book, the opposition of the 'Aryan' and 'the Jew' as well" (Achinger 2013: 124). In the first part of the book, Weininger develops a critique of dichotomous conceptions of gender difference, arguing that the basis and reason for sexual attraction is the existence of both male and female aspects and qualities of mind in men and women. Thus the starting point of the work lies in the assumption of a general human bisexuality: "Between Man and Woman there are innumerable gradations" (2003: 13), expressed in "intermediate sexual forms" (2003: 13). In the second part, however, he creates the "ideal Man M" and the "ideal Woman W" as ontologically different and "begins to identify M and W with empirical men and women [...] and largely adheres to a dualist model of gender, governed by strict polarity" (Achinger: 2013: 130). His fears are focused to begin with on female sexuality, and women embody more or less the threat of the modern sexualization of life. As a genophobic, Weininger particularly fears the dissolution of traditional images of chaste masculinity and sees male chastity being held up to ridicule:

> It is now apparent from where this demand for "seeing life," the Dionysian view of the music hall, the cult of Goethe in so far as he follows Ovid, and this quite modern "coitus-cult" comes. There is no doubt that the movement is so widespread that very few men have the courage to acknowledge their chastity, preferring to pretend that they are regular Don Juans. Sexual excess is held to be the most desirable characteristic of a man of the world, and sexuality has attained such pre-eminence that a man is doubted unless he can, as it were, show proofs of his prowess. (Weininger 1906: 242)

These men are in the process of submitting to the female values of sexuality, understanding masculinity only sexually and no longer "purely" and in an ethical sense. Although Weininger adopts the thesis of bisexuality, the poles of

the gender struggle are sharply distinguished for him: "W, the female principle is, then, nothing more than sexuality; M, the male principle is sexual and
something more" (Weininger 1906: 78). As the embodiment of sin, woman
threatens the entire culture, for she represents "negation, the opposite pole
of the Godhead, the other possibility of humanity" (Weininger 1906: 218). In
Berlin of 1918, too, Walter Rathenau, Weimar's first foreign minister, had similar thoughts about radical moral decline in the German Republic when he
lamented that "women [seduce] to hedonism" and that the "insecure sense
of maidenhood," which slumbers in every woman, is perverted into "the disposition of the prostitute ("den "haltlosen Mädchensinn, der in jedem Weibe
schlummere, zum "Dirnensinn" verkehre"). "Here is the blame," so Rathenau's
fearful fantasy, "for the rising up of primitive, negro-like desires, tamed for
millennia, in the women of our time, whose misery and degradation will hor-
rify their grandchildren." (Rathenau 1918, in Lubich 1997: 251)

For Weininger, one thing is certain: in this fatherless "final battle of the
sexes," redemption and salvation of the higher Christian culture is to be
hoped for only in the absolute asceticism of the man, for "only if the man
redeems himself from sex [...] can he redeem woman" (Weininger 1906: 250).
For Weininger, not even the chastity of men is sufficient surety, and at the
end of his six hundred-pages work he calls for the abolition and sublation of
the sexes, because "death will last so long as women bring forth, and truth
will not prevail until the two become one, until from man and woman a third
self, neither man nor woman, is evolved" (ibid: 250). In a very similar way
to Hans Blüher, Otto Weininger was driven by the shock-like self-reflection
brought about by the thesis of bisexuality. For Weininger, the homosexual,
converted Jew, this self-reflection ultimately turned into self-hatred. In Sex
and Character he adopts and reinforces the equation of women with (male)
Jews that was already widespread in the antisemitic discourse of the time.
He develops the figure of the "effeminate Jewish man" as a deviant antithesis
of the Aryan male. For him it was ominously certain that "the male has everything within him, and, as Pico of Mirandola put it, only specializes in this or
that part of himself. It is possible for him to attain to the loftiest heights, or
to sink to the lowest depths; he can become like animals, or plants, or even
like women, and so there exist woman-like female men." (Weininger 1906:
144). He sees the same possibility of adaptation with respect to Judaism. For
Weininger, Judaism is therefore neither a "race" nor a "people," but a spiritual
possibility for every human being:

> I must, however, make clear what I mean by Judaism: I mean neither a race
> nor a people nor a recognized creed. I think of it as a tendency of the mind, as
> a psychological constitution which is a possibility for all mankind, but which
> has become actual in the most conspicuous fashion only amongst the Jews.
> (Weininger 1906: 222)

As the virile man is confronted by the effeminate man, so too the modern
Aryan man is confronted by the Jew: as a psychological possibility of himself.
Christianity, as the author further emphasized in this passage of his book,
already used Judaism to define itself by opposition. Weininger, and this is an
essential part of understanding his work, was an antisemite and himself a
Jew. As already mentioned, shortly after the publication of his book, at the
age of twenty-three, he took his own life. In *Sex and Character*, antisemitism
and misogyny come together inextricably in the thesis of the femininity of
the Jews. Introductory to the chapter on "Judaism" (224), Weininger declares:
"But some reflection will lead to the surprising result that Judaism is satu-
rated with femininity, with precisely those qualities the essence of which I
have shown to be in the strongest opposition to the male nature." At the end
of his work, Weininger sees women and male Jews as without "mind" (225)
and even "without an I" (225), and therefore without "intrinsic value" (225).
According to him femininity and Judaism converge in secular-liberal modernity: "Judaism," he writes (239), "has reached its highest point since the time of
Herod. Judaism is the spirit of modern life." To determine what this "Jewish"
element of modernity primarily consists in, Weininger intones the conservative litany of the decline of culture and morals, and ends as follows: "Our age
is not only the most Jewish but the most feminine. It is a time when art is
content with daubs and seeks is inspiration in the sports of animals; the time
of a superficial anarchy, with no feeling for Justice and the State. [...] It is the
time when coitus has not only been approved but has been enjoined as a duty"
(ibid.: 239).

What the Jewish homosexual is to Blüher, the Jewish man in general is
to Weininger: a paradoxical figure. "More womanish" and hence sexually less
potent than the Aryan man, but also "more womanish" and therefore "always
more absorbed by sexual matters than the Aryan, although he is notably less
potent sexually and less liable to be enmeshed in a great passion" (Weininger
227). It is not sexuality as such, however, but the drive and urge to "coitus" and
"match-making" in which, for Weininger, the ambivalent "essence" of women

with the equally questionable "essence" of the Jews converge (all terms from 227).

Woman, according to Weininger, strives with all her power to copulation. "For all this it is again manifest that femaleness and match-making are identical" (ibid: 212). "Match-making" is also "an organic disposition of the Jews" (cf. 227). If nothing else, their lack of understanding for all asceticism suggests this. Like "women," the "I-less" Jew is incapable of a life separated from the other people and demarcated by boundaries, and is instead as a "breaker down of limits" (227) and an "inborn communist" (ibid.), at once a mass man and a master of formlessness. Above all, however, he is a match-maker, because "Men who are match-makers have always a Jewish element in them" (ibid.). For Weininger, here the point of greatest correspondence between femininity and Judaism has been reached. Like the supposedly excessive sexual desire of Jews, woman's overwhelming desire for sexual union does not stop, in Weininger's emotionally charged imagination, with the private sphere but presses beyond into the social. Proceeding from her own coitus, which in match-making becomes the practice of "coitus in general," woman strives for union:

> Whether as a mother seeking reputable matrimony, or the Bacchante of the Venusberg, whether the woman wishes to be the foundress of a family, or is content to be lost in the maze of pleasure-seekers, she always is in relation to the general idea of the race as a whole of which she is an inseparable part, and she follows the instinct which most of all makes for community. (Weininger 1906: 212)

While the fear of comingling that Weininger expresses in this passage draws on antisemitic and misogynous discourses, it also points to a more general social ferment in a "crisis of modernity". It is no accident that, at the end of Weininger's project of salvation and purification, redemption consists in the extinction of the feminine and "woman." As we know, Blüher did not follow Weininger's model here. On the contrary, as demonstrated in the previous chapter, his response to the crisis of patriarchal masculinity and the women's movement was a new model of power that simultaneously appropriates homoerotism and projects femininity on the "homosexual Jew": the male band (Männerbund) as the elite of a purely male society.

Bibliography

Achinger, Christine (2013): "Allegories of Destruction: 'Woman' and the 'Jew' in Otto Weininger's *Sex and Character*." In: *The German Review*, 88, pp.121-149.

Anderson, Benedict (2006 [1983]: Imagined Communities: Reflections on the Origin and Spread of Nationalism, London: Verso.

Beachy, Robert (2015): Gay Berlin. Birthplace of a Modern Identity, New York: Alfred A. Knopf.

Braun, Christina von (1989): "Männliche Hysterie – Weibliche Askese. Zum Paradigmenwechsel der Geschlechterrollen." In: Christina von Braun (ed.): Die schamlose Schönheit des Vergangenen. Zum Verhältnis von Geschlecht und Geschichte, Frankfurt a. M.: Verlag Neue Kritik, pp. 51-80.

Brude-Firnau, Gisela (1995): "A Scientific image of Woman? The Influence of Otto Weininger's *Sex and Chracter* on the German Novel." In: Nancy A. Harrowitz/Barbara Hyams (eds.): Jews & Gender: Responses to Otto Weininger, Philadelphia: Temple University Press, pp. 171-182.

Brunotte, Ulrike (2015): Helden des Todes. Studien zur Religion, Ästhetik und Politik moderner Männlichkeit, Würzburg: Ergon.

Brunotte, Ulrike (2013): Dämonen des Wissens. Gender, Performativität und Materielle Kultur im Werk von Jane Ellen Harrison, Würzburg: Ergon.

Bublitz, Hannelore (1998): Das Geschlecht der Moderne. Genealogie und Archäologie der Geschlechterdifferenz. Frankfurt a. M. : Campus.

Connell, Raewyn (1995/2005): Masculinities, Cambridge (UK): Polity.

Detering, Heinrich (2002): Das offene Geheimnis. Zur literarischen Produktivität eines Tabus von Winckelmann bis zu Thomas Mann, Göttingen: Wallstein Verlag.

Foucault, Michel ([1978] 1979): History of Sexuality, Vol. 1, New York: Viking Press.

Gilman, Sander (1995): "Otto Weininger and Sigmund Freud: Race and Gender in the Shaping of Psychoanalysis." In: Nancy A. Harrowitz/Barbara Hyams (eds.): Jews & Gender: Responses to Otto Weininger, Philadelphia: Temple University Press, pp.103- 120.

Hausen, Karin (1978): "Die Polarisierung der 'Geschlechtercharaktere' – eine Spiegelung der Dissoziation von Erwerbs- und Familienleben." In: Heide Rosenbaum (ed.): Seminar: Familie und Gesellschaftsstruktur. Materialien zu den sozioökonomischen Bedingungen von Familienformen, Frankfurt a. M.: Suhrkamp, pp. 161-191.

Hohendahl, Uwe (2002): "Die Krise der Männlichkeit im späten 18. Jahrhundert. Eine Problemskizze." In: Zeitschrift für Germanistik, Neue Folge XII, 2/2002, pp. 263-275.

Koschorke, Albrecht (2000): Die Männer und die Moderne. In: Wolfgang Asholt/ Walter Fähnders (eds.): Der Blick vom Wolkenkratzer. Avantgarde – Avantgardekritik – Avantgardeforschung, Amsterdam/Atlanta: Edition Rodopi.

Le Rider, Jacques (1993): Modernity and Crises of Identity: Culture and Society in Fin-de- Siècle-Vienna. New York: Continuum.

Lubich, Frederick A. (1997): "La loi du père vs. le désir de la mère. Zur Männerfantasie der Weimarer Republik." In: Walter Erhart/Britta Herrmann (eds.): Wann ist der Mann ein Mann? Zur Geschichte der Männlichkeit, Stuttgart/Weimar: Metzler, pp. 249-270.

Mosse, George L. (1996): The Image of Man: The Creation of Modern Masculinity, Oxford: Oxford University Press.

Nagel, Joane (2010): " Masculinity and nationalism: gender and sexuality in the making of nations." In: Ethnical and Racial Studies, vol. 21, Nr. 2, pp. 242-269.

Rack, Jochen/Heinrich, Klaus (2006): "Wir und der Tod. Ursprungskult oder Bündnisdenken über die Mitbestimmung der Toten." In: Lettre International, 72, pp. 100-103.

Rathenau, Walter ([1918] 2018): Gesammelte Schriften in 5 Bänden, Bd. III, Berlin: Ingtank.

Richter, Simon (1992): Laocoon's Body and the Aesthetics of Pain. Winckelmann, Lessing, Herder, Moritz, Goethe. Detroit: Wayne State University Press.

Weininger, Otto (1906 [1903]): Sex and Character. New York: The Echo Library, G.P. Putnam's Sons.

Winckelmann, Johann Joachim ([1755], 1765): Reflections on the Painting and Sculpture of the Greeks. (Translated by Henry Fuseli) London: Millars, in the Strand.

Winckelmann, Johann Joachim (1969 [1755]): Gedanken über die Nachahmung der griechischen Werke in der Malerei und Bildhauerkunst. Stuttgart (1969).

4. Against Effeminization. Sigmund Freud's Theory of Culture between Male Band Discourse and Antisemitism[1]

The Rhetoric of Race and Gender

This chapter examines through various text extracts the implications that being Jewish and the "Jewish Question" had on Sigmund Freud's theory of culture. The main focus falls on the influence of fin de siècle antisemitic discourses that conceived of the Jewish difference in terms of gender-determined distinctions. According to this conception, Jewish men were seen as unmanly or effeminate and therefore unfit to become good doctors or scientists. Moreover, their entry into the public sphere – that is, their attempt at assimilation – was looked upon as threatening the entire gender order. My analysis is in line with several older studies on Freud's confrontation with the antisemitism prevalent in his time – for example, Carl Schorske's reconstruction of antisemitic pressures on Freud's work (1973), Jacques Le Rider's study on antisemitism, antifeminism and the gender crises in fin de siècle Vienna using the case of Otto Weininger (1982), and Peter Gay's biography of Freud (1987).

But the works that have treated most thoroughly the effect of the prevailing early twentieth century medicalization of antisemitism on Freud's work are two early studies by Sander Gilman *The Case of Sigmund Freud: Medicine and Identity at the Fin de Siècle* (1993a) and *Freud, Race and Gender* (1993b). The scientific antisemitism prominent in medicine at the time aimed, among other things, at portraying male Jews as effeminate and diseased. They were denied the possession of masculinity and thus too the aptitude to be a scientist.

---

1   The translations of this chapter is done by Jonathan Uhlaner.

Freud's personal and scientific struggle to define a "heroic" Jewish masculinity was therefore closely linked throughout his life, up to and including his late work on *Moses and Monotheism* (*Der Mann Moses*, 1939), with his fight against the dominant antisemitism. As Gilman observes:

> To understand the complex issue of what Jewishness meant to Freud, it is necessary to examine the implications of the stereotype of the Jewish male, especially the Eastern Jewish male, in the science of his time. The very term "Jew" is as much as a category of gender, masculine, as it is of race. The relationship between the Jew and that of the woman (as parallel categories to the Christian and the male) became a central element in the structuring of Jewish identity. (Gilman 1993b: 8)

As we have already seen in Chapter one, Gilman and Daniel Boyarin also examine psychoanalysis in the context of "Freud's Jewish Question" (Geller 2007: 17). Both view Freud's theory of "normal," that is, heterosexual masculinity, as a reaction to the *fin de siècle* antisemitic dispositive of effeminization, but in very different ways. Gilman sees Freud's longing for masculinity as the product of a universalizing shift: "it is the concept of gender into which the anxiety of the Jewish body and mind are displaced" (Gillman 1993b: 11), while Boyarin (1995) interprets Freud's construction of the heroic-heterosexual Jew as a homophobic reaction to the antisemitic stereotype of the effeminate-homosexual Jew. Geller in turn recognizes in Freud's "ideal of the fighting Jew – of masculine Judaism" (2008: 159) above all an act of defense and outdoing. For all three researchers, the enterprise of Freudian psychoanalysis is the struggle of an assimilated Jew from Eastern Europe for "heroic," "Aryan" masculinity, and thus for recognition as a scientist and citizen with the same rights as others.

The present chapter places Freud's theory of the founding of cultures, particularly the model of the civilization-establishing community, the male associations or clan of brothers, in the context of the antisemitic discourses of the time. As shown from different perspectives in Chapters two and three, around 1900 political masculinity had become a battleground of German identity politics. The first step in this chapter will be to place Freud's theory of the founding of cultures in the context of contemporary debates and discourses in religious studies and anthropology. This reflection on the history of scholarship is then supplemented by considering the influence that virulent discourses and political activities in German-speaking countries of the time about and of male bands (*Männerbünde*) had on Freud's cultural theory. Attempting to place Freudian psychoanalysis also in the context of turn-of-the-century an-tisemitism and homophobia does not, of course, amount to a biographical re-duction. To quote Boyarin, it is rather "to put psychoanalysis on a Foucauldian couch of culture and poetics of critique" (1995: 137, note 1).

Context within the History of Scholarship

The research perspective of the *performative turn* in cultural studies (Fischer-Lichte 2008) brought about a renaissance in the theory of ritual at the end of the 19th and beginning of 20th centuries. The development of the modern academic canon of subjects around 1900 not only in religious studies, com-parative anthropology, ethnology and folklore, but also sociology and theater studies, was already unfolding in colonial contact zones and in productive engagement with indigenous rituals (cf. Brunotte 2017).

It was the religious studies scholar from South Africa, David Chidester who began to relocate the discipline of comparative religion in the context of colonial frontier discourses. While his earlier book, *Savage Systems* (1996), explores comparative religion in a colonized periphery and his newer study *Empire of Religion* (2014) focuses on the metropolitan center, both books ap-ply the same fruitful methodological and theoretical approach. *Savage Systems* argues that "comparative religion was at the forefront of the production of knowledge within these new power relations" (Chidester 1996: 1). The re-searcher later shows that a frontier comparative religious studies *avant la lettre* was already practiced by European travellers, missionaries, settlers, and colo-nial agents in open frontier zones and closed systems of colonial domination. With reference to Mary Louise Pratt's concept of the colonial contact zone (Pratt 1992), for Chidester the colonial frontier was a fiercely contested zone "where knowledge was produced and impacted in both directions" (Chidester 2014: xiv); it was a space in which to explore and dominate indigenous soci-eties (the colonies) and to understand recent developments in Europe. Ever since the rise of merchant capitalism and colonialism, knowledge of "alien" re-ligions and indigenous civilizations had been inextricably linked to the project of European expansion, while also fostering discourses on similarity and dif-ference. With reference to Freud's *Totem and Taboo* (1912-1913), therefore, we can and must ask to what extent the theory of the then under the keyword of *totemism* much discussed founding act of violence, patricide, and the canni-balistic act as well as the later ritual sacrifice of the "primal horde" (*Urhorde*), which was developed in comparative religious studies around 1900, also possessed a contemporary diagnostic potential.

In view of the possibility that a new reading of classical turn-of-the-century theories of ritual, freed from the theoretical trench warfare of the time, could prove productive, the only slight interest within psychoanalysis to take up again Freud's contribution to the theory of sacrifice, ritual and culture is astonishing. Thus, the editor of the book *Hundert Jahre Totem and Taboo*, Eberhard Haas, emphasizes "that this discussion has shifted from the internal space of psychoanalysis to other cultural sciences" (Haas 2012: 7). Religious studies and cultural theory, for example, re-discovered Freud's reflections on sacrifice and ritual. In 1972, two important studies were published that focused on the subject of religion and sacrificial violence and recognized the importance of *Totem and Taboo*. In *Homo Necans* (1972), the Swiss classicist Walter Burkert examined ancient Greek sacrificial rituals and their recurring patterns of action going back to the time of hunter-gather societies; and in *Violence and the Sacred* (1972), the French Romance and cultural studies, scholar René Girard developed a cultural theory of the mimetic crisis and the scapegoat. While the foundations of their theories of sacrificial violence could not be more different, both scholars nevertheless confirmed Freud's hypothesis of an original founding act of violence and of a sacrificial cult. At the same time, we now know that *Totem and Taboo* cannot be understood merely as a contribution to the prehistory of the human species and ethnology. It is also and especially a text about the indissoluble intertwining of modernity and the "archaic," of civilization and violence:

> Freud himself had a very high opinion of this last essay [i.e., *Totem and Taboo*, U.B.], both as regards its content and its form. It contains his hypothesis of the primal horde and the killing of the primal father and elaborates his theory tracing from them the origins of almost the whole of later social and cultural institutions. He told his present translator, probably in 1921, that he regarded it as his best written work. (Strachey 1955, The Standard Edition of the Complete Works of Sigmund Freud [hereafter cited as SE followed by volume and page number], 13: xi)

But what exactly made the psychoanalyst believe so strongly in the "truth" of *Totem and Taboo* that he repeatedly applied its theory of culture, right through to his work on *Moses and Monotheism*? Mario Erdheim has suggested reading *Totem and Taboo* as a cultural-theoretical essay on collective violence, its internalization and ritualization, and its recurrence in modern times. Freud's cultural theory was "not about the savages over there, but about the savages here, not from the earliest beginnings of society, but since the establishment of our own institutions" (Erdheim 1992: 23). If we follow this reading, then, in addition to the central theme of patricide and regicide, we must also consider that of the establishment of culture by the clan of brothers. In general, of course, Freud's text goes beyond this. His "scientific myth" of patricide and brotherhood ties in first of all with the religious tradition of myths of origin, which, beginning with the biblical myth of Cain and Abel, themselves reflect on the relationship between crisis, founding violence, and ethics. At the same time, *Totem and Taboo* belongs to the Enlightenment tradition of the socio-philosophical narratives of foundation, in which authors such as Thomas Hobbes and John Locke speculate about the relationship between deadly savagery and civil self-government. Like these socio-philosophical essays, the phylogenetic narrative of psychoanalysis is and remains a scientific myth about the founding acts of culture.

Around 1900, at a time when the utopias of progress were being shaken by the massively developing potential for violence in the so-called civilized societies of modernity, Freud set at the beginning of the "prehistory of the species" an act of murder, and then sought the erotic forces that create culture and upon which all sociality rests. At the origin of human culture and all higher social orders, *Totem and Taboo* posits an egalitarian male society, thus adopting the Enlightenment postulate of fraternity. This male society is supposed to function as a collective *doppelgänger* of the family hero Oedipus. Freud thus combined his reflections on the ontogenesis of incest, patricide, and self-control with an imaginary phylogeny of humanity. In doing so, he proceeded from the colonial ethnographic knowledge of his time: *Totem and Taboo*'s theoretical narrative of foundation, which will be the subject of the first part of this chapter, is in constant critical discussion with, above all, the theoretical systematizations of this material by religious studies scholars, ethnologists, anthropologists, and sociologists such as William Robertson Smith, James George Frazer, J.J. Atkinson, Andrew Lang and Edward Westermarck, Gustave Le Bon, and Émile Durkheim. When Freud ends the book with the famous sentence from Goethe's *Faust*, "In the beginning was the Deed" (Freud, 1953-74, SE, 13: 161), he confidently placed himself alongside the then new anti-idealistic approaches in the theory of religion advocated by Robertson Smith, Jane E. Harrison, and Émil Durkheim, which focused on the social performance of collective rituals.[2] Like Darwin in his construct of the "primal horde," these researchers set forth evolutionistically coded founding scenarios; presented as originary models of society and figures of communalization and domination, they communicated with topical questions of modernization in the guise of origin myths. Hans Kippenberg rightly sees the "presentation of the history of religion closely interwoven with the diagnosis of the dangers of modern civilization [...] in this early study of religion" (Kippenberg 1997: 269). As in the pioneering sociological works of contemporaries such as Ferdinand Tönnies, and Max Weber, or those of the ethnologist and folklorist Heinrich Schurtz, the previously mentioned religious studies researchers were concerned with performative practices and cohesive forces of society, community, and family – but also with the crowd, the (male) band, and forms of traditional and charismatic authority. However, Freud wrote his patchwork story of the primal horde and clan of brothers also in the face of *fin-de-siècle* cultural and scientific antisemitism, whose subtle effect on his work emanated from the brutal political antisemitism of the Christian Social Party, which had governed Vienna under the Lord Mayor Karl Lueger since 1897.

As already mentioned in Chapter two, the social model, the male fantasy, and the right-wing populist battle cry of the male band (*Männerbund*) was initially linked to German colonial undertakings in Africa (especially to ethnographic material from "German Southwest", today's Namibia and "German East Africa", today's Tanzania, Rwanda and Burundi). In 1902, Heinrich Schurtz, who was an assistant at the Bremer Übersee-Museum, published the book *Altersklassen und Männerbünde* (Age-Classes and Male Bands), introducing to ethnological research the concept and social model of the male band, alliance, or society. He believed that his findings in indigenous (then called "primitive") societies in Africa and all over the world were equally relevant to European societies and subtitled his bestselling book, "A Depiction of the Fundamental Forms of Society," staking an obvious claim to universal significance. Evolutionary theorists had interpreted male societies in contemporary indigenous African cultures as merely "prehistorical" forerunners of European civilization. Schurtz's thesis, which was enthusiastically received in Germany and Austria, differed from this interpretation in two respects: first,

---

2   Freud omits Harrison from the ranks of his "predecessors." Her work is mentioned here, however, because she was of crucial importance as a theorist of ritualism. For further information about Harrison, see Brunotte 2013 and 2015.

Schurtz included examples of male bonding from 19th century Germany; secondly, he called on his readers to appropriate the primitive colonial model of elite "male societies" in order to solve the modern problem created by the gender crisis and women's suffrage. His construct of the primitive "male society" saw male bands and secret societies as associated with the initiation of boys, bound together by religion and cultic practices, watching over the communal norms and directing the cult of the dead (*Totenkult*). In Schurtz's model of male bands, evidently conceived in opposition to Bachofen's idea of "mother right" and of traditional patriarchal domination, political masculinity attained socio-cultural relevance and power.

As Chapter two has explained from a different perspective, it was especially the young Berlin lay analyst Hans Blüher who popularized the ethnological discourse of the male band. In the 1910s, he became a bestselling author as an historian and theorist of the *Wandervogel* movement. Sexualizing Schurtz's ethnographic theories, he declared a homoerotic male society to be the chief engine of all higher cultural development. In its ethnic-national turn, particularly after 1918, misogynistic male band discourse increasingly took on antisemitic features. It now shifted from the indigenous cultures of the African continent (known to Schurtz via ethnographic findings from the German colonies), to an imaginary primordial Germanic warrior band. At the same time, Blüher and other adherents of the male band thesis radicalized the racist distinction, already virulent in the cultural discourse of the day, between "effeminate, Jewish homosexuality" and "virile, healthy, Aryan inversion." After the loss of the German colonies, the figure of the Germanic cult and warrior community gained explosive political power in the Weimar Republic, in which neo-Germanic leagues and "hordes" were becoming more and more active. Freud's cultural theory, especially his concept of the "primal horde" and the "clan of brothers," reacted, as this chapter is intended to show, in an overdetermined way to these developments.

Like *doppelgängers*, both social formations, the primordial horde and the clan of brothers, pervade Freud's cultural-theoretical and religious-philosophical texts from *Totem and Taboo* (1912-13) and *Group Psychology and the Analysis of the Ego* (1921) to *Moses and Monotheism* (1939). The description of the clan of brothers is thereby marked by an ambivalence: it fluctuates between murderous cannibalistic mob and a civilization-founding contractual community. The clan of brothers stands in doppelgänger-like proximity to the primal horde in some places, only to assume the role of its direct, democratic opponent in others.

Against Circumcision: Oedipus as Hero of Masculinity

Recent poststructuralist, postcolonial, and gender-theoretical interpretations of Freud's psychoanalysis place the author and his work in the cultural-historical context of the *fin de siècle* period, which was marked by modern gender crises and antisemitism. As a result, not only has Freud's theory of the Oedipus complex, in particular the underlying assumption that castration anxiety is the eye of the needle through which all male development must pass and that women are constitutionally deficient beings, but also his theory about the foundations of culture has received a new interpretation. The latter intervention is mainly owing to the pioneering work of the American Freud researcher and religious studies scholar Jay Geller, which he presented in his books *On Freud's Jewish Body. Mitigating Circumcision* (2007) and *The Other Jewish Question* (2011). In the last twenty years or so, as mentioned in the introduction and in Chapter two, particularly Sander Gilman's *Freud, Race and Gender* and *The Case of Sigmund Freud* (both from 1993) and Daniel Boyarin's *Unheroic Conduct. The Rise of Heterosexuality and the Invention of the Jewish Man* (1997) have treated the extent to which the overdetermined gender and antisemitic ascriptions that shaped Jewish identity around 1900 consciously or unconsciously influenced Freud's work. The focus of these investigations fell on Freud's struggle for heroic, that is, normative-normalized (cf. Foucault 1990) and, above all, "hegemonic masculinity" (cf. Connell 1995/2005). Following this work and seeking to locate Freud's theory of religion and identity in the context of the political identity crises at the end of the 19th century, we must first note the double-bind in which an assimilated Central European Jew found himself: on the one hand, the European states demanded complete assimilation to the dominant culture, to the point of obliterating all signs of Jewishness; on the other hand, the antisemitic cultural discourse rested on the assumption that Jews are constitutionally incapable of overcoming their "sinister" difference. This difference was physically inscribed in the sex of Jewish men through circumcision. As Geller states:

> In the imagination of Central Europe, a society in which individual identity and social cohesion are principally (but by no means exclusively) determined by sexual division of labor and its gender-coded spheres, "circumcised" male Jews are identified *with* (not *as*) men without penises, that is, *with* (not *as*) women. (Geller 2007: 199)

Freud, who felt himself to be a European citizen and identified himself with secular cultural values, especially the enthusiasm for Greek antiquity that marked the hegemonic culture, was keen to ensure that psychoanalysis should not be thought Jewish but instead acknowledged as a positivistic-objective and universal science. For him, the struggle for recognition was therefore also the struggle of a marginalized, that is, feminized, Jewish masculinity to take part in German hegemonic masculinity, which is imagined as neutral. At the same time, Freud described his position as a Jew struggling for recognition with the image of virile combat:

> This is how he states it in his *self-portrayal* and repeats it in his 1926 address to the Viennese Jewish association B'nai B'rith: "Being Jewish had become indispensable for me on my difficult path in life [...]. [...] as a Jew, I was prepared to go into the opposition and to forego agreement with the "compact majority." (Geller 2008: 161)

In Freud's portrayals of his childhood and adolescence, too, "being Jewish is described as a test of masculinity imposed by the anti-Semitic majority" (ibid). This includes above all the traumatic childhood memory of his father's humiliation at the hands of Christian ruffians against whom the father was unable to defend himself. Drawing on Freud's work, especially the establishment of the Oedipus complex as a universal model of male psychological development, Boyarin reconstructs the "virile struggle" of an Eastern European Jew, who has come to Western Europe and tries to cleanse himself of the antisemitic stigma of the "effeminate Jewish male" (Boyarin 1997: 27). For Boyarin, Freud's ignominious childhood memory of his father's unheroic behavior in his hometown of Freiberg even acquires the status of an "initiatory story of modernity" (ibid: 33). In the *Interpretation of Dreams*, Freud sets a different memory of his youth before his "unheroic" father's reminiscence. It is of the Carthaginian general and hero of his boyhood Hannibal, who fought against the Roman Empire in the Punic Wars. If this was just a simple youthful crush at first, Freud later acknowledged consciously and all the more his admiration for the "Semitic hero":

> But Hannibal [...] had been the favorite hero of my later school days. Like so many boys of that age, I had sympathized in the Punic wars not with the Romans but with the Carthaginians. And when in the higher classes I began to understand for the first time what it meant to belong to an alien race, and anti-semitic feelings among the other boys warned me that I must take up

a definite position, the figure of the Semitic general rose still higher in my esteem. To my youthful mind Hannibal and Rome symbolized the conflict between the tenacity of Jewry and the organization of the Catholic Church. And the increasing importance of the effects of the anti-semitic movement upon our emotional life helped to fix the thoughts and feelings of those early days. (Freud 1953, SE, 4: 196).

As if to tone down the trauma-inducing recollection of his father by identification with the victorious Carthaginian general, Freud frames his memory with a story about Hannibal:

> I may have been ten or twelve years old, when my father began to take me with him on his walks and reveal to me his views upon things in the world we live in. Thus, it was on one of these occasions that he told me a story to show me how much better things were now than they had been in his days. "When I was a young man," he said, "I went for a walk one Saturday in the streets of your birthplace; I was well dressed and had a new fur cap on my head. A Christian came up to me and with a single blow knocked off my cap into the mud and shouted: 'Jew! Get off the pavement!' "And what did you do?" I asked. "I went into the roadway and picked up my cap", was his quiet reply. This stuck me as unheroic conduct on the part of the big, strong man who was holding the little boy by the hand. I contrasted this situation with another which fitted my feelings better: the scene in which Hannibal's father, Hamilcar Barca, made his boy swear before the household altar to take vengeance on the Romans. Ever since that time Hannibal had had a place in my phantasies. (Freud 1953, SE, 4: 197)

However much has been written about this Freudian anecdote, Boyarin argues that its status as an historical document has not hitherto been sufficiently appreciated. It bears witness to how much the shift of the Eastern Jewish population to the modern, Western-bourgeois way of life was linked to questions of *male gender*. At the turn of the century, male Jews were not only humiliated, according to Gilman (1993b), but were further at the same time feminized by the humiliation. Against this, Freud directed his own, psychoanalytic concept of gender. For this purpose, he went back to the religious tradition, not of course to the Jewish or Christian one, but to pagan religion of Greek antiquity – to the Greek myth of Oedipus. This story, which was to become fundamental to Freud's construction of hegemonic masculinity in Connell's sense (Connell 2005), is about a father "who refused to be dislodged from a road" (Boyarin 1997: 39). The supposed stranger, who as the imaginary father in the psychoanalysis threatens castration, is killed in the myth by his heroic son Oedipus. Oedipus, who kills his father Laius unwittingly, also does not know that he has married his mother, Jocasta. For Gilman, Geller, and Boyarin, the invention of psychoanalysis, with the (at least initially) unambiguously heterosexual hero Oedipus, who desires his mother and hates his father, at its center, was also a defense against the antisemitic effeminization of Jewish men. According to the psychoanalytic theory, not only male Jewish bodies, marked as different by circumcision, were threatened by castration in Oedipal development; to become men, *all* boys must pass through the needle's eye of the castration threat. As described in detail in Chapter two, the production of sexualities called "perverse," "including the homosexual" and its pathologization, further radicalized the "racialization and gendering of antisemitism" (Gilman 1993b: 163). Gilman summarizes: "The image of the Jew and the image of the homosexual were parallel in the *fin de siècle* medical culture" (ibid). Thus, Freud attempted to consolidate his male identity in figures of heroic struggle against antisemitic hostility:

> Probably the most vivid depiction of Jewish masculinity setting itself off against non-Jewish cowardice appears in the memory of Freud's son Martin of a summer excursion in 1901. He describes how his father confronted a crowd that blocked the path of Martin and his brother Oliver and showered them with anti-Semitic taunts: "Father, without a trace of hesitation, jumped out of the boat and marched towards the hostile crowd, always staying nicely in the middle of the street [...] ten men armed with sticks and umbrellas [and] the women in the background cheering the men on with shouts and gestures. In the meantime, father, swinging his stick, attacked the hostile crowd, which gave way and promptly dissolved, clearing the path for him." (Geller 2008:161-162).

The cultural and political significance of models of masculinity, especially for Jews interested in assimilation, who, like Freud, sought to free themselves from the stigma of the effeminized Jewish man, should indeed not be underestimated. Masculinity, also in the sense of an ideal self-government trained on the body images of antiquity and embodied in noble proportions, was, as George Mosse (1996) was one of the first to show, an ethical and aesthetic norm constitutive for the European process of nation-building. In addition, at the latest in the modern, partly antisemitic, race and gender-coded crisis debates of the *fin de siècle*, masculinity became a decisive reference category for inclusion and exclusion. As shown in chapter three, the supposedly neutral, autonomous subject of the Enlightenment and later of the state and the nation was encoded from the start as heterosexual, white, and male. Along with his cultural masculinity, the sociability of the (male) Jew therefore also became problematic. Analogous to women, as Gilman emphasizes, or liable to queer/feminine connotations, as Boyarin (1997) and Geller (2007) point out, the Jewish man came culturally close to homosexuals defined as deviant. As an ultimately indefinable gender that fluctuated between "an abject, male or oversexed femininity, a homosexualized or 'less-than-virile' masculinity" (Boyarin 1997: 8), the male Jew put the entire bourgeois gender order into question.

Transformations of Violence in Sacrificial Ritual

In *Totem and Taboo*, Freud forges an evolutionary link between Darwin's patriarchal "primal horde" and the bourgeois family, and between his own theory of the Oedipus complex and the origin of religion and culture. As a result, in the central theorem of his general theory of identity, the castration complex and castration no longer function as a metonymy of Jewish circumcision but as the needle's eye of "normal" and therefore "healthy," that is, heterosexual German, masculinity. In Gilman's interpretation, Freud's theory of castrated femininity is a reaction to the antisemitism of the time. Instead of the Jewish man, women are now made to bear the stigma of castration. The merit of Gilman's reading, according to Stefanie von Schnurbein, is to "track down the diversity of the category of masculinity to the point [...] in Freud's work where the category gives itself out as most universalistic: in Freud's reflections on the castration and Oedipus complex and the deficient physical constitution of women" (Schnurbein 2005: 289).

In *Totem and Taboo*, Freud derived not only the origin of religion but also the origin of social life and culture in general from the phylogenetic primal drama of father and sons. The idea of patricide or regicide therefore initially suggested itself as the central theme of his treatise. In this, Freud was moving in the mainstream of the ethnological and classical Greek and Roman research of his day. Karl-Heinz Kohl has pointed out the contemporary virulence of the topic not only in James George Frazer's *Golden Bough* (1890) but also in research by orientalists, classical philologists, ethnologists, and anthropologists around 1900. For Kohl, the regicide narrative is a "collective obsession" of the time:

> What fascinated the ethnologists and scholars of the late 19th and early 20th centuries about sacred regicide was undoubtedly the fact that in this institution certain political constellations of their own epoch could be recognized as in a distorting mirror. The long 19th century, which according to Hobsbawm began with the French Revolution and ended with the assassination of the Austrian heir to the throne in Sarajevo, was not only an age of revolutions, but also of monarchies. Few epochs have seen the coming, and often enough the violent going, of so many kings and emperors. (Kohl 1999: 72-73)

In *Totem and Taboo*, along with the primal horde and patricide, the topos of the band of brothers assumes almost equal importance. Like the sociologist Émile Durkheim, Freud was on the lookout for what holds modern, increasingly divergent society together at its innermost core. Both had read Gustave Le Bon's *Psychologie des Foules* (*The Crowd: A Study of the Popular Mind*) (1895), but each drew different conclusions from their readings. Both were interested in the interplay between social order, emotion(s), and religion, and followed the Biblical critic and Semitist William Robertson Smith in his theory of sacrifice as an act of communion between the worshippers and the god, symbolized and materialized in consuming the flesh and the blood of a sacred victim. This theory saw the earliest communal social form as produced first and foremost by the collective, totemic sacrificial feast – by an act of killing and communion. Both Durkheim and Freud, however, further adopted Edward Burnett Tylor's earlier theory of sacrifice, which was steeped in the totemism enthusiasm of the time. With reference to the role of violent killing and the common meal, they therefore also drew attention to the aspects of gift and (drive) renunciation in the sacrificial process. At this point at the latest, the scientific paths and interests of the two researchers parted ways, for, as Edward Evans-Pritchard (1968: 103-104) comments with polemical exaggeration: "For Freud the father is God, for Durkheim society."

In fact, Freud's psychoanalytic enterprise can also be read as an attempt to save the traditional family, whose central position around 1900 was called into question by various modern developments, above all the youth movement, the *Wandervogel*, and various suffrage movements. Suppressed in Evans-Pritchard's polemic is the immense role that all the previously mentioned religious-sociological approaches give to the performative, group-emotional processes, which are borne by ritual communalization. For with

Robertson Smith, Harrison and especially Durkheim and his close colleague at the *Collège de Sociologie* Marcel Mauss, the focus of reflection on the theory of ritual shifted. From the (post) Enlightenment figure of Frazer's "primitive thinker," who seeks to control the natural law of fertility through rituals, researchers' interest moved to the communally "energized society." In Durkheim's view, this society not only represents itself in the event of the festal (sacrificial) ritual, but further, as it were, creates itself anew. Henrik Versnel gets to the heart of the idea thus: "[...] however the ritual may relate to external data like fertility of the soil, what counts is *what the participant himself experiences*, his own emotion. The mythical images, therefore, are products, first and foremost, of spontaneous, collective emotions" (Versnel 1993: 26). In these decidedly social-cultural approaches, external nature is more or less abandoned as a frame of reference for rituals in favor of an affectively and performatively formed social space. Rituals are emphatically treated as media of mass excitement, festive self-perception, (sacrificial) violence, and communalization.

Like the other pioneers of the theory of sacrifice, the establishment of culture and ritual, whose materials and approaches Freud put to use, he too starts from the construction of a "primitive" collective, which he localizes in Darwin's primal horde. To evade the reproach that this is a *petitio principii*, and that the rituals, which first create collective institutions, ethics and the experience of the sacred always actually presuppose them, Freud constructed his "scientific myth" of the primordial patricide. He then projected this myth onto the beginning of human history as the oedipal founding legend of civilization and society. As already observed, *Totem and Taboo* is also and especially a text about the indissoluble intertwining of modernity and the "archaic," civilization and violence. The so-called "primitiveness" of the original violence harbors the possibility of its return in the modern age.

In *Thoughts for the Times on War and Death* (Freud, SE, 14), the culture theorist and mass psychologist Freud recognized the persistent virulence of regressive developments in modern culture in the fanatical war enthusiasm of 1914, as Andreas Hamburger observes: "What is noticed, but still unexplained, is the mass effect that brings about cultural regression and turns unconscious fantasies into a real 'gang of murderers'" (Hamburger 2005: 73). Freud will then examine the role of this regressive mass effect in *Group Psychology and the Analysis of the Ego* (1921). There he interprets the cultural relapse into barbarism that can occur through the medium of the masses in the form of a return of the archaic primal horde:

The leader of the group is still the dreaded primal father; the group still wishes to be governed by unrestricted force, it has an extreme passion for authority; in Le Bon's phrase it has a thirst for obedience. The primal father is the group ideal, which governs the ego in place of the ego ideal. (Freud SE, 17: 127)

Totem and Taboo first appeared in 1912/13 as a series of articles in *Imago*. Shortly before the outbreak of World War I, Freud presented his theory of modern, Christian society's indissoluble nexus with violence in the guise of a theory of a criminal act of archaic founding: as in the origin myths of the Bible, Greek mythology, and Romulus and Remus, at the beginning of the phylogenetic narrative of psychoanalysis stands murder. In *Totem and Taboo*, however, Freud also advocated the theory, inspired by Robertson Smith, that social organization, moral restrictions, and religion began with the *ritualization* of an archaic killing in a sacrificial communal cult.

Bringing Darwin's primal horde theory together with the findings of early ethnographic and archaeological research, Freud thus had two models of archaic social organization to account for the origin of society: on the one hand, the mythical father of the equally unverifiable mythical primal horde, who forced his sons into exogamy; and, on the other, early forms of democratic male bands. Freud writes:

The most primitive kind of organization that we actually come across – and one that is in force to this day in certain tribes – consists of **bands of males** [*Männerverbände*]; these bands are composed of members with equal rights and are subject to restrictions of the totemistic system, including inheritance through the mother. (Freud SE, 13: 141, emphasis in original)

The question that Freud asks himself in the fourth chapter of *Totem and Taboo* is the following: "Can this form of organization have developed out of the other one? And, if so, along which lines?" (ibid). To answer the question, he adopts Atkinson's assumption in *Primal Law* (Atkinson 1903: 220-22; quoted in *Totem and Taboo*) that the sons excluded by the father band together to kill him. Freud then returns to the totemic sacrificial ritual: the killing of the sacrificial animal, which represents "God," and the communal meal. For Robertson Smith, the sacred act was first and foremost an act of fellowship between the deity and his worshipers, the "totem meal" a performative *communio* of believers with their god. In *Totem and Taboo* Freud directly quotes Robertson Smith: "It can be shown that, to begin with, sacrifice was nothing other than 'an act of fellowship between the deity and his worshipers' [Smith 1894: 224; quoted in Freud SE, 13: 133]. For Freud, however, the homicide that preceded these festive communions of the sacrificial ritual gained a decisive importance. For this crime consists in the horde's killing the primal father and together cannibalistically feasting on his body, an act which the community of brothers then performatively repeats and puts into ritual form. This ritual form "… was the beginning of so many things – of social organization, of moral restrictions and religion" (ibid). Because, Freud continues, the collective act triggers the decisive, creative "sense of guilt and remorse" in the perpetrators (Freud, SE, 13: 144). The collective establishment of the new, ethically constituted body of society is possible only through the dynamic of this feeling of guilt, inspired by belated pangs of paternal love and "deferred obedience" (ibid: 145). In the ritual, the social body and the totem god of the father cult take the place of the dead body of the father. Freud makes not the mother's body, as Melanie Klein will later do (Klein 1962), but the body of the mythical father the receptacle of ambivalent endeavors. In agreement with Klein, however, for whom the feeling of guilt in the "depressive position" is the decisive engine of individual and cultural creation, we could also speak here of founding violence and reparation: "Society was now based on complicity in the common crime; religion was based on the sense of guilt and the remorse attaching to it; while morality was based partly on the exigencies of this society and partly on the penance by the sense of guilt." (Freud, SE, 13: 146) Freud, however, was concerned not only with a theory of foundational murder and its ritualization in the religious cult of father/god/totem and sacrifice, but also, as Mario Erdheim has emphasized, the "dialectic of rebellion and obedience" (Erdheim 1992: 38). We could even add, quoting the title of Klaus Heinrich's book, that the theory is about the "difficulty of saying 'no'" (1985), understood here as the problem of a successful revolution of the sons. The collective of the community of brothers, founded after the collective murder of the father-king, thereby also gained potency for a diagnosis of modernity.

At the beginning of human history, Freud set the bloody revolt of the sons and brothers. The ambivalence of the "no" to the father – that is, the simultaneity of hate and love – ultimately drives the sons into self-submission to the commandments of the dead. They renounce the women who were withheld from them by the primal father, thus avoiding mutual slaughter and building an ethically stable community based on their emotional bonds. And yet, at this point we must ask if the feeling of guilt is really sufficient to explain the collective renunciation of women and the binding forces of the new self-government. Here Freud introduces "social fraternal feelings" (Freud, SE, 13: 146):

> In addition to the affectionate spate of feelings towards the father trans-
> formed into remorse, the murderous tendencies remain, limited only by the
> "social fraternal feeling,"' from which the "sanctification of the blood tie" and
> the imperative of solidarity, specifically the prohibition against fratricide,
> develop. (Hamburger 2005: 66)

But what are these decisive "social fraternal feelings," which lead to the covenant and the contract with the dead father, and which Freud, unlike Enlightenment philosophers, rightly wants to explain with more than only the rational and utilitarian advantages of cooperation?

Self-Sacrifice and Self-Government

Through a patchwork of cultural-historical narratives, *Totem and Taboo* aims to confirm the ontogenetically developed oedipal pattern of male development as a collective, even phylogenetically, operative model. The posited connec-tion between primitive primal horde and bourgeois family not only makes modern individuation overlap with the prehistoric foundational sacrifice, but also changes the meaning of the sacrifice itself. While Robertson Smith con-ceives of the sacrifice as a killing and a community meal within the frame of totemism, and René Girard sees the function and performance of the sacrifi-cial ritual culminating in the transformation of destructive, chaotic violence into sacred, creative, and ultimately reconciling sacrificial violence, from the point of view of the individual members, the sons and brothers, it is an initi-ation ritual whose performative execution transforms the participants them-selves – from a more or less closely connected group of "savage" cannibalistic sons, suppressed by the primal father, into a civil community of young men living in fraternal bonds. In the original German text of *Group Psychology and the Analysis of the Ego*, Freud even speaks, using religious-sounding terminol-ogy, of a *Brüdergemeinde* (communion of brothers) (Freud GW, 1972, 13: 136), which the English translation downplays by always speaking of a "community of brothers" (Freud SE, 18: 65-143). The newly constituted society is now based on the ability of this community of brothers to renounce their instincts and to govern themselves.

In the chapter on Odysseus in the *Dialectic of Enlightenment* (1947), Adorno and Horkheimer argue in a very similar way about the formation of the individual. There the authors see the mythical foundation of the bourgeois subject prefigured in Odysseus' self-control and drive renunciation, especially in his adventure with the Sirens. Alluding to Max Weber's paradigm of the disenchantment of nature and the theory of a culture-founding renunciation of drives in *Totem and Taboo* (1912-13), they point to the figure of the sacrifice as primarily constituting the autonomous (male) self. For Adorno and Horkheimer, the shipwrecked traveler Odysseus is a link to a modern model of self-sacrifice, interwoven with the overcoming of a "crisis", which is represented as a story of the triumph of rational self-government. Famously symbolized in his adventure with the Sirens, Odysseus overcomes and disenchants the mythical powers of nature and the religious past with the help of his cunning. Adorno and Horkheimer call his well-known ruse of self-preservation an "adaptation to death" (Adorno/Horkheimer 2002: 48). Bound to the mast of his ship and his comrades' ears plugged up with softened beeswax, the hero can listen to the fatally seductive song of the Sirens but is restrained from following his impulse to go to them, let alone to touch them. For Adorno and Horkheimer, "Odysseus bound" embodies a model of male subjectivity that is built on the disenchantment of nature – inner and outer nature. For them, Odysseus' heroic self-control and empowerment implies a model of constitutive self-sacrifice: sacrifice of the self found the self. In their own words: "The human being's mastery of itself, on which the self is founded, practically always involves the annihilation of the subject in whose service that mastery is maintained" (ibid: 43). It is the "internalization of the sacrifice," they continue, "which, as permanent self-suppression, performs the self-mutilation of the man in any case" (ibid: 43 and 56). The authors refer, of course, solely to the repression of the heterosexual libido, most obvious in the Siren episode. Freud proceeds in a very similar way in interpreting the father drama of his ancient hero Oedipus. When inventing the Oedipus complex, the psychoanalyst disregarded the bisexuality of Laius, whose pederastic actions are handed down in myths.[3]

---

3   In ancient mythology, Laius, later the father of Oedipus, was cursed by Pelops for making homosexual-pedophilic advances on his son Chrysippus.

Democratic Male Bands (Männerbünde) and Negation of the Mother

The primal patriarchal family, Freud was aware, is a myth. In view of the ethnological research of his time, he admitted in *Totem and Taboo* that the Darwinian primal horde, with its autocratic primal father at its center is a mythic conjecture: "This earliest state of society has never been an object of observation" (Freud SE vol. 13: 141). Yet not all the social collectives that participated in the founding acts were merely "scientific myths." Freud's theory of cultural institutions was based on the oldest known form of social organization at the time: the "bands of males; these bands are composed of members with equal rights and are subject to the restrictions of the totemistic system, including inheritance through the mother" (Freud SE, 13: 141). Contemporary ethnological research had twice discovered egalitarian male groups in non-European indigenous societies and brought to light numerous findings, not least the integration of these groups into matrilineal cultures. Here, to begin with, we should note the ethnological verification of Johann Jacob Bachofen's cultural and historical speculations on the archaic "matriarchy" (1861) by the Scottish ethnologist John McLennan in *Primitive Marriage* (1865). This ethnographic authentication of matrilineal systems shook the belief in the originality and naturalness of the monogamous-patriarchal family. Then, in 1877 Lewis Henry Morgan's *Ancient Society*, based on studies of the kinship structure and political organization of the North American Iroquois, succeeded in proving that acephalous societies, that is, those without a central authority, can function very well. And here, too, matrilineal inheritance was combined with equality within the (male) tribe, clan or group. "Morgan never wearies," notes Uwe Wesel, "of describing the freedom, equality, and brotherhood [of the Iroquois] and their deeply democratic character." (Wesel 1999: 22)

Because of its strong fixation on the culture-building relationship between father and son, and its author's compulsion to apply the Oedipus complex as a performative model of the individual and social development of manhood to the history of the species, Freud's analysis failed to appreciate the powerful and *active* role of the mother/mothers and her attached mother cults, which is well documented in myths and cultic lore. For Freud, "a longing for the father" (*Vatersehnsucht*) was "at the root of every form of religion" (Freud SE, 13: 149), and he was just as certain that the Oedipus complex contains the roots of religious feelings. Yet he admitted that, in the evolution from bands of brothers to patriarchy and father-religions, "a place is to be found for the great mother-goddesses, who may perhaps in general have preceded the father-gods" (ibid).

He granted the institutions of maternal law a certain, if unclear, role in the establishment of religion, ethics and social organization by the community of brothers. The collective establishment of the prohibition against incest after the murder of the primal father transforms the competitors, fighting for libidinal satisfaction and power, into an acephalous male community which first worshiped mother goddesses. "For a long time afterwards [the killing of the father], the social fraternal feelings, which were the basis of the whole transformation, continued to exercise a profound influence on the development of society [...]. The patriarchal horde was replaced in the first instance by the fraternal clan" (Freud SE, 13: 146).

The blind spot in Freud's theorizing (cf. di Censo 1996), which here again becomes apparent, extends not only to the "dark continent" of female sexualities but also to the hypotheses about matriarchal rule and mother cults suggested by the mythic material. In addition to Erich Neumann's phenomenological study *The Great Mother* (1974), Melanie Klein (1962), André Green (2004), and Julia Kristeva (1982) in particular studied the clue that Freud ignored. Missing from the drama of *Totem and Taboo*, which leads to the catastrophe that culminates in the killing of the king, are the women. They play a role solely as objects of the mythical struggle between father and sons: "A drama in which there are no women puts the absence of women center stage. [...] This systematic omission or reduction of the mothers to the incest taboo as a 'culturally necessary negation' is a further key to the interpretation" (Hamburger 2005: 70). In *Totem and Taboo*, only an "exclusive society of brothers creates structure," and in general the work confines itself to depicting the endeavor to "create an autonomous male order" (ibid).

In his theory of the founding of culture, Freud, as we have seen, repeatedly uses models of male-masculine communalization, ranging from the primal horde to the community of brothers. He thus intentionally adopts a powerful discursive and political topos of the time, the male band (*Männerbund*). The discourse about the male band around 1900 focused on the question of the binding emotional forces that constituted and held these bands together. In this discussion Freud played an active part, and not only through his correspondence with Hans Blüher and his reception of recent ethnological research. Following Geller's argument (2003 and 2007), we need a more complex reading, for the origins of the patchwork of human prehistory that Freud sewed together from *Totem and Taboo* to *Moses and Monotheism* lie less in British colonialism, contemporary ethnography, or Austrian family norms than in his theory of the foundation of culture, which should be seen as a reaction to the then virulent male band discourse and the antisemitically tinged homophobic "male fantasies" (Theweleit [1977/1979]) that had penetrated as far as the Viennese metropolis.

> Yet, as the tale traversed his corpus from *Totem and Taboo* to *Moses and Monotheism*, Freud would continually tinker with the relationship within the band of brothers, especially with the role played by homosexuality. [...] the changes in Freud's depiction of homosexuality in his accounts of social origins – the increasingly sharp distinction between homosociality and homosexuality that ultimately culminated in the foreclosure of homosexuality from Freud's narrative – may be connected with the anti-Semitic, *völkisch* turn of Männerbund theories as well as the racialization of homosexual identities. (Geller 2003: 90)

By 1900, normalized masculinity functioned as a central reference category for inclusion and exclusion. It is therefore not surprising that in the fierce debates about cultural crises of the time the supposedly moral "degeneration" of society is always at the same time described as a "male gender crisis" (Fout 1992: 388). As explained in Chapter three, "at the center of this was a feminization of culture that appeared nightmarish" (Bublitz 1998: 19; cf. Brunotte 2004). As a powerful cultural antidote against the threat, exacerbated in visionary male fantasies, a variety of youth movement-inspired youth groups, male societies and fellowships of comrades rose up around 1900 in Germany and invented the homoerotic male band as a new salvific form of community.

The Invention of the Neo-Germanic Male Band through Colonial Transfer

The male band, understood as a ritually produced, initiatory communitas in Victor Turner's sense (1989), was, like Robertson Smith's communion, a product of the "imaginary ethnography of the 19th century," as the subtitle of Fritz Kramer's book *Inverted Worlds* (1977) has it. Ethnographic research into ritual already found itself in the pull of *völkisch* discourse in Wilhelmine Germany and Lueger's Vienna and thus under the pressure of expectation that its discoveries should contribute to inventing a Germanic counter-tradition radically opposed to modernity. Schurtz also had developed his consequential plea for the socially progressive role of male bands explicitly against the backdrop of the current European debates about the origin of the family, society, and state, debates in which Freud also took part. According to Schurtz, neither kinship nor family unions but rather the voluntary "artificial unions" of young, unmarried men are the ultimate "bearers of almost all higher social development" (Schurtz 1902: 61). After the Great War, the "ritualist school" of German studies and classical archaeology in Vienna took up Schurtz's hypothesis of male societies as dynamic forces of civilization. In a kind of scholarly version of colonial mimicry, non-European models of "savage" male societies, with their ecstatic initiation cults, warrior rituals and secretive cults of the dead, were projected onto early Germanic history. In a large-scale "reinvention of tradition" (Hobsbawm/Ranger 1983), researchers replaced the image of the naive Germanic peasant with that of the untamed, frenzied ancient Norse berserker. In German studies, this move to dress an allegedly primeval Germanic tradition in the costume of the colonial native began in 1927 with the "discovery" of the Germanic warrior band as a national identity myth by authors such as Lily Weiser and Otto Höfler. Drawing on the work of Schurtz, they imagined a sacred and heroic male band that sometimes transformed itself into a ferocious army of the dead. Höfler in fact broke completely with Schurtz's universalist approach, which had not distinguished between male societies in the colonized regions and in Europe. He elevated the wild "Germanic Aryan" to the status of a unique phenomenon; for him, the ancient Germans could not be compared with a savage tribe at all. Höfler emphasized the special capacity for development among the "savage" Germanic tribes, owing in his view to the fact that "it is in these male bands that the most unique gift of the Nordic race has its home, the power to form states" (Höfler 1934: 357). Precisely this ethno-nationalist turn in theories about male bands led, after the defeat of 1918 and the loss of Germany's colonies, to radicalizing the typological comparison of "healthy," Aryan masculinity and "sick," Jewish homosexuality. Geller summarizes:

> In the wake of [...] the loss of Germany's overseas colonies, some postwar German ideologues and ethnographers recolonized their tribal past with homogeneous communities led by cultic bands of male warriors, while others endeavored – far too successfully – to restore those idealized Männerbünde in the present. Moreover, [...] public dissemination of a racial typology of homosexualities [increased] the opposition between the healthy inversion characteristic of manly Germanic men and the decadent homosexuality of effeminate Jews. (Geller 2003: 90-91)

Both developments would influence not insignificantly Freud's theories about the role of Männerbünde and Männerverbände ("male bands and men's associations"), *Brüderclans* ("clans of brother"), *Brüdergemeinden* ("communions of brothers"), *totemistische Brüdergemeinschaften* ("totemistic brother communities") (Freud GW, 13: 151), or the "brother group" (*Brudermasse*: thus his choice of terms in the original German of *Massenpsychologie und Ich-Analyze* (Freud GW, 13: 136 and 151-152). Unfortunately, the English translation makes the nuances almost invisible (Freud SE, 18: 122 and 135).

It was, however, the Berlin Wandervogel and later bestselling author Hans Blüher who took up Schurtz's theory of the power of male bands to establish culture and first sexualized it and later made it antisemitic. To begin with, Blüher radicalized Schurtz's bourgeois theory of sociability, which was based on a neutral "sociability instinct" (Schurtz 1902) in men, by tracing the formation of male bands to male-masculine eros. He thus declares homoeroticism to be a culture-creating potency. In his *Familie und Männerbund* of 1918, Blüher writes:

> An instinct to socialize, if something like this could even exist as an original, instinctual element, would contain the accidental, the occasional, the nonbinding [...] We can already feel from afar that this concept is inadequate to explain the grave fate that came upon the human species. [...] The trace of the human formation of states reaches rather all the way down into eros [...]. Male bands [...] are products of sexuality, namely of male-masculine sexuality. (Blüher 1918: 21-22)

With this idea about the crucial role of male-masculine eros in the formation of communities and the founding of states, Blüher ultimately wanted to develop a cultural theory that was as fundamental as Freud's: not repressed or sublimated heterosexual eros or eros in general is the origin and engine of all higher cultural development, as psychoanalysis has it, but rather ennobled or transformed homoeroticism. Not the family but the male band is the nucleus of all higher civil associations.

Blüher and Freud: Homosexualities and the Longing for Masculinity

As John Neubauer (1996: 123-148) has reconstructed, Freud was in lively correspondence with Hans Blüher, twenty years his junior, at the time he was writing *Totem and Taboo*. In their letters they carried on a debate about the psychological and cultural "nature" of homosexuality, especially in the German youth movement, but also in society at large. The twenty-three-year-old Blüher was one of the leading thinkers of the youth movement and the gay liberation movement *avant la lettre*. As shown in Chapter three, he also belonged to a group of various friendship circles [*männerbündische Zirkel*], which Andrew Hewitt (1996) and Claudia Bruns (2008) refer to as "masculinists." From 1914 at the latest, these groups represented the previously mentioned clearly racially tinged binary concept of an Aryan, and hence pure, virile, "healthy" sexual inversion, and a Jewish, hence effeminate and "sick" homosexuality. Blüher had begun his career as an ardent admirer of Freud, whose *Three Essays on the Theory of Sexuality* (1905) and *Civilized Sexual Morality* (1908) had made a lasting impression on him. In both texts, Freud speculates about the relationship between progressive renunciation of drives and cultural evolution. Blüher was particularly fascinated by Freud's view that inverts or homosexuals should not be viewed as a "degenerate" group and therefore separate from the "normal" members of a culture, as was common in the medical-cultural discourse of the time, but that they represented rather a variant of sexuality which all human beings pass through at some stage in their development, since all human beings are fundamentally bisexual. In a part of footnote 1 in *Three essays on the Theory of Sexuality*, added in 1915, Freud wrote:

> Psychoanalytical research is most decidedly opposed to any attempt at separating off homosexuals from the rest of mankind as a group of a special character. By studying sexual excitations other than those that are manifestly displayed, it has found that all human beings are capable of making homosexual object-choice and have in fact made one in their unconscious. [...] Thus, from the point of view of psychoanalysis the exclusive sexual interest felt by men for women is also a problem that needs elucidating and is not a self-evident fact. (Freud SE, 7: 145-146, note 1)

In the same essay, Freud not only emphasizes sociability but also, with a view to antiquity, the special intelligence and cultural achievement of homosexuals (Freud always uses the term "inverts") in history. Blüher, who as a lay analyst interested in sexual science advocated depathologizing homosexuality, was fascinated by this position, which was very advanced for the time. In his first letters to the father of psychoanalysis, Blüher testified to his enthusiasm for

Freud's thought, which for him was a "true illumination."[4] His reverence for the psychoanalyst was also justified by the fact that Freud vehemently opposed the common use of the term "degeneration" with regard to inversion and inverts. Freud writes:

> The attribution of degeneracy in this connection is open to the objections which can be raised against the indiscriminate use of the word in general. [...] If we cast our eyes round a wider horizon, we shall come in two directions upon facts which make it impossible to regard inversion as a sign of degeneration ... one must almost say [that inversion is] an institution charged with important functions – among the people of antiquity at the height of their civilization. (Freud SE, 7: 138 and 139)

In his analysis, Geller links the debate between Freud and Blüher about the "health" of inversion and the culturally crucial role of homosexual sublimation with the concept of the "community of brothers," which changed significantly in Freud's work between 1912 and 1929. In *Totem and Taboo*, at the beginning of his reflections about the social fraternal feelings on which the first, democratic social form rests, Freud speaks of "homosexual feelings" as a binding agent of male bands. (Freud SE, 13: 144; 18: 124, note 1). As long as they were distinguished by their masculine character, Freud gives both the inverts and the democratic male associations of his foundation myth a positive connotation (cf. Brunotte 2004; Bruns 2011). Claudia Bruns therefore sees "[...] clear affinities" in Freud's early theories of homosexuality "to masculinist positions in the Männerbund discourse" (Bruns 2008: 300). In *Three Essays on Sexuality*, the psychoanalyst expressly distances himself from the thesis of the femininity of inverts, set forth at the time chiefly by Magnus Hirschfeld, and argues "that there can be no doubt that a large proportion of male inverts retain the mental quality of masculinity" (Freud SE, 7: 144). And he continues: "It is clear that in Greece, where the most masculine men were numbered among the inverts ..." (ibid). In 1905 Freud also speaks of the high cultural sociability of homosexuals when, again with a view to antiquity, he remarks that inverts should not be called "degenerate" because homosexuality is sometimes found in people "whose efficiency is unimpaired, and who are indeed distinguished by especially high intellectual development and ethical culture" (Freud SE, 7: 139). In 1908 Freud reaffirmed the positive assessment of homoeroticism

---

4   The correspondence was first published and annotated by John Neubauer in 1996; see Neubauer 1996: 123-148; here letter to Freud of May 2, 1912, ibid: 133.

when, in *Civilized Sexual Morality and Modern Nervous Illness*, he wrote: "The constitution of people suffering from inversion – the homosexuals – is, indeed, often distinguished by their sexual instinct's [*Trieb*, drive] possessing a special aptitude for cultural sublimation" (Freud SE, 9: 190). This position is easily recognized in *Totem and Taboo*'s depiction of homosexual bonds within the clan of brothers and their importance for the patricide and later the founding of culture. There Freud says that, after committing the fateful murder, the sons establish the prohibition against incest (and all other commandments and institutions) in order to continue the civil community that gave them the strength to act in the first place: "In this way they rescued the organization, which had made them strong – and which may have been based on homosexual feelings and acts, originating perhaps during the period of their expulsion" (Freud SE, 13: 144).

On the other hand, in one of his letters to Blüher and in other texts, Freud also speaks of the suffering of his inverted patients and their excessively strong identification with the mother, bringing with it the danger of feminization. In the end, he came close to adopting the then widespread thesis that inversion is caused by neurosis and that "healthy" psychological development must go beyond the phase of same-sex object choice. The question about the culture-creating function of male societies and the role of homosexuality therein will nevertheless occupy Freud into 1939 and *Moses and Monotheism*, not least because of the increasingly virulent Männerbund discourse in the society around him:

> In particular, the development of the (homo)sexualised and later racialized version of the Männerbund initially disseminated by *Wandervogel* [...] Hans Blüher may explain the persistent return of Freud's construct of the primal horde throughout the rest of his writing life. (Geller 2003: 94)

While Freud was working on *Totem and Taboo*, the young Blüher was writing his analysis of the contemporary generational strife. The sensational third volume of his *Wandervogel* trilogy was to appear in 1914 under the title *Die deutsche Wandervogelbewegung als erotisches Phänomen* (The German *Wandervogel* Movement as an Erotic Phenomenon), and Freud was one of the first outsiders to read the manuscript. But perhaps it is less this early reading than the increasingly ethno-nationalist and antisemitic political reality of male bands and men's associations that explains the vacillation in Freud's concept of the clan of brothers. The more clearly Blüher placed the inverted male bands at the center of his *völkisch* theory of state formation, the more clearly Freud distanced himself from these discourses and thoughts. Moreover, Freud's and Blüher's disagreement about the "health" of inverts was never resolved in their correspondence, above all because Freud ultimately clung to the neurotic genesis of homosexuality as an expression of an overly strong bond with the mother. That these tensions led to a break between the two owed chiefly to the previously mentioned political reasons. For Blüher came to espouse more and more openly misogynistic, antisemitic and ethno-nationalist positions. A quotation from the second volume of Blüher's main work, *Die Rolle der Erotik in der männlichen Gesellschaft*, (The Role of Eros in Male Society) published in 1921, illustrates the inextricable link between gendered, antisemitic and socio-political classifications and fault-lines in Männerbund discourse. Although already quoted in Chapter two, it bears repeating here:

> With the Jews it is as follows: they suffer at one and the same time from a weakness in male-bonding [*Männerbundschwäche*] and a *hypertrophy of the family*. They are submerged in the family and familial relations, but as to the relations among men, the old saying holds true: *Judaeus Judaeo lupus*. Loyalty, unity, and bonding are no concern of the Jew. Consequently, where other people profit from a fruitful interaction of the two forms of socialization (i.e., the family and the *Männerbund*), with the Jews there is a sterile division. Nature has visited this fate upon them and thus they wander through history, cursed never to be a people [*Volk*], always to remain a mere race. They have lost their state. (Blüher 1919b: 170; emphases in the original; English translation in Hewitt 1996: 123, 125)

Geller argues that the mystery of the stateless survival of the Jews was for Blüher to be found in their devotion to sexuality and family. Here is the corroborating quotation from Blüher: "There are people who are simply exterminated as peoples and therefore disappear, but this cannot be the case with the Jews, for a secret process internal to their being as a people constantly displaces the energy typically directed toward male bonding onto the family. Consequently, the Jews maintain themselves as race through overemphasis of the family" (Blüher 1921: 170; English translation in Hewitt 1996: 125). Thus the "weakness of male bonding" amongst the Jews culminates for Blüher in the paradox of their simultaneous (heterosexual) hypersexualization *and* effeminization. After the break between Freud and Blüher, the latter wrote a series of anti-Jewish treatises, in which he describes Jewish thought as materialistic and corrupt. Thus, in *Secessio Judaica*, we read: "even [Freud's] valuable

thoughts become fruitful only when they pass through a German brain ...."
(Blüher 1922: 24)

Brother Clan and Brother Group: the Importance of Homoerotic Bonds in Freud's Theory of Culture

At the beginning of human culture and all higher social orders there is an egalitarian male society. Fundamental passages on the theory of culture in *Totem and Taboo* revolve around the aggressive, socially creative, and emotional potentials of this form of organization, which Freud sometimes calls "male community" (*Männergemeinschaften*), sometimes "clan of brothers" (*Brüderclan*), sometimes "band of brothers" (*Brüderbund*), sometimes "communions of brothers" (*Brudergemeinde*), and, in *Group Psychology and the Analysis of the Ego*, with a view to the jointly committed murder, even "brother mobs" (Brudermasse) (Freud GW, 13: 152).[5] Unfortunately, as has already been noted, almost all the differently connoted terms for the *Brüderclan*, with the exception of "male bands" (*Männerbünde*), were translated into English as "community of brothers" or "clan of brothers."

The clan of brothers runs through Freud's work from *Totem and Taboo* and *Group Psychology and the Analysis of the Ego* to his late religious-philosophical essay *Moses and Monotheism*. In 1939, as a designation for these fraternities in this last work, Freud even makes use of the then highly charged term *Männergemeinschaft* ("male community") (Freud 1965: 169; Freud SE, 23: 131). What kind of social and erotic feelings bond together male societies, and what indirect or open role homosexuality thereby plays, occupied his thoughts from the beginning. On page 144 of *Totem and Taboo*, he speaks plainly of "homosexual feelings" (Freud SE, 13: 144). A little further in the text, he avoids speaking of open homosexuality or even of homoeroticism as the bonding force of the community of brothers, and now emphasizes familial and homosocial feelings of solidarity as the elements upon which civil culture is based:[6]

> The social fraternal feelings, which were the basis of the whole transformation, continued to exercise a profound influence on the development of so-

---

5   Inadequately rendered in SE as "brother groups."

6   I use the term "homosocial" in Eve Kosofsky Sedgwick's sense; cf. Sedgwick, *Between Men*.

ciety. They found expression in the sanctification of the blood tie, in the emphasis upon the solidarity of all life within the same clan. (Freud SE, 13: 146)

The reference to the hatred of the father and the heterosexual desire for his wives as the prime motive for the crucial murder further diminishes the culture-creating potency of homosexual bonds. In the final section of *Totem and Taboo*, Freud then has his evolutionary model of cultural history culminate in the modern, oedipally-structured family with the father as its chief. We find a similar avoidance of homosexual libido and homoerotic ties in Freud's foundation narrative of the family hero Oedipus. Here, too, the psychoanalyst deals very selectively with the ancient mythical-literary material. Robin N. Mitchell-Boyask studied Freud's notes on the mythic sources and concluded: "The Oedipus he chose was the result of long and careful deliberation. Freud's exclusion of Laius's homosexuality and its consequences marks Freud's insistence on the experiences of the specifically Sophoclean hero and their implication for all individual men." (Mitchell-Boyask 1994: 34) In a separate chapter of *Group Psychology* on the subject of identification, Freud seeks to shed more light on the central hinge between individual and group psychology. The early oedipal father-identification serves thereby as both a model and an antidote for the dissolution of the individual ego in the mass, a concept which was tinged with feminine connotations even before Le Bon. For Le Bon, precisely the characteristic of pulling the bourgeois self into the maelstrom and delivering it to the unconscious and the emotions makes the masses feminine, because "[c]rowds are everywhere distinguished by feminine characteristics, but Latin crowds are the most feminine at all" (Le Bon 2002 [1896]: 13). By contrast, for Freud nothing is more important to emphasize about the father-identification than its masculinity. And in the same place we find a tellingly open remark about the menacing "feminine" attitude of the son. The young Oedipus can act the part of the destroyer of the sphinx and a resistance hero because:

> We may say simply that he takes his father as his ideal. This behavior has nothing to do with a passive or feminine attitude towards his father (and towards males in general); it is on the contrary typically *masculine*. It fits very well with the Oedipus complex, for which it helps to prepare the way. (Freud SE, 18: 105)

In *Group Psychology*, which treats the analysis of modern mass formations, Freud returns to *Totem and Taboo*'s primordial horde and clan theory of brothers and sisters, and now parallels the primordial horde with the masses in order to explain the transformation from individual psychology into mass psychology:

> The primal father had prevented his sons from satisfying their directly sexual impulsions; he forced them into abstinence and consequently into emotional ties with him and one another which could arise out of those of their impulsions that were inhibited in their sexual aim. He forced them, so to speak, into group psychology. (Freud SE, vol. 18: 141)

Here, Freud speaks of the fact that in the artificial masses, church, and army as well as in the masses in general, there "is no room for woman as sexual object" and "it seems certain that homosexual love is far more compatible with group ties, even when it takes the shape of uninhibited sexual impulses" (ibid). In a note in the same text, we now find a narrative about the drive-motivated patricide that qualifies the oedipal construction. No longer solely the desire for incest, but now also mutual homosexual desire and love triggered the impulse to parricide: "It may perhaps be also assumed that the sons, when they were driven out and separated from their father, advanced from identification with one another to homosexual object-love, and in this way won freedom to kill their father." (ibid, note 1) The fluctuations in Freud's conception of the clan of brothers and the affectional bonds at work therein, noticeable since *Totem and Taboo*, are reflected in *Group Psychology* not least in the choice of words. At the beginning of the German text, Freud speaks of "der Umwandlung der Vaterhorde in eine Brüdergemeinde" (Freud GW, 13: 136; "the transformation of the paternal horde into a community of brothers," Freud S, 18: 122), *Brüdergemeinde* or "communion of brothers" being a seemingly religious term (Freud SE, 18: 122), and later, entirely following Robertson Smith, of the *Brüdergemeinschaft* (Freud GW, 13: 152; "totemic community of brothers," Freud SE, 18: 135). If, however, we pursue the changing names of the "group of brothers" or "fraternal clan" throughout the text, the contrast between community of brothers and mob (German *Masse*) of brothers (in the English translation unfortunately always "group") dissolves to the extent of their becoming completely identical at one point: the "fraternal clan" becomes the *Brudermasse* (Freud GW, 18: 152; "group of brothers," Freud SE, 18: 135). Again, the English translation levels the important linguistic nuance. In the extreme case of the "mob of brothers," the otherwise clearly drawn boundaries between "savage" primordial horde, feminine-tinged regressive crowd (cf. Le Bon) and a civilizing "male band" performatively establishing a society, are done away with in the original German.

In Freud's narrative of the patricide that creates culture, the clan of brothers is supposed to pursue a decidedly *male game* (that is to say, a heterosexual one) of incestuous desire and father hatred. *Totem and Taboo* tells the tale of how the group of rebellious sons, on whose shoulders cultural development will rest, was strengthened by homoerotic social bonding. With this idea, Claudia Bruns also thinks that "he [Freud] tied in directly with Blüher" (Bruns 2008: 303). And in the previously cited comment in *Group Psychology*, Freud even speculated, as we have already seen, that the homosexual bonds of brotherhood could also have been a factor in triggering the impetus to patricide. At the moment in *Totem and Taboo*, when the ambivalence of the paternal bond leads to establishing the "father cult" and all ethical principles, Freud naturally no longer spoke of homoeroticism as the central binding agent, but rather only of "societal fraternal feelings" (Freud SE, 13: 146).

Fight against Antisemitism

In the renewed resurgence of the primordial horde theory in *Moses and Monotheism*, Freud's attempt to definitively cleanse the male band that created culture of all vestiges of homosexual and even homoerotic libido gained in explosive political force. In addition to the great religious-historical subject of the foundation of monotheistic father-religion by the people of Israel, the book, which was first published in its entirety in 1939 by an Amsterdam publisher, also treats the then highly topical question of the cultural reasons for antisemitism. In view of the powerful male band then ruling Germany, and as a response to its racist antisemitism, Freud was very keen to avoid any connection between psychoanalysis or the Jewish tradition with *Männerbund* ideologies.[7] Geller has emphasized that Freud was concerned with two things: "to silence the association of male Jews with effeminate homosexuals," but at the same time to "distanc[e] himself and the Jewish people from the now Aryan-identified [...] Männerbund" (Geller 2003: 111).

---

7   While elements characteristic of the male band shaped the National Socialists and
     emerged particularly in the early days of the SA, historical research has in general re-
     frained from classifying the NSDAP as a Männerbund; cf. Winter 2013.

According to *Moses and Monotheism*, the mob or clan of brothers of the "primitive" Israelite ex-slaves, a "stiff-necked people" (Freud SE, 23: 36) that resembles *Totem and Taboo*'s community of brothers, murdered their leader Moses. In the course of founding a religion, a civilized brother clan then concludes its covenant with God by establishing the Decalogue. This was the "triumph of intellectuality over sensuality, or strictly speaking, an instinctual renunciation [*Triebverschicht*]" (Freud 1965: 150), "with all its necessary psychological consequences" (Freud SE, 23: 113). The spiritualizing effect of the imageless Jewish religion, Freud emphasizes, then helped the Israelites "to check the brutality and the tendency to violence which are apt to appear where the development of muscular strength is the popular ideal" (ibid: 115). In this variant of the story of patricide and the band of brothers, the sons' heterosexual desires are now expressly stressed, and every hint of a possible homosexual bond is obliterated: "The lot of the sons was a hard one: if they roused their father's jealousy they were killed or castrated or driven out. Their only resource was to collect together in small communities, to get themselves wives by robbery" (Freud SE, 23: 81). Thus every association of the Israelite band of brothers with homosexuality is erased. In this way, Freud eliminated from his theory of culture and religion any proximity to the homoerotically bonded Männerbund in Blüher's sense.

Looking back from *Moses and Monotheism*, readers with an interest in religious studies in particular must be surprised that *Totem and Taboo* contains almost no reference to the Jewish religion. In this work, Christianity, as the religion of the son, seems to have emerged solely from pagan cults. Particularly symptomatic here is that the story of the *Akedah*, or binding of Isaac, which is fundamental to Judaism, is missing in Freud's list of founding sacrificial myths of religion and culture. This is all the more striking as in the religious narrative God first demands the sacrifice of the only son, only then to relent at the last moment and allow substitution by a sacrificial animal and the commandment of circumcision. Thus, the story is not only about Abraham's test of faith and the establishment of the covenant, but also about the binding of Isaac as one of the instituting legends of the fleshly signs of covenant that every Jewish man bears on his genitals – circumcision. In *Totem and Taboo*, the single mention of circumcision is found in a footnote on the death of Attis by castration (Freud SE, 13: 153, note 1). In *Moses and Monotheism*, circumcision is identified as an Egyptian tradition and thus relocated to a different culture. If Freud renders Jewish religious history and the Israelite culture of circumcision as good as invisible, he nevertheless gives them well-nigh central importance in the psychoanalytic theory of antisemitism. For Freud, cultural antisemitism, which at the same time implies the effeminization of the Jewish man, rests among other things on the unconscious assumption of a connection between circumcision and castration. In a famous footnote in an *Analysis of a Phobia in a Five-Year Old Boy* (1909), Freud boldly declares the circumcision of the Jews to be a psychological cause of antisemitism. The case study of little Hans was to play a role not only in the verification of the theory of the Oedipus complex, but also served in *Totem and Taboo* as a reference for the infantile return of totemism. Referring to Otto Weininger, Freud explains:

> The castration complex is the deepest unconscious root of anti-Semitism; for even in the nursery little boys hear that a Jew has something cut off his penis – a piece of his penis, they think – and this gives them a right to despise Jews. And there is no stronger unconscious root for the same sense of superiority over women. Weininger, in a chapter [of *Sex and Character*] that has attracted much attention, treated Jews and women with equal hostility and overwhelmed them with the same insults. Being a neurotic, Weininger was completely under the sway of his infantile complexes; and from that standpoint what is common to Jews and women is their relation to the castration complex. (Freud SE, 10: 36, note 1)

The article about little Hans, who was actually the little Herbert Graf, is a case analysis that Freud carried out together with the child's father, Max Graf, a Jewish member of the Wednesday Psychological Society. In Freud's psychoanalysis, it was to gain the status of central empirical evidence for the correctness of the Oedipus complex as a universal model of normal male development. Thus, the positive emphasis on the homoerotic bonds of the male associations that founded civilization and the avoidance of everything Jewish in the religious-historical institution of circumcision in *Totem and Taboo* throw light on Freud's still epic struggle for assimilation and recognition around 1912/13. The blank space in *Totem and Taboo* points at the same time to Freud's postcolonial outsider position in Austro-German culture of the time. As Geller was the first to show, the role that male societies play in Freud's prehistory of culture and religion, and the question of what affects and emotions hold these societies together, cannot be separated from the historical context of an increasing antisemitism fed by Männerbund propaganda and male fantasies. They are also directed against the antisemitic feminization of the Jewish male:

The changes in Freud's depiction of homosexuality in his accounts of social origins – the increasingly sharp distinction between homosexuality and homosociality, which ultimately culminated in the foreclosure of homosexuality from Freud's narrative of origins – may be connected with the anti-Semitic, *völkisch* turn of *Männerbund* (male-band) theories as well as the racialization of homosexual identities. (Geller 2003: 90-91)

This chapter has placed Freud's cultural-theoretical reflections on foundational male associations, sacrifice, and patricide in historical context. It has focused on the various connotations of the social model of the clan of brothers and set them against the backdrop of waxing antisemitism. Following Erdheim's recommendation (1992), the chapter has read Freud's culture-theoretical essay *Totem and Taboo* with a view to its diagnostic power and as a reaction to his own time. After National Socialism had extended its domain to Austria, Freud had to complete *Moses and Monotheism*, his last commentary on (civilizing) foundational violence, on the community of brothers and the history on antisemitism, in London exile. In the end, the victorious "Aryan male band" and a murderous *völkisch* ideology had driven the father of psychoanalysis out of Vienna.

Bibliography

Adorno, Theodor W./Horkheimer, Max (2002 [1947]): Dialectic of Enlightenment. Philosophical Fragments, Stanford (California): Stanford University Press.

Assmann, Jan (1998): Moses der Ägypter. Entzifferung einer Gedächtnisspur, München: Hanser.

Blüher, Hans (1918): Familie und Männerbund, Leipzig: Der Neue Geist.

Blüher, Hans (1919 [1917]): Die Rolle der Erotik in der männlichen Gesellschaft. Eine Theorie der menschlichen Staatenbildung nach Wesen und Wert, Vol. 1: Der Typus Inversus, Jena: Diederichs.

Blüher, Hans (3rd ed.. 1921 [1919]): Die Rolle der Erotik in der männlichen Gesellschaft. Eine Theorie der menschlichen Staatenbildung nach Wesen und Wert, Vol. 2: Familie und Männerbund, Jena: Diederichs.

Blüher, Hans (1922): Secessio judaica. Philosophische Grundlegung der historischen Sicht des Judentums und der antisemitischen Bewegung, Berlin: Der weiße Ritter.

Blüher, Hans (1953): Werke und Tage. Geschichte eines Denkers, München: Paul List.

Böhme, Hartmut (2011): "Die Antike nach Freud." In: Claudia Benthien/ Hartmut Böhme/Inge Stephan (eds.), Freud und die Antike, Göttingen: Wallstein, pp. 423-456.

Boyarin, Daniel (1995): "Freud's Baby, Fliess's Maybe: Homophobia, Anti-Semitism, and the Invention of Oedipus." In: GLQ: A Journal of Lesbian and Gay Studies I-2 (Winter-Spring): pp. 115-147.

Boyarin, Daniel (1997): Unheroic Conduct. The Rise of Heterosexuality and the Invention of the Jewish Man, Berkeley: University of California Press.

Brunotte, Ulrike (2004): Zwischen Eros und Krieg. Männerbund und Ritual in der Moderne, Berlin: Wagenbach.

Brunotte, Ulrike (2017): "Classical Ritual Theories." In: Richard King (ed.), Religion, Theory, Critique. Classic and Contemporary Approaches and Methodologies, NewYork: Columbia University Press.

Brunotte, Ulrike (2020): "Queering Judaism and Masculinist Inventions: German Homonationalism Around 1900." In: Marco Derks/Mariecke ban den Berg (eds.),Public Discourses About Homosexuality and Religion in Europe and Beyond, Cham (Switzerland): Palgrave Macmillan, pp. 125-146.

Bruns, Claudia (2008): Politik des Eros. Der Männerbund in Wissenschaft, Politik und Jugendkultur (1880-1934), Köln/Weimar/Wien: Böhlau.

Bruns, Claudia (2011): "Kontroversen zwischen Freud, Blüher und Hirschfeld. Zur Pathologisierung und Rassisierung des effeminierten Homosexuellen." In: Ulrike Auga et al. (eds.), Dämonen, Vamps und Hysterikerinnen. Geschlechter- und Rassenfigurationen in Wissen, Medien und Alltag um 1900, Bielefeld: transcript, pp. 161-184.

Bruns, Claudia (2018): "How gay is Germany? Homosexuality, politics and racism in historical perspective." In: Achim Rohde/Christina von Braun/ Stefanie Schüler- Springorum (eds.), National Politics and Sexuality in Transregional Perspective. The Homophobic Argument, New York: Routledge, pp. 88-104.

Burkert, Walter (1972): Homo Necans, Berlin/New York: De Gruyter.

Burkert, Walter (1983): Anthropologie des religiösen Opfers. Schriften der Carl Friedrich von Siemens Stiftung, München.

Bublitz, Hannelore (1998): Das Geschlecht der Moderne. Genealogie und Archäologie der Geschlechterdifferenz, Frankfurt a.M./New York: Campus.

Chidester, David (1996): Savage Systems: Colonialism and Comparative Religion in Southern Africa. Charlottesville: University Press of Virginia.

Chidester, David (2014) Empire of Religion: Imperialism and Comparative Religion. Chicago: University of Chicago Press.

Connell, Raewyn (2005 [1995]), Masculinities, Berkeley: University of California Press.

DiCenso, James J. (1996): "*Totem and Taboo* and the Constitutive Function of Symbolic Forms." In: Journal of the American Academy of Religion LXIV/3, Vol. 64, No. 3 (Autumn), pp. 557-574.

Durkheim, Émile (2001[1912]): The Elementary Forms of Religious Life, Oxford University Press.

Erdheim, Mario (1991): "Zur Lektüre von Freuds *Totem and Taboo*." In: Mario Erdheim (ed.), Sigmund Freud: Totem und Tabu Einige Übereinstimmungen im Seelenleben der Wilden und der Neurotiker, Frankfurt a.M.: Fischer pp. 7-42.

Evans-Pritchard, Edward (1968 [1881]): Theories of primitive Religion, Oxford: Oxford University Press.

Fischer-Lichte, Erika (2008): The Transformative Power of Performance. A New Aesthetics, New York: Routledge.

Foucault, Michel (1990 [1984]: History of Sexuality, Vol. I, New York: Vintage.

Fout, John C. (1992): "Sexual Politics in Wilhelmine Germany: The Male Gender Crisis, Moral Purity, and Homophobia." In: Journal of History of Sexuality 2(3), pp. 388-421.

Freud, Sigmund (1972-1976): Gesammelte Werke [henceforth GW], Anna Freud (ed.)5th-7th ed., 18 vols. Frankfurt/M: Fischer.

Freud, Sigmund (1976, 6th ed. [1900]): Die Traumdeutung, GW, Bd. 2/3, pp. 1-722.

Freud, Sigmund (1972, 5th ed. [1905]: Drei Abhandlungen zur Sexualtheorie, GW, Vol. 5, pp. 127-145.

Freud, Sigmund (1973 [1908]): Die kulturelle Sexualmoral und die moderne Nervosität, GW, Vol. 7, pp. 143-169.

Freud, Sigmund (1973 [1909]): Analyse der Phobie eines fünfjährigen Knaben, GW, Bd. 7, pp. 343-377.

Freud, Sigmund (1972, 5th. ed. [1912/13]): Totem and Taboo, GW, Bd. 9, 5. Aufl., pp. 2-194. Freud, Sigmund (1972, 7th. ed. [1921]): Massenpsychologie und Ich-Analyse, GW, Vol. 13, pp. 71-161.

Freud, Sigmund (1965 [1939]), Der Mann Moses und die monotheistische Religion, Frankfurt a.M.: Suhrkamp.

Freud, Sigmund (1953-74): The Standard Edition [henceforth SE] of the Complete Works of Sigmund Freud. Translated and edited by James Strachey, 24 vols., London: Hogarth Press and Institute of Psycho-Analysis. (Titles listed in order of appearance in the SE, with original date of publication in parentheses.)

Freud, Sigmund: The Interpretation of Dreams, 4-5: 4-627 [1900].

Freud, Sigmund: Three Essays of the Theory of Sexuality, 7: 1-122 [1905].

Freud, Sigmund: "Civilized Sexual Morality and Modern Nervous Illness." 9: 177-204 [1908].

Freud, Sigmund: "Analysis of the phobia in a Five-Year-Old Boy." 10: 1-147 [1909].

Freud, Sigmund: Totem and Taboo, 13: 1-161 [1912-13].

Freud, Sigmund: "Group Psychology and the Analysis of the Ego." 18: 65-143 [1921].

Freud, Sigmund (1939): Moses and Monotheism, 23: 1-137 [1934-1939].

Freud, Sigmund/C.G. Jung: Briefwechsel (1974), William Mc Guire/Wolfgang Sauerländer (eds.), Frankfurt a.M.: Fischer.

Gay, Peter (1987): A Godless Jew. Atheism and the Making of Psychoanalysis, London: Yale University Press.

Geller, Jay (2003): "Freud, Blüher, and the Secessio Inversa. Männerbünde, Homosexuality, and Freud's Theory of Cultural Formation." In: Daniel Boyarin/Daniel Itzkovitz/Ann Pellegrini (eds): Queer Theory and the Jewish Question, New York: Columbia University Press, pp. 90-120.

Geller, Jay (2007): On Freud's Jewish Body. Mitigating Circumcision, New York: Fordham University Press.

Geller, Jay (2008): "The queerest cut of all: Freud, Beschneidung, Homosexualität und maskulines Judentum." In: Ulrike Brunotte/Rainer Herrn (eds): Männlichkeiten und Moderne. Geschlecht in Wissenskulturen um 1900, Bielefeld: transcript, pp. 157-172.

Gilman, Sander L. (1993a): The Case of Sigmund Freud, Baltimore/London: Johns Hopkins University Press.

Gilman, Sander L. (1993b): Freud, Race, and Gender, Princeton: Princeton University Press.

Girard, René (1992, [1972]): Das Heilige und die Gewalt, Frankfurt a.M.: Fischer.

Green, André (2004): Die tote Mutter, Gießen: Psychosozial-Verlag.

Haas, Eberhard Th. (2000): "Opferritual und Behälter. Versuch der Rekonstruktion von Totem and Taboo: Weitere Übereinstimmungen im Seelenleben der Wilden und der Neurotiker." In: Psyche 54 (11), pp. 1110-1140.

Haas, Eberhard Th. (2012): "Editorial." In: 100 Jahre Totem and Taboo. Freud und die Fundamente der Kultur, Gießen: Psychosozial, pp. 7-13.

Hamburger, Andreas (2005): "Das Motiv der Urhorde. Erbliche oder erlebte Erfahrung in Totem und Tabu." In: Ortrud Gutjahr (ed.), Kulturtheorie, Würzburg: Königshausen & Neumann, pp. 45-85.

Heinrich, Klaus (1985): Versuch über die Schwierigkeit nein zu sagen, Frankfurt a.M.: Roter Stern.

Hewitt, Andrew (1996): Political Inversions. Homosexuality, Fascism, and the Modernist Imaginary, Stanford: Stanford University Press.

Höfler, Otto (1993 [1934]): Kultische Geheimbünde der Germanen, Vol. 1, Frankfurt a.M.: Verlag der Manufactur.

Kippenberg, Hans (1997): Die Entdeckung der Religionsgeschichte. Religionswissenschaft und Moderne, München: Beck.

Klein, Melanie (1994, [1962]): Das Seelenleben des Kleinkindes, Stuttgart: Ernst Klett.

Kohl, Karl-Heinz (1987): Abwehr und Verlangen. Zur Geschichte der Ethnologie, Frankfurt a.M.: Qumran.

Kohl, Karl-Heinz (1999): "Der sakrale Königsmord. Zur Geschichte der Kulturmorphologie." In: Paideuma. Mitteilungen zur Kulturkunde 45, pp. 63-82.

Kramer, Fritz (1977): Verkehrte Welten. Zur imaginären Ethnographie des 19. Jahrhunderts, Frankfurt a.M.: Syndikat.

Kristeva, Julia (1982 [1980]): Powers of Horror. An Essay on Abjection, translated by Jennifer Curtiss Gage, Ithaca (NY): University of California Press.

Le Bon, Gustave (2002 [1895]): The Crowd: A Study of the Popular Mind, Mineola, New York: Dover Publications.

Le Rider, Jacques (1982): Le Cas Otto Weininger: Racines de l'antifeminisme et l'antisemitisme, Paris: Presses Universitaire de France.

McLennan, John (2015 [1865]): Primitive Marriage, Oxford: Andesite Press.

Mitchell-Boyask, Robin N. (1994): "Freud's Reading of Classical Literature and Classical Philology." In: Sander Gilman et al. (eds), Reading Freud's Reading, pp. 23-46.

Morgan, Lewis H. (1985 [1877]): Ancient Society, Chicago: University of Arizona Press.

Mosse, George L. (1996): The Image of Man, The Creation of Modern Masculinity, Oxford (UK): Oxford University Press.

Neubauer, John (1996): "Sigmund Freud und Hans Blüher in bisher unveröffentlichten Briefen. " In: Psyche. Zeitschrift für Psychoanalyse und ihre Anwendungen 50, pp. 123-148.

Pratt, Marie Louise (2007): Imperial Eyes: Travel Writing and Transculturation, New York: Routledge.

Schorske, Carl (1973): "Politics and Patricide in Freud's Interpretations of Dreams." In: American Historical Review 78, pp. 328—347.

Schurtz, Heinrich (1902): Altersklassen und Männerbünde. Darstellung der Grundformen der Gesellschaft, Berlin: Georg Reimer.

Sedgwick, Eve Kosofsky (1993): Between Men. English Literature and Male homosexual Desire, New York: Columbia University Press.

Smith, William Robertson (2005 [1889/1894]) Lectures on the Religion of the Semites, London: Adam and Charles Black.

Strachey, James (1955): Editor's Note to Vol. XIII, The Standard Edition of the Complete Psychological Works of Sigmund Freud, pp. II- XV.

Theweleit, Klaus: (2013 [1977/1979]): Male Fantasies, Vol. 1: Women, Flood, Bodies. Cambridge (UK): Polity Press.

Turner, Victor (1989, [1969]): Das Ritual. Struktur und Anti-Struktur, Frankfurt a.M.: Campus.

Versnel, Henrik S. (1993): Transition and Reversal in Myth and Ritual, Leiden/ New York/Köln.

von Schnurbein, Stefanie (2005): "Sander Gilman: Freud Identität und Geschlecht." In: Martina Löw/Bettina Mathes (eds.), Schlüsselwerke der Geschlechterforschung, Wiesbaden: Verlag für Sozialwissenschaften, pp. 283-295.

Wesel, Uwe (1999): Der Mythos vom Matriarchat. Über Bachofens Mutterrecht und die Stellung von Frauen in frühen Gesellschaften, Frankfurt a.M.: Suhrkamp.

Winter, Sebastian (2013): "Sippengemeinschaft statt Männerbund. Über die historische Genese der Männlichkeitsentwürfe in der SS und die ihnen unterliegende Psychodynamik." In: Anette Diedrich/Ljiljana Heise (eds), Männlichkeitskonstruktionen im NS, Formen, Funktionen und Wirkungsmacht von Geschlechterkonstruktionen im Nationalsozialismus und ihre Reflexion in der pädagogischen Praxis, Bern: Peter Lang: pp. 25-81.

5. The "Jewess Question"[1]. The Figure of the *"Beautiful Jewess"* between (Self-)Orientalism and Antisemitism

The first three chapters focused on "effeminization" as a central discursive tool for othering the male Jew at the beginning of the twenties century. Mainly chapter four moreover analyzes the influence of a masculinist homophobic antisemitism in selected works of Jewish scholars, in particular that of Sigmund Freud, and asks how he reacted to and in what ways he internalized and resisted antisemitic attributions.

As already said in the introduction the "femininity puzzle" of the book's title unfolds in two ways: it firstly analyzes the role of effeminization of the male Jew and his "modern queer sexualization" (Boyarin 1997) in racialized discourse and it secondly pays attention to the transgressive and liminal forms of femininity that were attributed to Jewish women, especially in their allosemitic orientalization as "Beautiful Jewess" in 19th century arts, opera and literature. Especially in French literature and nineteenth century art, the figure of the Jewess was "ubiquitously conflated with the Oriental woman, and recognized by her stylized sensual beauty: her large dark eyes, abundant hair and languid expression" (Valman 2007: 4). Ingres, who was famous for his *Grande Odalisque* (1814) and his orientalist depictions of the Harem did also produce an orientalized image of the rich Parisian Jewess. As suggested by Carol Ockman (1995: 67) his portrait of the *Baronne de Rothschild* (1848) uses "orientalist" and "ethnic stereotyping" (ibid.) to refer to her Jewish femininity.

Ockman also discusses the enthusiastic description of the portrait by the art critic Gustave Geofroy to underline her analysis. He wrote:

---

1   Cit. Valman 2007: 1.

The artist's model, seated on a divan, faces front, as if she were engaged in an attentive little chat, with knees crossed, the left hand lightly supporting her chin, the right arm thrown across her body with abandon, and holding a closed fan. [...] Two large eyebrows a *l''orientale* are outlined on her forehead [...] and, in like manner, her eyes sparkle with life and wit. (Geofroy 1848: 447, quoted from Tinterow 1999: 425)

Fig. 7: Jean-Auguste-Dominique Ingres: Portrait of the Baronne de Rothschild (1848), Private Collection.

Public Domain, Wikimedia Commons

Focussing on the similar pictorial representation of women in classical orientalist paintings, Ockman especially mentions the description of the exuberant
delicacy of her dress, the eyes and eyebrows a *l'orientale* and the "sensuality"
(ibid. 77) to emphasize her thesis that the artist and the viewer as well as many
French authors from Balsac via Flaubert to Huysmans were using the same
coded language to create the Jewess as a "femme Orientale" (Ockman 1995:
68-69, see also Fournier 2011).

This chapter will again follow an allosemitic (Bauman 1998: 143-156) approach to embrace the ambivalence and instability of the figure of the "Beautiful Jewess" in German literature. European orientalism had different societal and cultural frames in France and the UK, which were the main objects
of investigation in Said's book *Orientalism*, it was an explicit political-colo-
nial setting and colonial discourse. According to Said's widely criticised thesis (overview, cf. Polaschegg 2005 and Riegert 2009), Germany as a country
without many colonies, did not play an important role in the scholarly and
political enactment of orientalism. Referring back to the prestigious German
orientalist and Biblical scholarship (Erwin 1981-82: 108-9, Lewis 1993), but also
to processes of internal orientalization as tools of Germany's "colonial fantasies" and minority politics (Zantop 1997), this chapter explores discourses
on the "Orient" as a prominent way to discursively construct the Jewess as
Internal Other, but also her self-empowering role in German-Jewish self-orientalization. During the 19th century, self-orientalization became a tool in the
hands of Jewish artists for negotiating the emancipation of women and Jews.
Moving beyond Said's dictum that orientalism is "a strange, secret sharer of
Western anti-Semitism" (Said 1978: 27-28), in this chapter I investigate the
plural history of topical discourses, hybrid figures and recurrent narratives,
symbolizing internal religious and cultural differences. Building on different
discursive junctures between Jewishness and women (femaleness) the chapter
analyses the "Beautiful Jewess" as an exemplary liminal figure, torn between
different cultures and religions.

Historically, Jews have often been regarded "concurrently as occidental *and*
oriental" (Kalmar/Penslar 2005: xii) in the Western world. The liminal position
of the Jews in European imagination is all the more relevant when it comes to
the gendered dimension of orientalist discourse. Starting from the presupposition of her situatedness on a cultural frontier, the chapter concentrates
on the depiction of the "Beautiful Jewess" in literature. It analyses how literature explores the ambivalences of the stereotype and opens up third spaces
of reflection. Narrative and scenic discourses on the orient are analyzed as a

multilayered and ambivalent ensemble of relational references. A special focus lies on the role of gender in the representation of the Jews as "internal Orientals" (Aschheim [2010] 2017: 13).

The *"Beautiful Jewess"* as European Fantasy

The figure of the "Beautiful Jewess" became a literary preoccupation in nineteenth-century Europe. These literary constructions functioned as the gendered and emotional embodiment of the "Jewish Question" (cf. Valman 2007). Following approaches of postcolonial and gender studies, the chapter investigates the extent to which the "Beautiful Jewess" can be analyzed as a "figure of the third" (Holz 2005; Eßlinger et al. 2010), i.e. as a paradox figure of a non-identity, a marker of borderlines and as a placeholder for hybrid knowledge. Since the Enlightenment period, the "Jewish Question" referred to the debate on whether the Jewish religious minority could be integrated as equal to the Christian majority and how the Jews assimilated as citizens in the modern nation-states. The "Jewish Question" became a litmus test for Enlightenment ideals of emancipation and demonstrated the ambivalence of modern European universalism. At the latest since the nation-building process in the nineteenth century, Jewish identity has posed "a number of insurmountable difficulties" (Mufti 2007: 41). According to Susannah Heschel, the German discourse on the "Jewish Question" can be interpreted as a "proto-colonist enterprise" (Heschel 1999, 62-63). Her analysis is concentrated on the intertwinement of "identities of colonizer and colonized" (64). Susanne Zantop (1997) also demonstrates that the absence of colonies did minimize neither Germany's influence on orientalist discourse nor the bearing that colonial discourse had on German constructions of national identity. Focussing on the case study of Johann David Michaelis (1717-1791), Jonathan Hess (2012) points out that influential German orientalists and Protestant theologians were responsible for the anti-Judaic orientalization of contemporary Jews. "Such attitudes," however, as Steven E. Aschheim (2017: 13) argues, "were not limited to overt Jew-haters." Thus Herder called the Jews "the Asiatics of Europe," Voltaire designated the ancient Jews as "vagrant Arabs infested with leprosy," and even the champion of Jewish rights, Christian Wilhelm Dohm, spoke of Jews as "Asiatic refugees."

Despite these trends within the debate on the "Jewish Question" in the European national-building processes, Kalmar and Penslar warn of the consequences to equate colonialism with antisemitism when it comes to the study of orientalism: "Orientalism is an instance of colonial discourse, but it is also more than that. This holds true for Orientalism in general and certainly for Orientalism where it concerns the Jews" (Kalmar and Penslar 2005: xviii). Especially the nineteenth century witnessed a plurality of romantic-poetic idealizations of the "Orient" and moreover poetic and scholarly self-orientalisations of the Jews (see Wittler 2015: 63-81). In her ground-breaking book, *Der andere Orientalismus* (2005), Andrea Polaschegg "highlighted the weakness of Said's homogenizing conception and advanced in its stead a pluralistic, relational, and dialectic conception of oriental and colonial discourses" (Brunotte, Ludewig, Stähler 2015: 7). Focussing on case studies of poetic and literary orientalization, this chapter follows Victor Turner's approach to the liminal space "betwixt and between" (Turner 1967), Bauman's (1991) and Klaus Holz' (2005) ambivalent "figure of the third" as well as Homi Bhabha's assumption of a "third" or "hybrid space" of relational identity constructions (Bhabha 1994). In his essay on stereotypes and colonial discourse Bhabha states that even a stereotype is not a fixed image, which is entirely knowable, but a figure that is overdetermined, opague, and ambivalent:

> Likewise the stereotype, which is its major discursive strategy, is a form of knowledge and identification that vacillates between what is always "in place", already known, and something that must be anxiously repeated ... as if the essential duplicity of the Asiatic or the bestial sexual license of the African that needs no proof, can never really, in discourse, be proved. It is this process of *ambivalence*, central to the stereotype that my essay explores as it constructs a theory of colonial discourse. (Bhabha in Newton 1997: 293-301, 293)

As already mentioned the chapter investigates the extent to which the "Beautiful Jewess" functions as a "figure of the third" (Eßlinger et al. 2010, Holz 2005). To go beyond the fixed dichotomy of anti-Jewish and philosemitic discourse, Zygmunt Bauman's term "allosemtism" (Bauman 1998: 143-156) is preferable. A guiding question will be the following: how does the metaphorical language of literature make use of the ambivalence of the orientalist and the antisemitic stereotypes to open up new spaces of reflection? Following my own research (Brunotte 2015) as well as Valman's, and Sicher's approaches, the chapter asks how narrative figurations – especially the Jewish daughter and her father – of cultural and religious differences are gendered (Valman 2007; Sicher 2017). It will show in particular the intertwinement of idealized and demonized femininity and orientalization within literary constructions of the "Beautiful Jewess".

Wilhelm Hauff's "Jud Süss" (1827): German-Jewish Identity Struggles

Sander Gilman claims that "The Jew was always defined as a masculine category" (1998: 67) in European antisemitic discourse; "the Jewish body served as a model for the body of the alien. This fantastic body of the Jew was marked by its ugliness, his visible and invisible otherness" (1999: 3-4). Yet, as Barbara Hahn has argued on the basis of Bernard Picart's *Cérémonies et costumes religieuses* (1727–1743), Jewish women were seldomly as clearly marked as Jewish men were (Hahn 2005: 33). Along with the emancipation of the Jews – yet in the early nineteenth century at the latest – however, the Jewish woman, as the "Beautiful Jewess" became a literary, artistic, and theatrical figure in Europe. This figure, which expanded into the European imagination, also got a seismographic function. Eric Fournier (2011: 9) notes her allosemitic quality:

> More than other representations of the Jewish world, this ambivalent figure of the Other did in fact appear with an intensified plasticity, which was capable of expressing, in frenetic manner, the entire range of judgements and opinions about Judaism, from philosemitism to Antisemitism.

French artists and authors were prominent in Europe not only for their creation of the oriental Odalisque, but also of the "Beautiful Jewess". The most famous example, and paradigmatic for this time, was Formenthal Halévy's and Eugène Scribe's Opera *La Juive* from 1835, whose central character is the Jewish daughter Rachel. In her story all the key motifs relevant to the tragic liminal position of the young Jewish woman are present: the recurring narrative of the miserable daughter of an often "tyrannical", traditional Jewish father who has fallen in love with a Christian man, her martyrdom and her uncertain identity. The inherent ambiguity of the "Beautiful Jewess" in this case is even more striking: Rachel believes herself to be a Jewish woman but is in reality a Christian and the daughter of the very Cardinal, who condemns her to death at an Inquisition trial. All these motifs reveal and exaggerate her tragic *liminal* character. As Nadia Valman claims: "The tragic force of *La Juive* turns on the fact that the truth of Rachel's self is invisible... even to her... Unlike the figure of the Jew, whose physique is indelibly marked by the sign of his religious and racial difference, the body of the Jewess is unreadable" (Valman 2007: 3). Shifting the focus to the figure of the female Jew allows for breaking with fixed images and accounts in antisemitic discourse. The objects of investigation, literature and the arts support this purpose by opening up imaginary third spaces of reflection. I begin *in medias res* with an example from German literature: Wilhelm Hauff's novella *Jud Süß* (literally "Süss the Jew"), published in 1827. Though rarely read today, the novella is a watershed work in German cultural history. It established the story of Josef Süss-Oppenheimer, a financial advisor under Duke Karl Alexander of Württemberg in the early eighteenth century, as a literary subject. As Jefferson Case states:

> In course of the next 150 years, some 100 to 200 literary and artistic works up to Veit Harlan's notorious Nazi film, were to retell the tale of Süss-Oppenheimer's mercurial rise from Heidelberg ghetto and spectacular 1738 execution, after a notoriously unfair trial, for the crime of high treason. Hauff's novella prefigures both the would-be philo-Semitic and anti-Semitic treatments of the Süss-Oppenheimer's story and, as such, rehearses the entangled logic of emancipation and chauvinism so prominent in German nineteenth century. (1998: 724)

As an example of my thesis, I shall analyze the Carnival scene in the novel. Lea, the much younger sister of the Court Jew and financial manager Joseph Süß-Oppenheimer, and her lover the young Gustav Lanbek, enter the ball-room separately. The subtle colour resemblance of their oriental costumes and masks is the only clue to their relation. Not recognizing Gustav in costume, several young men ask him tauntingly: "Do you only have your "Allah" as your battle cry, or do you know any other little slogans?" (Hauff [1827] 6). When Gustav removes the Saracen mask, "the readers and his surrounding friends bear witness to a cultural metamorphosis" (Polaschegg, 2005: 170):

> Blond ringlets crept out from under the turban and artlessly framed his un-powdered brow. A bold arched nose and dark, eyes gave his face an expression of enterprising force and a profound seriousness that stood in startling contrast to his hair's softness and gentle hue. (Hauff, translation into English by Krobb 1993: 267)

Shortly thereafter, Lea removes her mask in the presence of her lover and her maid. Yet, instead of the woman undergoing a metamorphosis, the costume itself transforms. As Krobb argues, "Already at the beginning she is introduced as an Oriental woman. [...] in contrast to the other costumes, which are costumes, the foreign dress underlines her real self" (Krobb 1993: 127). Her lover now gazes upon a second orientalist image, which, through allusions to the Hebrew Bible, is introduced to the viewer and the reader as an expression of cultural authenticity. The other differences, however, emphasise the attractiveness of an erotically charged, exotically pagan yet idealized femininity:

> One could say her face was the culmination of oriental features. That symmetry in its delicate features, those wonderfully dark eyes shaded by long silken lashes; those boldly arched, shining black eyebrows, and those dark curls that fell about her pale brow with such pleasing contrast; and the meeting point of these features: tender red lips further accented by dainty white teeth; the turban, wound about her curls, the rich pearls gracing her neck, the charming and yet so modest costume of a Turkish lady—these produced, together with those features, such an illusion that the young man believed he was seeing one of those marvellous inventions described by Tasso, as painted by the fantasy that seizes the traveller on her return. "Truly!" he cried. "You resemble Armida the sorceress, and that is just how I would imagine the daughters of your tribe when you still lived in Canaan. Rebecca and Jephthah's daughter were just so". "How many times have I said this?" remarked Sara, the maid. "When I look upon my child, my Lea in her splendour; pocket hoops and crinoline, high heels and all the articles of fashion do not suit her nearly as much as this folk costume" (Hauff [1827] 1905: 56).

With her fascinating, exotic beauty and idealized femininity, Lea embodies different cultures and religions, bringing together the Hebraic figures of the biblical past with the German-Jewish present. The diversity of biblical and pagan references that contributes here to orientalizing the young Jewess is, first of all, connected to her Muslim-Turkish costume. The narrative description further alludes to the poetic form of the *Song of Songs* from the Hebrew Bible. As a Protestant theologian, Wilhelm Hauff certainly knew the *Song of Songs* very well. As Andrea Polaschegg demonstrates, it was in German Protestant theology and in line with its new historical-critical hermeneutic methods that the Hebrew Bible underwent a tripartite process of transformation: it was historicized, the Hebrew language was given a poetological quality, and, last but not least, the book was orientalized (see Polaschegg: 166). In his novella, Hauff follows the erotic-poetic line of the *Song of Songs* when describing Lea's physical beauty. He presents her features one by one: Lea's eyes, her hair, dark eyebrows, red lips – everything, except for her modestly veiled breasts, merges into the orientalized "costume of a Turkish lady" (Polaschegg 2005: 170).

Most relevant for the narrative process of her orientalization are the strong allusions to simultaneously Hebraic and orientalist female figures from the biblical past: first to Jacob's mother Rebecca, and then to the tragic daughter of the Ammonite Jephthah. Even in her idealization, however, the "magic" effect Lea has on her admirer "indicates her basic foreignness: she presents the ultimate expression of the Orient [...]". The unhealthy strangeness of Gustav's attraction to the "Beautiful Jewess" is re-emphasized on several occasions in the story, for example, when Hauff writes of the "magic spell that has been preserved through the daughters of Israel since the days of Rachel" (Hauff [1827] 1905:97, cited in Case 1998: 731).

In his introduction to *Orientalism*, Edward Said (1978: 27-28) stated that there is a similarity between orientalism and antisemitism and wrote: "I have found myself writing the history of a strange secret sharer of Western anti-Semitism. That anti-Semitism, and as I have discussed it in its Islamic branch Orientalism resemble each other is a historical, cultural, and political truth." Even if this equation is too narrow, it broadens the scope of Said's *Orientalism* and includes the power relations and knowledge production from Europe's internal colonial frontier. However, according to Said, Germany, a country with late and few colonies did not play an important role in the scholarly and political enactment of orientalism. Germany's influential oriental scholarship and its *Colonial Fantasies* (Zantop 1997) contradict this thesis. The orientalization of the Jews, which includes their idealization as well as their antisemitic degradation, started with the historization of Ancient Israel in biblical studies. In the course of this transference of the Ancient Jews and Old Israel to the "Orient", German literature and public media also established a discursive orientalization of contemporary German Jews (cf. Polaschegg 2005: 168). The orientalization of the "Beautiful Jewess" has multiple allosemitic layers. As apparent in the example of Hauff's Lea, there is a strong dimension of idealization in her description; a tragic dimension completes the picture. Hauff also attaches some uncanny, foreign oriental allusions to Lea by connecting her to Armida, a Syrian sorceress in Torquato Tasso's epic poem *Jerusalem Delivered* from 1575. "She was one of the most well-known oriental female figures in German literature, music and the arts in late eighteenth and early nineteenth century Germany" (Polaschegg 2005: 171). Her fame was even increasing due to Willibald Gluck's opera *Armide* (1686). Armida's story sounds like an early model of the later trope of the "Beautiful Jewess". Torquato Tasso's epic takes place at the time of the Crusades and the fight against Islam for a Christian Jerusalem. The Saracen sorceress intends to stop the Christian army by killing its leader Rinaldo. Yet, instead of doing him to death, she falls in love with him. Her love transforms her into a frontier or borderline figure (*Grenzfigur*) between cultures and religions. In the end, the Saracens lose the battle. In some versions of the story, Armida converts to Christianity. In every version, Armida, like Lea, is left behind alone at the end. Whereas Lea in the novella appears mainly as either a "naively innocent child or a tragic heroine nobly accepting her terrible fate," her comparison with the Syrian sorceress indicates her basic – oriental – foreignness (Case 1998: 731).

Hauff's Lea is further marked as a "Beautiful Jewess" through the intertextual realm of cultural associations invoked by the name "Rebecca." This name links her instantly with the well-known "Beautiful Jewess" of the early nineteenth century, the character of Rebecca from Sir Walter Scott's bestselling historical novel *Ivanhoe*, published in 1819. Like Lea, the English Jewess Rebecca falls in love with a Christian man, and both figures represent the young Jewess' struggling between two religions and cultures. In Hauff's novella her tragic destiny is connected to that of her older brother, Joseph Süß-Oppenheimer.

Like Scott's novel, Hauff's novella makes use of historical events from the past; especially the story of Süß-Oppenheimer, who left the Heidelberg ghetto, became the financial advisor of duke Karl Alexander of Württemberg and was executed after an unfair trial in 1738. Hauff's fictionalization strategies, however, start already with the transformation of the name Süss-Oppenheimer into the antisemitically connoted name "Jud Süß". Throughout the whole novel Hauff evinces an ambivalent attitude concerning the "Jewish Question", wavering between the rhetoric of antisemitism and that of tolerance. This becomes particularly evident when you analyze his use of the Antisemitic stereotype of the Court Jew (see Case 1998: 738-9). In the background of the novella a nationalist theme is at work. The novella describes the Court Jew Oppenheimer as the driving force behind the Catholic Duke's plans to drive the Protestant citizens of their power. Jud Süß becomes a scapegoat to solve internal tensions between a Protestant citizenry and a Catholic aristocratic ruler. Süß-Oppenheimer's accusation, trial and his execution made a new national unity possible. Against this backdrop, his much younger sister Lea, the passive victim, emerges as a martyr and tragic heroine. Her former lover, who now suddenly shows himself to be her brother's chief persecutor, rejects her and acknowledged the necessity of Jewish-Gentile apartheid. In his thoughts Lea is included in the general antisemitic prejudices concerning the "children of Abraham". She becomes a part of "the collectivized *Ahasverus* myth, the idea that the Jews as a people, because of some innate predatory viciousness, are fated to eternal homelessness" (Case 1998: 733). In the end she becomes a societal outcast and commits suicide.

The *"Beautiful Jewess"* as Mediating Figure

Florian Krobb considers the literary motif of the "Beautiful Jewess" to be a "pan-European phenomenon," in the characterization of which there is not always a clear-cut distinction between "the Jewish and the feminine" (Krobb 1993: 192). He also states that, in contrast to the Jewish man, the Jewish woman in (German-language) literature before the fin de siècle embodied not so much a negative difference, but functioned instead as an ambivalent mediating figure (Krobb 1993: 192; cf. Ludewig in Brunotte, Ludewig, 2015: 221-229 und Frübis 2018: 61-72). For Efraim Sicher "the Jew's daughter in its different variants and versions is a paradigm of conversion narratives [...], but the pattern holds long after the religious faith that motivated it has evaporated." (Sicher 2017: 2) As Nadia Valman has shown, using Sir Walter Scott's novel *Ivanhoe* as her starting point, this is even truer for Victorian (British) literature, in which the Jewess was not entirely Other:

> In protestant English culture, the Jewess was never so entirely Other, but closely connected to internal identity debates. That is already visible in Scott's Jewish heroine Rebecca of York. (...) Walter Scott's novel is considered as an Enlightenment historical narrative that seeks to explain the inauguration of the English nation in the Middle Ages as a rational rejection of superstitious hostility to racial and religious differences. Scott's argument for tolerance is focused through his representation of the Beautiful and heroic Jewess Rebecca. (Valman 2007: 10-11)

The story of the historical novel *Ivanhoe* takes place in the twelfth century, shortly after the Crusades in England. The knight Ivanhoe manages to successfully reconcile his Saxon heritage with the Norman Conquest. Admittedly, Rebecca's foreign beauty is as orientalized as Lea's, and her father is rich and lends money, but the story develops the "Jewish Question" differently from Hauff's Jud Süß. However, in contrast to Hauff's characterization of Lea, Rebecca is described as a strong and ethical character, and Isaac, her father, is not depicted as a villain. Moreover, the tension between the Jewish minority and the Christian majority culture is embodied by two men: Rebecca's Jewish father and the Christian Ivanhoe, the man she secretly loves. On the other hand, Rebecca's tragic liminal position between the Jewish religion and community and her love for the Christian knight is emphasized in the form of an inner struggle. Rebecca is depicted as a pious woman with a voice and will of her own.

In her orientalized beauty as well as her Jewish patriotism, Rebecca is presented as an idealized Jewess with higher spiritual qualities *and* as a woman of dangerous femininity. She risks her life to save the wounded Ivanhoe, and calls for peace and tolerance between the struggling parties. Scott uses narrative focalization to differentiate within the discourse on the Jews: through the eyes of the tyrannically depicted Norman nobility, her foreign, exotic beauty and her passion are demonized. She is almost raped and even accused of being a witch, but at the end Ivanhoe recues her. However, in Scott's novel, too, the Jewess remains ambivalent; she represents the ethos of enlightened tolerance and feminine tenderness, but she is also described as possessing a dangerously foreign beauty. At the end of the novel, Rebecca is invited to become a citizen of the new nation, but she refuses to renounce her Judaism. Rebecca rejects a possible conversion to Christianity and sacrifices instead her love to let the Ivanhoe enter into a strategic political marriage. Yet, as Valman (2007: 21) has emphasized:

> The principle for which Rebecca sacrifices Ivanhoe is ambiguous: she exhibits devotion not only to *his* greater destiny but also to the Jewish religion that prevents *her* participation in Christian social life. The philosophical and political problem of the "Jewish question" that this poses, for the novel, remains unresolved at its close.

This contrasts with Hauff's novella, since, in the end, Rebecca and her father are allowed to go into exile in Spain. As these two interconnected literary case studies show, in the nineteenth-century European cultural imagination, the "Beautiful Jewess" was a figure of the third; that is, a marker of borderlines, unsolved differences and tensions, and a placeholder for hybrid knowledge. In her often tragic destiny, torn between religions and cultures, secularism and traditional faith, she is an affective embodiment of the "Jewish Question." It was not only the literary figure of the Jewess, however, that recurred in novels, as well as in operas and in theatre plays all over Europe again and again, but also a specific narrative constellation. Andrea Polaschegg maintains:

> Since the beginning of the nineteenth century, it is the character constellation of a Jewish daughter with oriental signature, torn between an often

patriarchal Jewish father on the one hand, and a Christian-European knight on the other hand, that became the most successfully dramatized minimal-narrative nucleus of an often tragic story. (Polaschegg 2005: 173)

In this context, gender becomes relevant as a "useful category of historical analysis" (Scott 1986: 1053) and "the primary way of signifying relationships of power" (1069). Broader tensions of cultural and religious difference are "revealed in gendered representations" (Valman 2007: 7, cf. Sicher 2017). In the repeated master narrative, the "Beautiful Jewess" is the daughter (or in the exceptional case of Lea, the very much younger sister) of an often Antisemitically caricatured Jewish father, who functions as a compendium of all the negative prejudices against Jewish religion and culture. The complex ambivalence of "semitic discourse" (Cheyette 1993:8) is "most fully revealed in the opposite between 'Jew' and 'Jewess'" (Valman 2007:4). Characterized by her attractiveness and martyrdom the Jewess functions as a *pathos formula* of the cultural-political conflict of religious intolerance and Jewish emancipation, arousing empathy and even compassion in the reader and audience. Her story can end in conversion to Christianity, in total assimilation into a secular majority culture, in martyrdom or even suicide.

Oriental Fantasies and Jewish Self-Orientalization

The "Beautiful Jewess", as I have argued, was often merged with other fantasies generated by nineteenth-century orientalism. "Indeed, just as the scholarly apparatus of orientalism helped to naturalize Christian domination of colonized peoples, it equally provided a means of knowledge and power over Semites at home" (Valman 2007: 4). To describe these discursive strategies of "othering" the European Jews, Steven Asheim (Aschheim 2018: 13) coined the term the "internal Orientals". According to Kalmar and Penslar in their book *Orientalism and the Jews* (2005: xiii):

Orientalism has always been not only about Muslims but also about the Jew. We believe that the Western image of the Muslim Orient has been formed, and continues to be formed in inextricable conjunction with Western perceptions of the Jewish people. [...] It had been based on the Christian West's attempts to understand and manage its relation with both of its monotheistic Others, Muslims and Jews.

With the early nineteenth century, orientalism included the Muslim – mostly the Saracen and later Ottoman world – and the Jews, both seen as "Semitic." Ancient Israel and its Biblical religion were depicted as oriental and Biblical allusions played a significant role for the "othering" of contemporary Jewry in Europe. In the Carnival scene from Wilhelm Hauff's novel the author simultaneously employs and comments on a then-widespread ethnic stereotype in European music, literature, and painting. The physical beauty and sensuality of the Jewish woman, and sometimes even her clothing, were almost always described using orientalizing tropes and characteristics. As shown in this chapter, this often blurred the lines between the European Jewess as oriental and the depiction of oriental Jewesses. Probably the most famous examples in French orientalist painting is Eugène Delacroix's "Jewess from Tangier".

Fig. 8: Eugène Delacroix: Jewess from Tangier (1835).

Public Domain, Wikimedia Commons

As was demonstrated in this chapter the depiction of the Jewess and the role of oriental tropes were different in German and even more in English culture and literature, where the "Jewess was never so entirely Other" (Valman 2007. 4). In contrast to the visual stereotype, which was often fixed, in literature, the "Beautiful Jewess" got an individual character and a life story. As an often tragic heroine she was a "figure of the third." With the emancipation of the Jews, the "Beautiful Jewess" became a literary, artistic and theatrical figure in Europe. In his book *La Belle Juive* from 2011, Éric Fournier emphasizes the seismographic effect of this cultural invention. The figure of the "Beautiful Jewess", he states, "was capable of expressing the ambivalences around the "Jewish Question", that means the entire range of judgments and opinions about Judaism, from philo-Semitism to anti-Semitism" (Fournier 2011: 9). Around 1800, moreover, the famous Berlin Salonière, beautiful and highly educated women like Henriette Herz or Dorothea Schlegel, became the most famous "Beautiful Jewesses" in Prussia. "Even since they flourished [...], the Berlin Jewish Salons have been discussed as a symbolic space of the peaceful co-existence of enlightened individuals and, indeed, for a "Jewish-German" understanding" (Lund 2015: 33-62, 33). However, they were depicted to have an "Egyptian style" (54), even if most of them were converted to Christianity. As I have shortly mentioned before within the vast variety of European depictions of the figure of the "Beautiful Jewess" one aspect particularly remains striking: the literary trope sometimes blurs the clear-cut distinctions between "the Jewish and the feminine" (Krobb 1993: 192). The fascinating ambivalence of the figure raises the question of precisely how her Jewishness and her femininity work together in each case. As I (Brunotte 2015: 204) have argued in my previous work on the subject: "To describe the double difference of the imaginary Jewess, a *tertium comparationis* of her femininity and her Jewishness must be found. Her ambivalent orientalization served this purpose". (Brunotte 2015: 204). In the French colonial setting the Jews have always played an essential role in orientalist discourse,

> the "Beautiful Jewess" inscribes herself forcefully into the invention of the Orient (...) both as a discursive matrix and through a feeling of foreignness. (...) In the middle of this long list of exotic beauties – the Turkish, Egyptian, Greek, Moorish, Armenian, Abyssinian, and Coptic – the Jewess appears as the most troubling of all (Fournier 2011: 27).

Going beyond a postcolonial reading of internal *orientalism* does also include the topic of an active Jewish self-orientalization or at least the question "in

which ways German Jews co-created German Orientalism as a contested field"
(Wittler 2015:81). The Jewish response to orientalization was threefold, "first,
they rejected it wholesome; second, by idealizing and romanticizing the Orient and themselves as its representatives; and third they set up traditional
Jews as oriental, in contrast to modernized Jewry which was described as
"Western" (Kalmar/Penslar: xix). The most well-known visual expression of
a Jewish fascination with oriental style and culture – focussing on the Jewish culture in al-Andalus, was the Moorisch-style synagogues from Budapest
to Berlin and its most sophisticated literary articulation (was) in Heinrich
Heine's poem 'Jehuda ben Halevy', published in 1851 as part of his *Hebrew
Melodies.*" (Wittler 2015: 63) Mostly Bible-connected self-orientalization did
also provide Jews with discursive tropes to discuss the "Jewess Question". According to Kathrin Wittler self-orientalization became a tool for negotiating
the emancipation of women and Jews. Jewish authors used Biblical allusions
and self-orientalization to create agency and identity building and "to find a
balance between singularity and amalgamation" (ibid: 74).

*Fig. 9: Eduard Bendemann: Jews Mourning in Exile (1832),
Wallraf-Richartz Museum.*

Public Domain, Wikimedia Commons

Focussing on Fanny Lewald's novel *Jenny* from 1843, and especially the scene of a New-Year *tableau vivant* of Eduard Bendemann's monumental painting *Captive Jews in Babylon* (1832) at a New Year's Eve party, Wittler uses the narrative and pictorial figure of the "Beautiful Jewess" to demonstrate the role of Biblical self-orientalization for the emancipation of German Jews and women:

> Choosing to address the question of female and Jewish emancipation in her novel directly, Lewald presents her novel *Jenny* as an alternative of Michael Beer's drama *Der Paria* which the fictive protagonists of the novel deem an example of allegoric Orientalism and proof of Jewish cowardice. Settling her plot in present-day Germany and directly pointing to the oriental heritage of her fictive German-Jewish characters, thus promoting a kind of genealogical Orientalism [...], Lewald demonstrates her own courage as a female Jewish writer. (Wittler 2015: 80)

Wittler's study like that of Andrea Polaschegg (2005) and the case studies of my international research network RenGoo published in 2015 (Brunotte et.al 2015) highlight the weakness of Said's homogenizing conception and advances in its stead a pluralistic, relational, and dialectic conception of oriental and colonial discourse.

Concluding Remarks

The chapter has followed an intersectional and allosemitic approach to the "Beautiful Jewess" as a tragic figure that marks and transgresses cultural and religious differences. Throughout the nineteenth century this liminal figure represented the affective dynamics of the "Jewish Question." Biblical allusions, like in Fanny Lewald's *Jenny* connected her to the oriental Biblical heritage. The key narrative trope positioned her beside an antisemitic exaggerated father figure. Thus the "Jew's Daughter" (Sicher 2017) embodied an often idealized female that was "ripe for conversion" (ibid.: 1). In this chapter the different case studies "inform discourses about gender, sexuality, race, and nationhood" (Sicher 2017:2) as well as negotiations about the "Jewess question." As Valman showed for the British case, the idealized femininity, spirituality and her love for a Christian man played a significant role therein. Wittler has focused her research on the empowering role of German-Jewish self-orientalization and noted (Brunotte et. al. 2015: 10; Wittler 2015: 63-81) that "the use of Oriental styles, characters and topoi by German Jews, commonly understood as an "internalization" of antisemitic and/or orientalist aggressions, may be acknowledged as a self-determined contribution to the contested field of Orientalism." In mainstream European discourse, the figure of the "Beautiful Jewess", however, was often enough depicted as the daughter, "prisoner" and victim of a patriarchal Jewish father and his religion. In the "minimal-narrative nucleus" (Polaschegg 2005: 173) of her tragic story, she is waiting to be "saved" by a Christian or "secularized in other words civilized" white man. This narrative trope indeed shows similarities with the colonial master narrative – Said already pointed to Lord Cromer – of the brown woman who has to be saved by white men from her brown, patriarchal oppressors (cf. Spivak 1988). Even if the colonial dimension was not always explicit in nineteenth-century European narratives of the "Beautiful Jewess", it was often implicitly present. As shown by the example of Salome (and Judith) in chapter one and six, in the second half of the nineteenth century the Jewish daughter "leaves her father behind and becomes an independent agent of vengeance, a *femme fatale* who threatens European manhood" (Sicher 2017: 16).

Bibliography

Aschheim, Steven E. (2017): The Modern Jewish Experience and the Entangled Web of Orientalism. In Brunotte et. Al. (eds) *Internal Outsiders – Imagined Orientals? Antisemitism, Colonialism and Modern Constructions of Jewish Identity*. Würzburg: Ergon Verlag, pp. 11-34.

Bauman, Zygmunt (1998): "Allosemitism: Premodern, modern, postmodern." In: Cheyette, Bryan/ Marcus, Laura (eds): Standford: Standford University Press, pp. 143-156.

Bhabha, Homi (1997): "The Other Question: The Stereotype and the Colonial Discourse." In: Newton, Karl M. (ed). *The Twentieth Century Literary Theory. A Reader*, London: Palgrave Macmillan, pp 293-301.

Brunotte, Ulrike et al. (eds) (2015): Orientalism, Gender, and the Jews. Literary and Artistic Transformations of European National Discourses. Berlin/ New York: de Gruyter.

Brunotte, Ulrike et al. (2015): "Introduction". In: Brunotte, Ulrike et.al. (eds.): Orientalism, Gender, and the Jews. Literary and Artistic Transformations of European National Discourses, Berlin/New York: de Gruyter, 1-16.

Brunotte, Ulrike (2015): *All Jews are womanly, but no women are Jews*. The "Femininity Game of Deception." Female Jew, femme fatale Orientale und belle Juive. In: Brunotte, Ulrike et al. (eds.): Orientalism, Gender, and the Jews. Literary and Artistic Transformations of European National Discourses, pp. 195-220.

Brunotte, Ulrike (2012): "Unveiling Salome 1900. Entschleierungen zwischen Sexualität, Pathosformel und Oriental Dance." In: Dennerlein B., Frietsch E. (eds). Munich: Fink Verlag, *Verschleierter Orient, entschleierter Okzident. (Un-)Sichtbarkeiten in Politik,Recht, Kunst und Kultur*, 2012, pp. 93–116.

Case, Jefferson S. (1998): "The Wandering Jew and the Hand of God: Wilhelm Hauff's "Jud Süss" as Historical Fiction." In: *The Modern Language Review*, Vol. 93, No. 3 (July), pp. 724-740.

Cheyette, Brian (1993): Constructions of the Jew in English Literature and Society: Racial Representations 1875-1945. Cambridge: Cambridge University Press.

Eßlinger, Eva et al. (eds): Die Figur des Dritten. Ein kulturwissenschaftliches Paradigma. Frankfurt am Main: Suhrkamp Verlag.

Fournier, Éric. (2011): La "belle" Juive. Seyssel: Champ Vallon.

Frübis Hannelore (2017): The Figure of the *"Beautiful Jewess"*. In: *Internal Outsiders* – Imagined Orientals ? Antisemitism, Colonialism and Modern Constructions of Jewish Identity. Würzburg: Ergon Verlag, pp. 61-72.

Gilman, Sander (1993 and 1998): Salome, Syphilis, Sarah Bernhardt and the "Modern Jewess." *The German Quarterly* 66.2, 1993, 195–211. Also published in Gilman Sander Love+Marriage=Death, and Other Essays on Representing Difference. Stanford: Stanford University Press, 1998, pp. 65-90.

Gilman, Sander (1999): Die verräterische Nase: Über die Konstruktion von "Fremdkörpern". In: Hürlimann A., Roth M. and Vogel K. (eds). *Fremdkörper – Fremde Körper: Von Unvermeintlichen Kontakten und widerstreitenden Gefühlen*. Ostfildern: Hatje Cantz, pp. 31-47.

Hahn, Barbara. The Jewess Pallas Athena: This Too a Theory of Modernity. Princeton: Princeton University Press, 2005.

Hauff, Wilhelm ([1827] 1905): Jud Süß [Süß the Jew]. In: Hauff, Wilhelm and Stern, Achim (eds.) Sämtliche Werke [Complete Works], Vol. 1. Leipzig: Max Hesses Verlag, pp.46-103.

Heschel, Susannah: "Jewish Studies as Counterhistory." In: Insider/Outsider. Eds. Biale, David/Galchinsky, Michael/ Heschel, Susanna, Berkeley: University of California Press, 1998, pp. 101-115.

Heschel, Susannah: "Revolt of the Colonized: Abraham Geiger's Wissenschaft des Judentums as a Challenge to Christian Hegemony in the Academy." In: New German Critique 77 (1999): pp. 61–85.

Hess, Jonathan (2012): German Jews and the Claim of Modernity. Yale: Yale University Press.

Holz, Klaus (2005): "Die antisemitische Konstruktion des "Dritten" und die nationale Ordnung der Welt." In: von Braun, Christina/Ziege, Eva-Maria (eds.): "Das bewegliche Vorurteil". Aspekte des internationalen Antisemitismus, Würzburg: Königshausen & Neumann, pp. 43-62.

Kalmar, Ivan Davidson and Penslar, Derek J. (2005): Orientalism and the Jews. Waltham, MA: Brandeis University Press.

Krobb, Florian (1993): Die schöne Jüdin. Jüdische Frauengestalten in der deutschsprachigen Erzählliteratur vom 17. Jahrhundert bis zum Ersten Weltkrieg. Tübingen: Max Niemeyer Verlag.

Ludewig, Anna-Dorothea (2015): "Between Orientalization and Self-Orientalization. Remarks on the Image of the "Beautiful Jewess" in Nineteenth and Early Twentieth- Century Literature." In: Brunotte, Ulrike et. al. (eds) Orientalism, Gender, and the Jews. Literary and Artistic Transformations of European National Discourses. Berlin/New York: de Gruyter, 221-229.

Lund, Hannah Lotte (2015): "Prussians, Jews, Egyptians? Berlin Jewish Salonières around 1800 and Their Guests. Discursive Constructions of Equality and Otherness." In: Brunotte, Ulrike et. al. (eds) Orientalism, Gender, and the Jews. Literary and Artistic Transformations of European National Discourses. Berlin/New York: de Gruyter, pp. 33-62.

Mufti, R. Aamir (2007): Enlightenment in the Colony: The Jewish Question and the Crisis of Postcolonial Culture. Princeton and Oxford: Princeton University Press.

Ockman, Carol (1995): "Two large Eyebrows a l'Orientale", Ethnic Stereotyping in Ingre's Baronne de Rothschild". In: Ockman, Carol: Ingre's Eroticized Bodies. Retracing the Serpentine Line. New Haven: Yale University Press.

Polaschegg, Andrea (2005): Der andere Orientalismus. Regeln deutsch-morgenländischer Imagination im 19. Jahrhundert. Berlin and New York: de Gruyter.

Riegert, Leo W. (2009): Subjects and Agents of Empire: German Jews in Post-Colonial Perspective. In: The German Quarterly. 82.3 (Summer), pp. 336-355.

Said, E. (1978): Orientalism, New York: Pantheon Books (Random House).

Sicher, Efrain (2017): The Jew's Daughter. A Cultural History of a Conversion Narrative, London (UK): Lexigton Books.

Scott, Joan (1986): "Gender: A Useful Category of Historical Analysis." The American Historical Review 91.5 (1986): pp. 1053–1075.

Spivak, Gayatri Chakravorty: "Can the Subaltern speak?" In: Marxism and the Interpretation of Culture, Cary Nelson and Lawrence Grossberg (eds.). Urbana: University of Illinois Press, 1988, pp. 271–313.

Tasso, Torquato ([1574] 2009): The Liberation of Jerusalem. Oxford: Orford World Classics.

Turner, Victor (1967): Betwixt and Between. The Liminal Period in Rites de Passages. In: Turner, Victor: Forest of Symbols. As pects of Ndembu ritual. Ithaca/London: Cornell University Press, 93-111.

Valman, Nadia (2007): The Jewess in Nineteenth-Century British Literary Culture. Cambridge: Cambridge University Press.

Wittler, Kathrin (2015): "Good to Think" (Re)Conceptualizating German-Jewish Orientalism. In: Brunotte, Ulrike et. al. (eds) Orientalism, Gender, and the Jews. Literary and Artistic Transformations of European National Discourses. Berlin/New York: de Gruyter, pp. 63-81.

Wittler, Kathrin (2019): Morgenländischer Glanz. Eine deutsche jüdische Literaturgeschichte 1750-1850. Tübingen: Mohr Siebeck.

Zantop, Susanne (1997): Colonial Fantasies: Conquest, Family, and Nation in Precolonial Germany, 1770–1870. In: Durham, NC: Duke University Press.

6. Seeing, Hearing and Narrating Salome. Modernist Sensual Aesthetics and the Role of Narrative Blanks

Guiding Questions

Since fin de siècle paintings, Oscar Wilde's play and Richard Strauss's opera, the figure of Salome has been embedded in modern visual regimes so centrally that she can be defined as "a sign of the visual as such" (Bucknell 1993: 503). Yet the name Salome is not mentioned in the biblical stories of the death of John the Baptist; her dance is without narrative description and is as yet unembellished by the seven veils. The name of the young woman, however, the stepdaughter of Herod Antipas, is found in Antiquities of the Jews (Greek 93-94), a work by the Jewish historian Flavius Josephus (born 37 in Jerusalem, died after 100 in Rome). His Salome had nothing to do with the dance and never demanded the Baptist's head. It is precisely these kind of narrative blanks and uncertainties in the canonical biblical stories and in ancient historical documents that have been filled in by the imagination, first by religious commentators in the Patristic literature and then by the arts (cf. Inowlocki 2016: 356-67). The figure of Salome became a religious and artistic icon of luxuriant interpretations in the nominally authoritative commentaries of early Christianity and later in Renaissance and Baroque art. In the nineteenth century her revival was increasingly effected through narrative media, folk stories and literature; around the fin de siècle, dance, paintings and opera made her into an intermedia popular icon. Only Wilde's play, and then Richard Strauss however, aestheticizes visual desire, producing an aesthetic spectacle of Symbolist and biblical metaphors. In the opening scene of Strauss's opera, Salome's visual-physical attraction is contrasted with the fascination of the disembodied 'holy' voice of the prophet, proclaiming God's message from the depths of the cistern.

This chapter proposes the hypothesis that it is from the absence, the blank space within the biblical narratives that modern, multi-media aesthetics draws its formula of self-reflection as 'purely aesthetic' and a sacralization of the aesthetic. The guiding questions will be: How have narrative gaps and specific narrative strategies opened a virtual space of imagination in the process of aesthetic response? How have they helped to transfer the imaginary of this response into a picture, image and iconic body? And how, if at all, has this synergetic transmission between different media and art forms been 'reflected upon'? Building on Becker-Leckrone's research, the chapter further asks if Salome's fetishized body has silenced her biblical and family story and rendered "its intertextuality virtually invisible" (1995: 242)? The case study at the end of the chapter refers to Strauss's opera as the Salome figure's most powerful and resilient global medium of presentation. The discussion focuses on the "work on myth" (Blumenberg 1985) done by Claus Guth in his production of Salome, performed at the Deutsche Oper in Berlin in January 2016. Guth uses empty spaces without singing and 'gaps' in the libretto to insinuate an interpretation that radically reverse the traditional one and triggers confusion, new 'mental images' and critical thoughts in the viewer (see also Høgasen-Hallesby 2014: 195). By stepping into the blind spots and revitalizing storytelling on stage, Guth's production makes it possible to break with a stereotypically repeated Orientalist opera plot and to retrieve Salome's hidden story.

Fragmented Storytelling and the *Pathos Formula*

The story of Herodias, her daughter, and their part in the gospel narrative of the death of John the Baptist in Matthew and Mark, ranks among the most influential of "fascination stories" in the Bible, to use Klaus Heinrich's (1995) term. From the very start, its narrative constitution is based on narrative gaps, parallel narratives and intertextuality, the last particularly with references to the biblical canon and Josephus' version of the story, which supplied the name of Salome. Its long durée and the transformation of the gospel story into the Salome myth are a consequence partly of the polysemy of the mythical and early patristic narrations, and partly of the affective impact of the figure of Salome as a Pathos formula. In Aby Warburg's Mnemosyne Atlas, Salome plays a significant role as an emotionally charged figure of cultural memory (for further information see Brunotte 2013) and in chapter eight of this book.

Megan Becker-Leckrone (1995) has analysed "the intertextual and 'fetishist' obsessions with the fin de siècle Salome figure." (Dierkes-Thrun 2011: 15) She asks how "a narrative has become a woman, how the gospel story has become the Salome myth, has become Salome?" (Becker-Leckrone 1995: 242) "The dancer got the name Salome for the first time from Isidore of Pelusium, who combined the story of the canonical gospels with the Josephus' report." (Rohde, 2000: 267) Certainly, as Barbara Baert (2014) has demonstrated, the influence of the early patristic commentaries on the imputations of Salome's moral corruption and the idea of her 'evil' dance should not be underestimated. In these narratives Salome was already an icon of the perennial interconnection between death, dance and (female) attraction. It was first Wilde, however, and after him Strauss, who gave the girl Salome a voice of her own and let her say that she wants the head of John to satisfy her own desire. Against this background, the question of how the many Salome narratives have become the story of a modern femme fatale and a fetishist body gains even more importance (Baert 2014: 251).

The name Salome is not mentioned in the bible; her dance is not described until the patristic interpretations; nor is there any biblical reference to the seven veils. It is precisely these kinds of "narrative blanks" or gaps in the biblical stories, to use a central term of Wolfgang Iser's (1978) theory of aesthetic response, that have been supplied by the imagination, first by religious commentators and then, mainly in the nineteenth century, by literature, opera and the other arts. As Helmut Pfeiffer has emphasized: "It is precisely out of the biblical 'blank' of the nameless narrative function that modern aestheticism acquires its formula of self-reflection that is the 'purely aesthetic.' And it is the 'void' of this 'purely aesthetic' which, around 1900, is filled by an epochal imaginary."[1] At the peak of its fascination, "the body of Salome was the obsession of late nineteenth-century European, especially French culture." (Hutcheon/Hutcheon 1998:206) Referring to Friedrich Nietzsche's aesthetic theory, encapsulated in his dictum "It is only as an aesthetic phenomenon that existence and the world are eternally justified." (1993: 32) Dierkes-Thrun notes that "Wilde realized the potency of vivid literary representations of eroticism

---

1   "Gerade aus der biblischen Leerstelle der namenlosen narrativen Funktion gewinnt der Ästhetizismus die Selbstreflexionsformel des 'rein Ästhetischen', um in dessen Leere ein epochales Imaginäres einströmen zu lassen" (Pfeiffer 2006: 310).

couched in terms of metaphysical longing, creating imagery that fused sexual lust with a desire for the divine and vice versa." (2011: 25) Thus, what occurred was an aestheticization of the sacred or a sacralization of the aesthetic; a process of reversal, in which the figure of Salome became the icon of decadence and in which aestheticism played an essential role. Dierkes-Thrun even goes a step further and claims: "In Oscar Wilde's Salome, it is religion for aesthetics' sake, not the other way round." (30)

Biblical Intertextuality

The following brief analysis of the style, intertextual relations and narrative function of the story of Salome/Herodias and the death of John the Baptist in the Bible focuses on the gospel of Mark, because, compared with its parallel in Mathew, Mark reported the story in an extensive, highly vivid and detailed fashion. In contrast to Matthew, who clearly integrates his much shorter version of the story into his narrative of Jesus activities, Mark, by referring to this past event, even interrupts the gospel's linear narrative flow, with its focus on Jesus' passion. I use the NRSV (1998), Mark VI, 17-29:

> For Herod himself had sent men who arrested John, bound him, and put him in prison on account of Herodias, his brother Philip's wife, because Herod; had married her. For John had been telling Herod, "It is not lawful for you to have your brother's wife." And Herodias had a grudge against him, and wanted to kill him. But she could not, for Herod feared John, knowing that he was a righteous and holy man, and he protected him. When he heard him, he was greatly perplexed; and yet he liked to listen to him. But an opportunity came when Herod on his birthday gave a banquet for his courtiers and officers and for the leaders of Galilee. When Herodia's daughter came in and danced, she pleased Herod and his guests; and the king said to the girl, "Ask me for whatever you wish, and I will give it." And he solemnly swore to her, "Whatever you ask me, I will give you, even half of my kingdom." She went out and said to her mother, "What should I ask for?" She replied, "The head of John the baptizer." Immediately she rushed back to the king and requested, "I want you to give me at once the head of John the Baptist on a platter." The king was deeply grieved; yet out of regard for his oaths and for the guests, he did not want to refuse her. Immediately the king sent a soldier of the guard with orders to bring John's head. He went and beheaded him in the prison,

brought his head on a platter, and gave it to the girl. Then the girl gave it to her mother. When his disciples heard about it, they came and took his body, and laid it in a tomb.

The story is clear enough: the nameless daughter of Herodias, the "girl" in the Greek text, is a mere "instrument" in the hands of her hating and power-hungry mother. She and her dance are still undescribed. It is obvious that for the narrator the dance, which is only mentioned in passing, is not of great importance. He focuses his narrative skills on the description of the wily mother and the misuse of her daughter. Moreover, the biblical commentaries are unanimous that this narrative is not a historical report of John the Baptist's death. The Jewish historian Flavius Josephus, who gave Herod's daughter the Hebrew name 'Salome' (Ant. 18.135-36), omits mentioning her in connection with the beheading of John the Baptist (Ant. 18.116-19). Of particular relevance to the narrative style of the story is its reduced but finely developed language. The narration is economical in the extreme, refrains from taking sides and yet describes the key emotions – Herodias' hatred and Herod's ambivalence. Nevertheless, the story relates not only the events but depicts the whole atmosphere of the scene and, in the second half, even constructs a quasi-dramatic pace hastening to the beheading.

Following the commentators, the detached and impartial narrative perspective resembles the concise style of a Hellenistic novella, a literary genre that uses fragments of folklore poetry (see Wellhausen [1923] 2010: 121; Pesch 1997: 337-44, 339; for more recent research on the Hellenistic novella and the Salome story, see also Baert 2014). These ancient novellas can be described, as Tolbert has observed, as "literature composed in such a way as to be accessible to a wide spectrum of society, both literate and illiterate" (1978: 70; see also Hägg 2012 and Neginsky 2013: 15). In Mark's introduction, however, the Christological message and function of John's death as the advance notice of Jesus' death are clearly mentioned. Moreover, there are some obvious intertextual relations to the Hebrew Bible: Herodias resembles Queen Jezebel, who tried to kill the prophet Elia, and Herod resembles King Ahab. The display of Herodias own daughter, however, a Judaic princess, before a male audience, and her misuse for political reasons, are without precedent. As many commentators have pointed out, even in Greco-Roman culture only prostitutes could attend the second part of a banquet, with its various notorious entertainments (Neginsky 2013: 12). Further, the spare and impartial narrative style stresses the cruelty of the events. The action reaches its dramatic peak in the scene where the girl presents the head of the prophet to her mother, like a precious gift on a platter.

In the biblical stories, Herodias' daughter is innocent. She has no independent relationship to, let alone, desire for the prophet. She is a young virgin and there is nothing about a desire for Baptist's death. In the long visual tradition of Salome paintings, it was the Italian Baroque painter Caravaggio who most intensely expressed her deep sadness in a painting of 1607/10 entitled: Salome with the Head of John Baptist.

Fig. 10: Caravaggio: Salome with the Head of John the Baptist (1610), National Gallery, Washington.

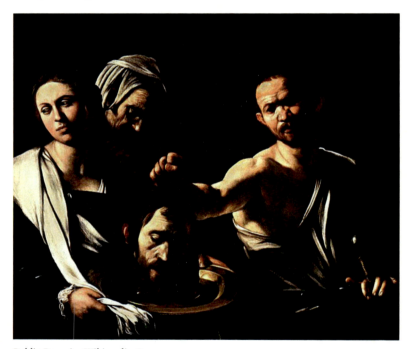

Public Domain, Wikimedia Commons

The first hint of the girl's independent significance in the early story can be seen in Herod's oath: "Whatsoever you shall ask of me, I will give it thee, unto the half of my kingdom." Here an intertextual approach, using the biblical concordance, uncovers an interesting layer of meaning. Some commentators have remarked that, by Herod's time, the expression "you can have even half of my kingdom" had become a "proverbial saying" without real meaning (Neginsky 2013: 21). Yet it is worth mentioning that the oath is a quotation from the book of Esther (Est. 5:3, 6; 7:2) of the Hebrew Bible, referring to the time of the Persian Diaspora. Esther, the Jewess behind the throne who could save her people, became the prototype for the "Beautiful Jewess" in the history of European-Christian reception:

> The Christian reading of biblical woman prefiguring the Virgin Mary, particularly Rachel and Esther (a figure at once redemptive and erotic), is familiar, and literary adaptations of the Book of Esther have a long history. Early modern depictions of Esther the queen intercessor set up a proactive woman who uses her beauty to effect salvation. [...] By nineteenth century, Esther, more than any other book of the Bible, had become a household reference and was invoked or adapted in numerous novels and plays. (Sicher 2017: 5)

Admittedly, the constellation of figures in the two stories, that of Esther and that of Salome, is very different: on the one hand the Jewish princess and girl Salome, upon whom a name is first conferred by Josephus, the stepdaughter of the Tetrarch of Galilee and a pawn in the hands of Herodias, her mother; on the other hand the young Jewess Esther, who resolutely represents and saves her people, in spite of being – and because – she is in the position of the Persian queen. In the first story a Jewish prophet and holy herald of Christ is killed by Herod; in the second, the head of a conspiracy against the Jews is executed by the Persian King. Yet by quoting the Persian king's oath in Mark's gospel story, the narrator creates an intertextual relationship between the two narratives: even though Mark's denomination of Herod as "king" is not without irony, both "kings are willing to give the power over half a kingdom…" to a young and beautiful Jewish woman. Moreover, both stories are characterized by an orientalized or, in Herod's case, hellenized setting, a banquet or a feast. Last but not least, the beauty of a young Jewess, woman or girl, becomes the decisive turning point of the narration.

Liminal Figures and Transgression

Taking into account the long-durée of the story up to modernity, these biblical narratives might be interpreted as already foreshadowing the figure of what has become known as the "Beautiful Jewess". The orientalization of female Jews even in the nineteenth century often refers to biblical figures. Anna Dorothea Ludewig (2014: 222-23) has emphasized the biblical precedent of the ambivalent figure of the "Beautiful Jewess":

> Eve, first woman and therefore first Jewish woman, is both the mother of humanity and the mother of sin. [...] The story of Abraham's wife, Sara, taken to the Pharaoh's harem on their journey to Egypt, can be viewed as representative. [...] Although he has already gathered a number of beautiful women in his harem, it is the Jewish woman, a 'stranger', who most captivates him. [...]. Also Ester, as many other Jewish women beside her, acts as a bridge, as an intermediary between the Jewish and the non-Jewish world.

Nevertheless, in nineteenth century literature and opera, the "Beautiful Jewess" was a liminal figure, which marked and crossed borders of gender norms, religion and culture (Valman 2007: 2). Whereas Esther is an unambiguous positive example, it was the Jewish heroine Judith whose ambivalent fascination best represents the possible ambivalence within the figure of the "Beautiful Jewess". In an extremely threatening situation for her people, Judith uses her beauty to seduce and then behead the Assyrian military commander, Holofernes, thus saving her village and her people from the aggressor. Even Judith, however, as a heroine of her people, could be interpreted within the traditional canon of patriotic and moral conduct; Salome's deed, however, transgresses against the religious core and, at least in Wilde's and Strauss's versions, could no longer be 'saved' by inclusion in a religious universe. Dierkes-Thrun writes: "In Wilde's hands, the legend of Salome hence becomes a thought experiment of taking the pursuit of beauty to its utmost extreme, following it literally into murder and death, while distorting the moral and religious dimensions into aesthetic surfaces, divesting them of their guiding and regulating functions." (2011: 29)

The depiction of Herodias and Salome as, "archetypical, corrupting women and relatives of Eve," in the words of Rosina Neginsky (2013: 3, 18), started very early. Christian commentators used the Salome story as a cautionary tale for educational purposes and to shape the view of woman in society. They creatively filled in the 'narrative gaps' and unsaid dimension of the biblical stories by producing the vivid picture of the self-assured and evil daughter in league with the wily mother. The central narrative blank within the biblical stories, as Barbara Baert (2014) maintains, was the dance. Focusing their imagination on Salome's dance, early commentators already employed graphic terms to describe and simultaneously demonize it. For

John Chrysostom, writing in the fourth century, Herodias and Salome are pure evil: "the feast is a satanic performance [...] with a dance that, in its shamelessness, overshadows even the performances of prostitutes."[2] (see also Levine 2008) Chrysostom concludes his denunciation thus: "Where there is dance, there too is the devil." (70) A Christian commentator of the twelfth century places Salome's dance in the pagan, Dionysian sphere and depicts it as an expression of wild bacchantic frenzy: "she was dancing 'shamelessly' and in the way of the maenads and corybants, jerking her hair through the air and exposing her body bit by bit to the audience." (Cermameus n.d.: 70-2) These early descriptions already demonized, paganized and so transformed Salome's dance into a scandalous image. In nineteenth-century Salomania, the pagan, mainly Dionysian subcode of the dance will remain, but now somewhat extended into the "oriental." Because Orientalism has been closely connected to visual culture, it was likely that opera, the monumental Gesamtkunstwerk, would become the most successful medium for presenting Salome. Here performance approaches image and the exotic is most strongly highlighted (Høgasen-Hallesby 2014: 187). Especially in Arnold Schönberg's opera Moses und Aaron (composed 1930-1932; premiered 1952), it is the "Dance around the Golden Calf" that presents not only the "almost overwhelming power of the graven image (pessel-temunah) [...], but [...] also central 'exotic' features of pagan rites and their bodily-sensual character...." (Assman n.d.: 19)

Transfigurations: the Visual and the Spiritual

The second part of this chapter focuses on the historical peak of European Salomania, the fin de siècle. During this time, the figure of Salome stepped out of the religious story of John the Baptist. According to Sicher (2017: 16) "In the second half of the 19th century, the Jewess [in general, U.B] leaves her farther behind and becomes an independent agent of vengeance, a femme fatale who threatens European manhood." The 19th century, a century in which women tried to re-enter the workforce and fought for political rights, "produced some 2,789 works of art and literature in which Salome was the central figure. This

---

2   John Chrysostom: "'Wo eben ein Tanz ist...' (...) O welch ein teuflisches Gastmahl! Welch ein satanisches Schauspiel! Welch sündhafter Tanz und noch sündhafterer Tanzlohn! (...) Wo eben ein Tanz ist, da ist auch der Teufel dabei." ([350-407] 2000: 68, 70)

image played a crucial role in creating the myth of women in the period." (Neginsky 2013: 74) During this phase of European art and popular culture Salome became iconic. At the same historical moment, when first literature seemed to assume the lead in her representation, the story was also transfigured (see Auerbach in Meyer and Largier 2015a: 155-6) into a highly popularized image and, finally, the fetishized and commercialized body of the dancing Salome.

> She is first of all an icon in western visual culture, in the many depictions of her holding or kissing the Baptist's severed head in various positions, as represented either in the vivid pictures of Gustave Moreau or in the refined black-and white lines of Audrey Beardsley. [...] Salome has [also, U.B.] come to demonstrate what western culture anxiously has to control: women, children, bodies, sexuality and the orient. (Høgasen-Hallesby 2014: 179)

In Wilde's play Salomé (1891), the act of looking, gazing and seeing is fundamental in two ways: as the dominant activity of the main characters, as well as the audience, and as a recurring theme of reflection and desire. Salome's story "is embedded in our visual imagination so effectively that, in a way, she [...] can be thought of as a sign of the visual as such." (Bucknell 1993: 503-26) The play explores the desire to 'unveil' the body, and it places this desire in a series of visual metaphors and visions that connects the sensual with the aesthetic and the sacred. Wilde's presentation of the Judean princess as desiring Jokanaan's ideal body and as searching in his new 'pure' religion for "spiritual rebirth," (see also Koritz 1994: 62). Anne L. Seshadri (2006: 24-25) even argues that in Wilde's play and even Strauss' opera "Salome served as a metaphor for the Jewish Question. Between the Jewishness of Herod's court, where the Jew was constructed as the unchanging racialized Other, and the Christ-like figure of Jokanaan stood Salome, signifier of transformable cultural Hebraism." Wilde connects her further with the tradition of the Carthaginian priestess Salammbô in Flaubert's eponymous novel, and also with that of Salome's dance in Flaubert's "Hérodias." In this highly sensualized story, published in 1877, "the young dancer mimics the searching, yearning movements of a lost soul for God." (Dierkes-Thrun 2011: 26) In a letter, Wilde himself compared his Salome to the virgin priestess and the mystic Santa Teresa of Avila: "My Salome is a mystic, the sister of Salammbô, a Sainte Thérèse who worships the moon." (quoted in Ellmann 1988: 376) During the second half of the play, however, her yearning becomes purely sensual. After Jokanaan's death, Salome at last kisses the lips of the severed head.

As is not unusual in Symbolism, the realm of aestheticized beauty and 'ideal art' abounds in spiritual and mythical references. Moreover, the play "thematizes a stark contrast between the verbal and the visual." (Wallen 1992: 124) The visual is connected with the ambivalent status of Salome as an 'acting icon': she is the one who is 'looked upon,' worshipped and desired, and who desires to see the body of Jokanaan. For her, 'seeing' is a bodily and sensual act. Holding the severed head of John the Baptist in her hands at the end of the play, she exclaims: "If you had looked at me you would have loved me." Jokanaan, on the other hand, represents the new (Christian) religion in a very puritan fashion: he refuses to look upon Salome, whom he condemns as "daughter of Babylon," and covers his eyes at the seductive beauty of her body. In an invisible, disembodied voice, rising out of the cistern, he praises the new religion and desires to hear only the words of his God. The modernist artistic "work on the myth" (Blumenberg 1985) reinvents and retells the biblical story, unearthing and elaborating the myth within its own cultural and historical context. In Wilde's "remaking of the iconic myth, a story about the death of John the Baptist [is] turned into the story of the dancing girl." (Høgasen-Hallesby 2014) It should be noted, however, that in the gospel stories of Matthew and Mark, the narrative flow is also interrupted as the 'girl' stages her body in dance.

In Western culture the dominance of the visual sense has been connected with the idea of a distancing, powerful gaze. This oft-gendered idea of the "gaze" (see Mulvey 1975/1999) is considered "superior to the other senses, in part because it was defined as being detached from what it observes." (Hutcheon/Hutcheon 1998: 15) When in 1905 Richard Strauss turned Wilde's play into an opera, Salome was given a singing voice, cast as a dramatic soprano, and merged with the figure of the diva. Opera as such is an embodied art form in which the voice cannot be imagined as disembodied. "Indeed," as Hutcheon and Hutcheon point out, "opera owes its undeniable affective power to the overdetermination of the verbal, the visual and the aural – not to the aural alone." (Hutcheon/Hutcheon 2000: 206) In Strauss's Salome, the body on stage gains even greater importance because, for nearly ten minutes, the singer does not sing at all, but only fills visual space with her dance.

Considering the late nineteenth-century self-reflective versions of the Salome story, it is possible to develop a more general theory about the relation between narration and imagination, the visible and the invisible, the body and the disembodied voice. All these opposites are connected to the question of how the biblical story, which in itself is already intertextually constituted, can be mediated and figured in modern art works and how artistic "work on the myth" has elaborated and developed new facets of sense in retelling and re-enacting myth. This chapter works with the hypothesis that the 'blank spaces' within the biblical narratives, in interplay with an increasingly colourful presentation of Salome and her dance in the authorized patristic commentaries and her mnemonic role as a pathos formula, have helped to create her fascination and the flourishing line of re-inventions and variations. It is out of these traumatic, unsaid and overdetermined tensions that modern aesthetics draws "its formula of self-expression as the – often sacralised – 'purely aesthetic.'" (Pfeiffer 2006: 310)

Aesthetic Response Theory and Mental Images

Wolfgang Iser's ground-breaking and influential theory of aesthetic response describes the interactive dynamics between text and reader. It asks how the "negations" or "gaps" in a narrative leave a virtual space for the imagination of the reader to produce (new) meaning. In the preface to his book The Act of Reading of 1978 (German edition: 1976), Iser wrote: "Effects and the responses are properties neither of the text nor of the reader; the text represents a potential effect that is realized in the reading process." (Iser 1978: ix) The act of reading becomes, not unlike the performative speech act in Austin's theory, a creative and transformative process. The reader-driven concretization and fictional actualization of the art work is described as an "affective" and "aesthetic effect" that "marks a gap in defining qualities of language. [...]. Thus, the meaning of a literary text is not a definable entity but, if anything, a dynamic happening." (22) This theory of "creative blanks" was influenced by Roman Ingarden's theory of literary indeterminacy. It also originated in collaboration and discussion with the philosopher Hans Blumenberg in the debates of the Constance group "Poetics and Hermeneutics." The theory of aesthetic response and Iser's later work on Literary Anthropology (1993) are closely connected with Blumenberg's considerations on the polysemy of mythical narration, as may be seen in Blumenberg's famous book Work on Myth (1985). There he maintains that mythical narrations circulate continuously and are constantly being re-told and re-invented in folk traditions, in art works and even in their academic interpretations. As Ben de Bruyn has observed: "The importance of Blumenberg's work for Iser's thinking on topics such as montage, metaphor, myth, reality, productivity and modernity cannot be stressed enough." (2012: 47) Iser focuses on the unsaid, invisible, undetermined or only implied meanings in literary narration, which, in the process of reading, trigger our imagination and can sometimes even induce the effect of shock (131). As a kind of productive "negativity" (225), these "blanks can function as a dynamic factor to bring forth – at least potentially – infinite possibilities" of remembrance, imagination and actualization. Narrative gaps or "empty spaces" allow the reader to reconsider their expectations and produce mental images: "it stimulates communicative [...] activities within us by showing us that something is being withheld and by challenging us to discover what it is with the help of 'processes of imagination.'" (Iser 1989: 140-1) "Blanks" are for Iser phenomena of tilting or tipping, in which a sudden shift of perspective occurs (1978: 212).

Since the 1980s, Iser's theory of aesthetic response has been applied to other media such as film (as he himself had already done), art works, visual culture and opera (see de Bruyn 2021). In his book An Anthropology of Images, Hans Belting (2011) demonstrates that Iser's anthropological reflections also apply to the analysis of visual culture. The art historian Christiane Kruse has also begun to develop Iser's theory of "narrative blanks" into a general theory of media (Kruse 2003: 291).

As pointed out previously in this chapter, there are already narrative gaps in the biblical story. In his book Intertextuality and the Reading of Midrash, Daniel Boyarin connects a narratological approach and ideas of narrative gaps to the interpretative re-telling and re-writing of the midrash: "The gaps are those silences in the text which call for interpretation if the reader is to 'make sense' of what happened, to fill out the plot and the characters in a meaningful way." (1990: 41) The midrash is very different from modern exegesis, but perhaps it can be connected to what we find in patristic literature and to artistic and narrative "work on myth" in Blumenberg's sense. The striking intertextuality of the Salome corpus in the gospel story, let alone its re-telling and re-invention up to modernity, is already a good example of the imaginative effect of its narrative "blanks." But the theory of the imaginative effect of narrative "blanks" can also help to understand the transformation and transfiguration of the textual corpus, first into an image and then into a dancing body.

Sensuality and Religion

The Church Fathers' narrative inventions of Salome and her dance were already full of visual, graphic and sexual imaginations. Thus, it is not surprising that, at least since 1000 AD, Salome, as a pathos formula (Brunotte 2013:), has been an icon of the visual arts and depicted first and foremost as a beautiful woman and a dancing body. The nineteenth century revived the sexualizing and demonizing patristic commentaries and transformed them, producing modern Salomania. The figure of Salome was popularized as the embodiment of the femme fatale and became the icon of the Symbolist movement, which sought to attain the 'divine' through art. At the peak of its cultural impact in Europe, Salomania embraced painting, photography and, in addition to the opera, various performances of the 'Dance of the Seven Veils' by female burlesque and barefoot dancers. It was above all the Canadian dancer Maud Allan who embodied Salome in Europe (see Chapter Seven). Even when Allan, in her "Vision of Salome," impersonated the oriental princess wearing only a daringly scanty costume, she meant to present Salome as an innocent girl fascinated by John the Baptist's religious message. As Amy Koritz notes, quoting Allan's autobiography, Allan tried "to express the 'ecstasy mingled with dread' that signalled her [Salome's] impending spiritual awakening." (1996: 67)

Wilde's presentation of the Judean princess as desiring Jokanaan's ideal body, and as searching for spirituality, introduces her as an icon of aestheticism. However, even when Salome's yearning for the Baptist's body becomes purely sensual, Wilde has her use variations of the erotic-spiritual language of Salomon's Song of Songs. After Jokanaan's death, Salome at last kisses the lips of the severed head. In the novel À Rebours (Against Nature), published in 1884, in which one of Gustave Moreau's famous pictures of Salome functions as symbol of decadence, Joris-Karl Huysman humanizes the "essential modernist crisis of faith [...] and inscribes empathy for the human condition into Moreau's Salome figures as well as into Des Esseintes's character ..." (Dierkes-Thrun 2011: 40) As in Flaubert's and Huysman's narrations, it was Salome's dance which became central in the multimedia re-inventions of Salome. It was also the nineteenth century in which narrative media entered into direct cooperation with the visual arts to re-tell Salome's story. In this connection it should be emphasized again that the famous "Dance of the Seven Veils," which even scholars have often projected onto the biblical story, was Wilde's invention. Wilde, however, created a dramatic blank and left the mental imagination of the dance to the reader and the theatre director. In his play there was no specific stage direction as to how the dance should be envisioned. On the other hand, Wilde's French version of the play, published in 1891, was inspired by Gustave Moreau's painting Salome Dancing before Herod (1876). Wilde was also inspired by the description of the painting that he encountered as an enthusiastic reader of the fifth chapter of Huysmans's novel. Midway through a description of the picture, the narrator Des Esseintes changes tense, steps out of the narrative past and creates the impression of the "absolute presence" of Salome's apparition: "She is almost naked! In the heat of the dance her veils have become loosened, the brocaded robes have fallen away, and only the jewels protect her naked body." (Huysmans [1884] 2008: 103-4 quoted in Neginsky 2013: 168)

Pictorial Narrativity and the Creation of an "Apparition"

As this example demonstrates, in Huysmans's novel there is already a tension between the narration and the visual, the said and the seen, narrative temporality and the "frozen image" of Salome. This tension becomes even more relevant in Wilde's play, where it functions as a medium to reflect on the relation between Salome and Jokanaan. Wilde's play is:

> built around a series of visual metaphors and explores the obsessive desire to gaze upon the body [...], the central tension of the play, between Iokanaan and Salome, revolves around his refusal to look at Salome and his desire to "listen but to the voice of the Lord God", whereas she demands to see and to touch Iokanaan. The play aligns the field of vision with the body and with sexual desire, in contrast to the verbal field, which is aligned with the immaterial and the suprasensual. (Wallen 1992: 124)

In this context, metaphors and processes of veiling and unveiling, secrecy and truth gain momentum. Here Iser's idea of "mental image" and Belting's use of this concept in his "anthropology of images" can be rendered productive. What is important for the analysis is that Iser's aesthetics of "narrative blanks" is itself full of visual metaphors. Iser even emphasizes "the picture character of the imagination (*Bildcharakter der Vorstellung*), which emerges in the reader out of the unsaid." (1994: 220) A few lines later he even goes so far as to say that "'[i]maging' depends upon the absence of that which appears in the image" (1978: 137). In fact, though it was Wilde's play that gave Salome's dance the famous name of the "Dance of the Seven Veils," it "leaves the dance undescribed" (Hutcheon/Hutcheon 1998: 215). Thus, Marjorie Garber rightly argues that "[i]n its non-description, in its indescribability, lies its power, and its availability for cultural inscription and appropriation" (1993: 341).

In modern literary tradition, it was Gustave Flaubert who first filled in this central "blank" of the biblical story. In his narrative *Herodias* (1877) he invented a highly sensual, orientalized description of Salome's dance. Neginsky maintains that this "description arouses the senses of all spectators present at the banquet [...]" and was also meant to "overwhelm the reader." (2013: 162) Drawing on iconographic traditions, Flaubert's narrative is a literary example of writing the visual, in which "the ways of plastic and literary expressions mutually enhance each other" (150, 164). According to James Heffernan, the modern use of *ekphrasis* focuses not on a simple description, but on a "verbal representation of a visual representation" (1993: 3-4); picturalism "is the generation in language of effects similar to those created by pictures." (Neginsky 2013: 150; see also Heffernan 1993 and Tooke 2000: 3) To increase the affective intensity of the scene, the chronological narration of events ceases. The "mode of representing temporal events as action stopped at its climatic moment [...]. It gave rise to the literary topos of *ekphrasis*, in which a poem aspires to the atemporal 'eternity' of the stopped-acting (...)." (Steiner 2004: 150) As in Huysmans's famous description of Salome's dance through the mouth of his protagonist Des Esseintes, a transfer of tense from past to present reinforces the impression of "eternity" and a nearly epiphanic immediacy. This creates the impression of frozen time. Especially the break in narrative flow produces an instantaneous experience of the instant, which takes on the form of a mental image and a living picture. In an article entitled 'The Fetishization of a Textural Corpus,' Becker-Leckrone (1995) argues that it is precisely through modern literature's use of theses narrative tools that the story of Salome has been transformed into an icon, body and fetish. "Des Esseintes' 'Salome'," she writes, "is, obviously, the woman rather than the story, a body rather than a text. 'She' is the object of his fascination, [...] his fetish." (240)

In sum, this section started with the idea that it is from the unsaid, the "blanks" within the biblical narratives, that modern aestheticism, in interplay with the imaginative patristic commentaries, draws its formula of self-reflection as the "purely aesthetic" (Pfeiffer 2006: 310). And it is exactly the epoch of fin de siècle aestheticism that used this biblical episode and its blank female figure to focus its reflection on the sensual and transgressive impact of aesthetic media. It was Wilde who invented the "Dance of the Seven Veils," but who, at the same time, played with the imaginary power of the blanks by leaving Salome's dance undescribed in his drama. Not without connections to the modern crisis of faith in the way it is represented in Wilde's play and in Huysmans's novel, the figure and the dance of Salome became an icon of Symbolism and of *decadence* (Brunotte 2012). Petra Dierkes-Thrun argues that Wilde's modern Salome embodied a "transformation of the religious aspect into a tool of seduction – and hence the fusion of the spiritual and the sexual." (2011: 31) The Symbolists also believed that art was a "'theurgical activity' [...], a vehicle for bringing the divine on earth through the soul." (Nezhinskaia 2010: 11) The creation of the *femme fatale* within Symbolist art and literature had therefore an ambivalent structure. Majorie Garber also maintains that "the Salome myth provides a much more equivocal narrative than the essentializing exaltation of 'the exotic, feminized Eastern Other.'" (Garber 1993: 340) It connects the sensual with the spiritual, the erotized female body with religion.

Strauss's Opera, Narrative Blanks and the Fetishizing of a Body

It was Richard Strauss's opera of 1905, the first modernist music drama, which completed and fixed the modern transformation of the Salome story in the orientalized fetish of the dancing femme fatale. The opera filled in the narrative blank of the "Dance of the Seven Veils," and by shortening Wilde's text in the libretto, silenced crucial parts of Salome's story. As Strauss confided to his diary in 1942, he wanted to write an oriental and a "Jewish opera" (Judenoper): "I've long found fault with oriental and Jewish operas because they lack an Eastern atmosphere and blazing sun. This lack inspired in me (for my own opera) really exotic harmonies, which shimmered in strange cadences, like shot silk." (Strauss 1949: 224)[3]

In her ground-breaking interpretation of 2008, Karla Hoven-Buchholz (356, title) asks the following question: "What veiled the unveiling of Salome?" Comparing Strauss's libretto and Oscar Wilde's play, which was used by Strauss in its German translation, she searches for the suppressed history and the untold narratives that were concealed and made invisible behind

---

3   Richard Strauss (1949: 224): "Ich hatte schon lange an den Orient- und Judenopern auszusetzen, daß ihnen wirklich östliches Kolorit und glühende Sonne fehlt. Das Bedürfnis gab mir (für meine eigene Oper) wirklich exotische Harmonik ein, die besonders in fremdartigen Kadenzen schillerte, wie Changeant-Seide."

the dance of the *femme fatale*. Her conclusion is that Strauss invented not only the orientalized "Dance of the Seven Veils" in his nearly ten minutes of dance-music, but also that, by cutting out important narrative parts of the play, he himself created narrative blanks which trigger a specific affective imagination in the audience (363-5). Hoven-Buchholz claims that it was these blanks together with Strauss's creation of an orientalized "Dance of the Seven Veils" that powerfully influenced the cultural imagination of the ancient and modern orientalized Jewish 'Other' and cast the figure of Salome as the sexualized, murderous *femme fatale* (see Seshadri 2006 and Brunotte 2014).

In contrast to the opera, Wilde's play does not omit Salome's story from the scene. It is at the same time an example of stylized Symbolist language *and* a reflection upon and parody of it. The author performs *and* presents the *habitus* of aestheticism. As we have seen, Wilde refuses to focus on the dance. For him Salome is a mystic and even tragic heroine. The opera, by contrast, focuses on the dance and Salome's final monologue addressed to the severed head. As Helmut Pfeiffer has stressed:

> Approximately a quarter of the entire opera of one hundred minutes is filled with the Dance of the Seven Veils [...] and the final monologue. This is a very great difference and shift in comparison with the text of Wilde's play, which was in any case a play to be read [...]. Especially the monologue with the head, which uses Wagnerian lyrical time extension, focuses on the exhibition of a woman whose [...] body has become a voyeuristic object: "[...]what the audience encounters is less a character singing than a woman, *as* woman, acting out a multiple debasement: scopic, erotic, artistic, linguistic." (Pfeiffer 2006: 334-5, Kramer in Pfeiffer 1990, pp.281)

For Hoven-Buchholz, by cutting out important parts of her story, Strauss did even more to intensify the creation of Salome as the body-icon of the *femme fatale*. Even in recent opera productions, these narrative blanks still have an affective impact on the audience by rendering her story unheard. For example, Strauss omits all narrative information about Salome's tragic and even incestuous position within the Herod-Herodias family. Wilde's play, Hoven-Buchholz emphasises, informs the reader that Salome knows how and where her father was murdered. Herod's brother, Herodias' former husband, was killed by Herod in exactly the same cistern in which John the Baptist is later imprisoned. Against this backdrop, her interest and 'love' for Jokanaan, his voice and message, acquires a different, a more childlike and *spiritual meaning* beyond the purely *sensual* one. Wilde invented a Salome in the image of a tragic heroine, a young girl torn between murderous and unresolved family dynamics, very much like Orestes or Hamlet (2008: 365, 366-70). In Strauss's opera *Elektra*, which was premiered two years after *Salome*, one has the strong impression that Hofmannsthal and Strauss were creating a continuation of Salome's story.

Fig. 11 and 12: Interpretation of Richard Strauss's opera "Salome" by Claus Guth, Deutsche Oper Berlin, January 2016.

Photos: Monika Ritterhaus, courtesy of the photographer.

Fig. 13: Interpretation of Richard Strauss's opera "Salome" by Claus Guth, Deutsche Oper Berlin, January 2016.

Photo: Monika Ritterhaus, courtesy of the photographer.

A very recent interpretation of Strauss's *Salome* (premiered January 2016) by Claus Guth, at the Deutsche Oper in Berlin, confirms Hoven-Buchholz analysis. Guth liberates the opera from all its oriental and sexualized readings and places Salome again in the thick of the fatal dynamics of family relations, especially the struggle between her mother and Herod. In his interpretation, Salome's behaviour is the result of trauma, abuse and failed communication. The audience must relinquish what generations of opera directors have made them believe about Salome the *femme fatale*. Guth used silent stretches within the singing and 'gaps' in the libretto for a radically reversed critical interpretation, which triggers new 'mental images' and thoughts in the audience. In particular, Guth's interpretation avails itself of the ten minutes of music normally reserved for the dance to narrate Salome's long history of abuse and suffering at the hands of her stepfather Herod.

He tells these stories by having them performed as in a puppet show by six children who are Salome's doubles. Dressed in the same costume as Salome, they range from a little girl of six to a young girl of approximately eighteen. They all have to 'dance' with Herod, and this dance immediately loses its seductive, 'erotic' meaning. Here the narrative is heard again behind and through the formerly fetishized body. In the retrieval of the suppressed story of a family and the untold narrative of Salome's abuse, the audience can discover even in Strauss's *Salome* a tragic heroine reminiscent of Orestes and Hamlet. Salome suddenly becomes a *pathos formula* not only of violence, perversity and passion, but also of trauma, suffering and the search for spiritual healing.

Bibliography

Assman, Jan (n.d.): Die Mosaische Unterscheidung in Arnold Schönberg's Oper Moses und Aaron. Available online: http://www.aroumah.net/agora /assmann03-schoenbergEF.pdf (accessed 2 January 2018).

Baert, Barbara (2014): "The Dancing Daughter and the Head of John the Baptist (Mark 6:14 29) Revisited. An Interdisciplinary Approach." In: Louvain Studies 38, pp. 5-29.

Bauman, Zygmunt (1991): Modernity and Ambivalence. Ithaka: Connell University Press.

Becker-Leckrone, Megan (1995): "Salome: The Fetichization of a Textual Corpus." In: New Literary History 26/2, pp. 239-60.

Belting, Hans ([2001; 2011] 2014): An Anthropology of Images: Picture, Medium, Body, Princeton: Princeton University Press.

Bucknell, Brad (1993): "On 'Seeing' Salome." In: English Literary History 2, pp. 503-26.

Blumberg, Hans (1985): Work on the Myth, Cambridge, Massachusetts: MIT Press.

Boyarin, Daniel (1990): Intertextuality and the Reading of Midrash, Bloomington: Indiana University Press.

Brunotte, Ulrike (2012): "Unveiling Salome 1900 – Entschleierungen zwischen Sexualität, Pathosformel und Oriental Dance." In: Elke Frietsch/Bettina Dennerlein/Therese Steffen (eds.), Verschleierter Orient – Entschleierter Okzident?, München: Wilhelm Fink Verlag, pp. 93-116.

Brunotte, Ulrike (2013): "Salome and the head of John the Baptist." In: Ulrike Brunotte, Dämonen des Wissens. Gender, Performativity und materielle Kultur im Werk von Jane Ellen Harrison, Würzburg: Ergon, pp. 217-44.

Brunotte, Ulrike (2015): "'All Jews are womanly, but no woman is a Jew'. The 'Femininity' Game of Deception: Female Jew, femme fatale Orientale, and Belle Jew." In: Ulrike Brunotte/Anna-Dorothea Ludewig/Axel Stähler (eds.), Orientalism, Gender and the Jews, Oldenburg: de Gruyter, pp. 195-220.

Ceramaeus, Theophanes ([12.Jh.] 2000): "Über die Enthauptung des ehrwürdigen Künders." In: Thomas Rohde (ed.), Mythos Salome. Vom Markusevangelium bis Djuna Barnes, Leipzig: Reclam, pp. 70-2.

Chrysostomos, Johannes ([350-407] 2000): "Wo eben ein Tanz ist..." In: Thomas Rohde (ed.), Mythos Salome. Vom Markusevangelium bis Djuna Barnes, Leipzig: Reclam, pp. 68-70.

de Bruyn, Ben (2012): Wolfgang Iser. A Companion, Boston and Berlin: de Gruyter.

Dierkes-Thrun, Petra (2011): Salome's Modernity. Oscar Wilde and the Aesthetics of Transgression, Ann Arbor: University of Michigan Press.

Ellmann, Richard (1988): Oscar Wilde, New York: Knopf.

Garber, Marjorie (1993): Vested Interests: Cross-Dressing and Cultural Anxiety, New York: Harper Perennial.

Hägg, Tomas (2012): The Art of Biography in Antiquity, New York: Cambridge University Press.

Heffernan, James A. W. (1993): The Museum of Words: The Poetics of Ekphrasis from Homer to Ashbery, Chicago: Chicago University Press.

Heinrich, Klaus (1995): Floß der Medusa. 3 Studien zur Faszinations-geschichte, Frankfurt/M.: Stroemfeld.

Høgasen-Hallesby, Hedda (2014): "Performing the Icon: The Body on Stage and the Staged Body in Salome's 'Dance of the Seven Veils'." In: Hyunseon Lee and Naomi D. Segal (eds.), Opera, Exoticism and Visual Culture, Bern: Peter Lang, pp. 179-202.

Høgasen-Hallesby, Hedda (2015): "Salome's Silent Spaces: Canonicity, Creativity, and Critique." In: The Opera Quaterly 31/4, pp. 223-41.

Hoven-Buchholz, Karla (2008): "Was verschleiert Salmes Tanz? Eine psycho-analytische Interpretation jenseits des Femme-fatale Klischees." In: Psyche –Zeitschrift für Psychoanalyse 62, pp. 356-80.

Hutcheon, Linda/Hutcheon, Michael (1998): "'Here's Lookin' at You, Kid': The Empowering Gaze in 'Salome'." In: Profession, pp. 11-22.

Hutcheon, Linda/Hutcheon, Michael (2000): "Staging the Female Body. Richard Strauss's Salome." In: Mary Ann Smart (ed.), Siren Songs: Representations of Gender and Sexuality in Opera, Princeton: Princeton University Press, pp. 204-21.

Huysmans, Joris-Karl ([1884] 2008): Against Nature, trans. by Brendan King, Cambs: Dedalus.

Inowlocki, Sabrina (2016): "Josephus and Patristic Literature." In: Honora Howell Chapman/Zuleika Rodgers (eds.), A Campagnion to Josephus, Oxford: Wiley Blackwell, pp. 356-67.

Iser, Wolfgang (1978): The Act of Reading. A Theory of Aesthetic Response, Baltimore and London: Johns Hopkins University Press.

Iser, Wolfgang (1994): Der Akt des Lesens. Theorie ästhetischer Wirkung, München: W. Fink.

Iser, Wolfgang (1989): Prospecting. From Reader Response to Literary Anthropology, Baltimore: Johns Hopkins University Press.

Iser, Wolfgang (1993): The Fictive and the Imaginary. Charting Literary Anthropology, Baltimore: Johns Hopkins University Press.

Koritz, Amy (1994): "Dancing the Orient for England. Maus Allan's 'Vision of Salome'." In: Theatre Journal 46, pp. 63-78.

Kramer, Lawrence (1990): "Culture and Musical Hermeneutics. The Salome Complex." In: Cambridge Opera Journal 2/3, pp. 269-94.

Kruse, Christiane (2003): Wozu Menschen malen. Historische Begründungen des Bildmediums, München: Fink Verlag.

Levine, Amy-Jill (ed.) (2008): A Feminist Companion to Patristic Literature, London: T&T Clark International.

Lohmeyer, Ernst (1967): Kirchlich-exegetischer Kommentar über das neue Testament, Das Evangelium des Markus, übersetzt und erklärt von Ernst Lohmeyer, Göttingen: Vandenhoeck & Ruprecht.

Ludewig, Anna-Dorothea (2014): "Between Orientalization and Self-Orientalization. Remarks on the Image of the '"Beautiful Jewess'"in Nineteenth- and Early-Twentieth-Century European Literature." In: Ulrike Brunotte, Anna-Dorothea Ludewig, and Axel Stähler (eds), Orientalism, Gender, and the Jews. Literary and Artistic Transformations of European National Discourses, Oldenburg: De Gruyter, pp. 221-29.

Meyer, Birgit (2015a): Sensational Movies. Video, Vision, and Christianity in Ghana, Oakland: University of California Press.

Meyer, Birgit (2015b): "Picturing the Invisible. Visual Culture and the Study of Religion." In: Method and Theory in the Study of Religion 27, pp. 333-60.

Mulvey, Laura ([1975] 1999): "Visual Pleasure and Narrative Cinema." In: Leo Braudy/Marshall Cohen (eds.), Film Theory and Criticism: Introductory Readings, Oxford: Oxord University Press, pp. 833-44.

Neginsky, Rosina (2010): Symbolism, its Origins and its Consequences, Newca upon Tyne: Cambridge Scholars Publishing.

Neginsky, Rosina (2013): Salome: The Image of a Woman who Never Was, Cambridge: Cambridge Scholarly Publishing.

Nietzsche, Friedrich ([1872] 1993): The Birth of Tragedy, trans. by Shaun Whiteside, London: Penguin Books.

Pesch, Rudolf (1976): Das Markus Evangelium. Einführung und Kommentar, Freiburg/Basel: Herder.

Pfeiffer, Hans (2006): "Salome im Fin de Siècle. Ästhetisierung des Sakralen, Sakralisierung des Ästhetischen. " In: Steffen Martus/Aandrea Polaschegg (eds.), Das Buch der Bücher – gelesen. Lesarten der Bibel in den Wissenschaften und Künsten, Bern, Berlin, Bruxelles etc.: Peter Lang, pp. 303-36.

Rohde, Thomas (ed.) (2000): Mythos Salome. Vom Markusevangelium bis Djuna Barnes, Leipzig: Reclam Verlag.

Seshadri, Anne L. (2006): "The Taste of Love: Salome's Transfiguration." In: Women and Music: A Journal of Gender and Culture 10, pp. 24-44.

Sicher, Efraim (2017): The Jew's Daughter. A Cultural History of a Conversion Narrative. Lanhm/Boulder/New York/London: Lexington Books.

Steiner, Wendy (2004): "Pictorial Narrativity." In: Marie-Laure Ryan/John W. Bernet (eds.), Narrative across Media. The Language of Storytelling, Lincoln and London: University of Nebraska Press, pp. 145-74.

Strauss, Richard (1949): Betrachtungen und Erinnerungen, hg. v. Willi Schuh, Mainz: Schott.

The NRSV (1998): Bible New Standard Version. Available online: http://www. devotions.net/bible/oobible.htm (accessed 2 January 2018).

Tolbert, Mary Ann (1989): Sowing the Gospel: Mark's World in Literary-Historical Perspective, Minneapolis: Fortress Press.

Tooke, Adrianne (2000): Flaubert and the Pictorial Arts. From Image to Text, Oxford: Oxford University Press.

Uehlinger, Christoph (2005): "Medien in der Lebenswelt des Antiken Palästina?." In: Christian Frevel (ed.), Medien im antiken Palästina: Materielle Kommunikation und Medialität als Thema der Palästinaarchäologie, Tübingen: Mohr Siebeck, pp. 31-61.

Valman, Nadia (2007): The Jewess in Nineteenth-Century British Literary Culture, Cambridge: Cambridge University Press.

Wallen, Jeffrey (1992): "Illustrating Salome: perverting the text?." In: Word & Image 8/2, pp. 124 -32.

Warburg, Aby (2010): "Mnemosyne Eileitung. " In: Martin Treml/Sigrid Weigel/Perdita Ladwig (eds.), Aby Warburg. Werke in einem Band, Berlin: Suhrkamp, pp. 629-39.

Wellhausen, Julius ([1923] 2010): Das Evangelium Marci, United States: Nabu Press.

7. "Dancing on the Threshold"[1].
Maud Allan and the English Salome Scandal

Maud Allan's misdeed

On February 16, 1918, the right-wing London journal *Vigilante* published an article under the insinuating title "The Cult of the Clitoris" (quoted in Hoare 1998: 90). The text warned against the harmful effects of a performance of Oscar Wilde's prohibited play *Salomé*. Staged by the private Independent Theatre Society, this was by no means a run-of-the-mill production. As a private theater performance, however, with only invited guests, it could pass the 1892 ban on Wilde's play.[2] The director was none other than the liberal, pro-German *Sunday Times* critic Jack (Jacob) Thomas Grein, and the role of Salome was assumed by the (in)famous and controversial dance artist Maud Allan. Skillfully blending political and sexual phobias, the conservative and patriotic Movement for Purity in Public Life exacerbated the ensuing public uproar once news of the performance had broken on February 10th (Kettle 1977). Early in 1918, a time in which a catastrophic Allied defeat still seemed possible and England remained gripped by war hysteria, the parliamentarian and leading figure of the Purity Movement, Noel Pemberton-Billing, advanced what was then held to be a thoroughly credible theory: together with the homophobic anti-Semite Harold Sherwood Spencer, Billing announced that a covert German military maneuver sought to debilitate the enemy's strength and patriotism via (homo)sexual infiltration.

Like the story of the "fifth column" that circulated during the Second World War, the combination of decadence and perversion was used to suggest

---

1   Heading in Dierkes-Thrun (2011: 15).

2   In 1892 the Lord Chamberlain prohibited public performances of the play because of its allegedly defamatory portrayal of biblical figures.

the existence of an "enemy within." Arnold White, a supporter of the Purity Movement, described German "sexual warfare" as follows: "The tendency in Germany is to abolish civilisation as we know it, to substitute Sodom and Gomorrah for the New Jerusalem, and to infect clean nations with Hunnish erotomania." (Hoare 1998: 89) This fear, virtually embodied in the wartime enemy, was part of a long-held national dialogue – the scandal designated by the name of Oscar Wilde. By the time of the First World War, more than thirteen years after his death and some twenty years after the original trial, Wilde was still seen as the personification of a culture of decadence, as suggested in this ambivalent and enigmatic statement from the turn of the century: "Wilde was a mythical figure: to some, a demon; to others a saint." (ibid: 15) In particular, Wilde was associated with his play *Salomé*, which had first been published in French and performed in continental Europe for some time before it was popularized by Richard Strauss's opera *Salome* (1905). For the British censor in 1918, the play symbolized the "degenerative" influence of liberal culture on puritanical England much more than at the time of its first prohibition by the Lord Chamberlain in 1892. That injunction was officially based on the general ban of biblical subjects from British theaters; the continued censorship of the play until 1931, two decades after the 1912 lifting of the ban on biblical plays, raises a few questions. With the help of sources from the archive of the British Library, Matthew Lewsadder (2002) has reconstructed the discursive field in which Wilde's *Salome* was consistently condemned by the Lord Chamberlain from 1892 to 1931. Lewsadder has shown that there was an "enigmatic relationship between Salome's active female sexual and essential carnal desire [...] as well as the embodiment of a subversive female sexuality [...] and the censorship of the play" (Lewsadder 2002: 520). For example, in a letter of 1892, written by the Examiner of Plays of the Lord Chamberlain's Office, Edward F.S. Pigott, to Spencer Ponsonby, the Controller of the Lord Chamberlaine's Office, Pigott stated that Salome's:

> Love turns to fury because John will not let her kiss him *in the mouth* – and in the last scene, where she brings in his head – if you please – on a "charger" – she *does* kiss his mouth, in a paroxysm of sexual despair. This piece is written in French – half Biblical, half pornographic – by Oscar Wilde himself. Imagine the average British public's reception of it. (Lewsadder 2002: 520)

In accordance with the Victorian moral discourse of "female passionlessness" (Cott 1978), with its idea that decent women "lacked sexual passion" and "were *less* carnal and lustful than men" (ibid: 221), Salome's sexual agency in Wilde's play was depicted as *unnatural, morbid, immoral, perverse* and "half pornographic." When J. T. Grein decided to produce an English translation of Wilde's *Salome* in 1918 it was again Salome's transgressive female sexuality and her open desire for John the Baptist, which was in the centre of the debate and the later legal controversy with Noel Pemberton-Billing at the Old Bailey. As will be demonstrated in the end of this chapter, Maud Allan, who took over the part of Salome in the private performance, was identified with Wilde's *Salome* and fell victim to a modern witch-hunt. Her own dance choreography of Salome's dance, with which she began in 1906, was, however, neither banned nor censored. On the contrary "Allan was highly acclaimed for the artistry of her dancing and her ability to transcend the indecency of Wilde's figuration of Salome." (Lewsadder 2002:527)

The Canadian barefoot dancer Maud Allan had begun her career as a Salome-dancer in Vienna and Berlin. As "the first influential modernist female interpreter of Oscar Wilde's play [...] she shot to international fame with 'The Vision of Salome' in London in 1908." (Dierkes-Thrun 2011: 83) Inspired not only by Wilde but also by Strauss and Max Reinhardt, her performance went beyond Loïe Fuller's Salome routine in her *pantomime lyrique* at the Comédie-Parisienne in March 1895. Following Allan's arrival in London in February 1908, the Canadian epitomized both exotic decadence and Edwardian "respectable" eroticism, while fostering the dissolution of the boundary between "high" and "popular" culture. Especially her solo dance in "The Vision of Salome" was "understood as a gender rebellion against women's traditional modesty" (ibid: 84). In this performance the avant-garde dancer played with intertwining the racial and gender stereotypes that made up the foundation of English orientalism and gender order. As Amy Koritz notes:

> Maud Allan's representation of an Oriental princess in "The Vision of Salome" invited discussions that invoked two discourses in particular, Orientalism and a separate spheres gender ideology. [It was especially] two potential threats this dance posed to its audience – female sexuality and the racial Other. Allan's dance was potentially transgressive in that it violated the supposed polarity between East and West by presenting her, a Western woman, as an Oriental. In addition, Allan violated the terms under which the separate spheres ideology assigned the "privileges" of (middle-class) femininity by appearing on a public stage in a daringly scanty costume. (1994: 65)

Moreover, the ambitious Allan had managed to make a name for herself as dancer in London avant-garde artistic circles and amongst (notably mostly pro-German) political advocates. Even Margot Asquith, the extravagant wife of Liberal leader Herbert Asquith, could be considered one of her fans. Before the war, during her husband's premiership, Asquith had opened the door of 10 Downing Street to cultural society "[...] and entertained the Souls with her risqué 'skirt dancing,' invented in Chicago by Loïe Fuller [...]" (Hoare 1998: 81). Mrs. Asquith was also present as a guest at exclusive private *Salome* evenings which had been taking place in the absence of men at the residences of famous female socialites since 1908, and at which not only the VIP of the evening, Maud Allan, but also the female spectators used to wear a "Salome costume."

Fig. 14: Maud Allan in her costume (1908), postcard.

MISS MAUD ALLAN AS 'SALOME.'

Public Domain, Wikimedia Commons

A *New York Times* report from August 8, 1908, (Cerniavsky 1991) describes one such event:

> Each of the ladies proceeded to outview her sisters in providing herself with a costume matching in all the undress effect of Miss Allan's scanty costume [...]. Salome's music was played [...] and some of the more graceful members of the party demonstrated that they had not only succeeded in matching Miss Allan's costume, but had learned some captivating steps in movements. (ibid: 176)

The stir created by the "Cult of the Clitoris" publicly spread a paranoid history of subterfuge that had already been peddled for some time by right-wing English political radicals. According to this idee-fixe, the German Kaiser Wilhelm II, in one of his most egregious acts of war, and under the influence of a homoerotic circle (see Chapter three of this book), was attempting to "seduce" the English nation into submission by employing an army of gay and lesbian secret agents. Writing in the *Imperialist* on January 26th, Billing stated that a top-secret "little black book" in the Kaiser's personal possession contained not only lurid details "regarding the propagation of evils which all decent men thought had perished in Sodom and Lesbia [...]" (quoted in Hoare 1998: 58), but also

> [...] the names of 47,000 English men and women. [...] It is a most *catholic list*. Privy Councillors, wives of Cabinet Ministers, even Cabinet Ministers themselves, diplomats, poets, bankers, editors, newspaper proprietors, and Members of His Majesty's Household [...] prevented from putting their full strength into the war by corruption and blackmail and fear of exposure. (ibid: 58; original emphasis)

Such sexual demonization of the adversary had for centuries been a conventional technique plied in war-mongering propaganda. The original rumors of homosexuality involving the Kaiser were connected to the Eulenburg-Moltke trials, which had generated much public interest between 1906 and 1908. As detailed in chapter three, the trials concerned the case of a close friend of the Kaiser who was accused of homosexuality and thus defamed. Together with the emergence of the early studies of sexuality like Krafft-Ebing's *Psychopathia Sexualis* from 1894 and Otto Weininger's bestselling book *Sex and Character* (1903) and the first European gay movement(s) in Berlin, these scandalous court cases carried their own political significance. The earliest Berlin sexologies were especially associated with the Jewish doctor, reformist and founder of the homosexual civil rights movement, Magnus Hirschfeld, and in 1897 the Scientific-Humanitarian Committee (Wissenschaftlich-humanitäre Komitee) was founded in Berlin. "Led by the Berlin medical doctor Magnus Hirschfeld, this group represented the world's first homosexual rights organization [...] and would soon help to make Berlin a center of sexology research and the capital of homosexual rights activism." (Beachy 2015: 40) As Eve Kosofsky Sedgwick observes: "Virtually all of the competing, conflicting figures for understanding same-sex desires [...] were coined and circulated in this period in the first place in Germany, and through German culture, medicine, and politics." (1993: 66) The result of this concentration of events in the German capital was the stronger association of Germany than other countries with an already emergent European discourse on "homosexuality."

Thus thirteen years after the destructive trial of Oscar Wilde in London, resulting in his becoming the first victim of a new English law criminalizing all "homosexual" activity, the concept of a new "Cult of the Clitoris" merged with an already existing, politically-charged case of homophobia. Together with Allan's disturbing representation of the "Oriental Other", male as well as female homosexuality represented a feared new danger to the English nation. This all the more because the national discourse employed a rhetoric of "homogeneous masculinity as definitive of Englishness" (Koritz 1994: 77). At the center of these paranoid fantasies, in which the English notions of gender roles and the clear distinction between "West" and "East" were both felt to be under threat, was the barefoot dancer celebrated across Europe, Maud Allan, and her performance of *Salome*.

Crossing Gender Boundaries: Femme Fatale and *"Beautiful Jewess"*

As will be shown in the following, the culturally charged discourse used to review and analyze Allan's dance in "The Vision of Salome" indicated an interconnective rhetoric of femininity and orientalism. Why, however, did this particular embodiment of the biblical figure from the time of John the Baptist's Judean ministry generate such an emotional response and trigger public outcry? To begin with, the figure of Salome was still associated with Wilde's play and scandalous trial. Another reason, perhaps, is the figure's compatibility with other cultural discourses and obsessions atthe turn of the century: orientalism and two cultural images of female difference – the *femme fatale* and the *"Beautiful Jewess"*. Since the beginning of the 19th century, and strongly mod-

eled after Sir Walter Scott's Rebecca in his highly successful historical novel
Ivanhoe: A Romance (1820), the "Beautiful Jewess" became a prominent literary
and cultural figure in Europe. As the "Beautiful Jewess", this culturally constructed Jewess was connected not only to physical but also to spiritual and
moral beauty (see Valman 2007: 1-21). "The Jewess continued to compel and
provoke writers precisely because she threw into disarray clear categories of
difference." (Valman 2007: 2) A radical shift in the literary and visual representation of the Jewess and the merging of the "Beautiful Jewess" with the
notorious figure of the sexualized femme fatale began in the second half of
the century alongside with growing antisemitism and reached its peak in the
fin de siècle. Karla Hoven-Buchholz, however, maintains that in the European bourgeois society of 1900, the figure of the femme fatale "had long since
ceased to represent the breaking of social taboo and instead belonged to the
negative inventory of bourgeois culture as the embodiment of evil that was
both warded off and indulged" (2008: 358).

As to the enduring fascination with Salome and her dance in turn-of-the-
century Europe, this thesis may be doubted. Further, for the first time in the
history of the figure, Wilde's Princess Salome performs her dance voluntar-
ily. She even requests for herself – or as Wilde has her say, "for mine own
pleasure" (Wilde 1967: 56) – the head of John the Baptist as reward. This detail
places the fourteen-year-old virgin in intimate proximity to transgressing a
taboo identified in Sigmund Freud's 1905 work *Three Essays on the Theory of Sexuality*, in which Freud dispels the illusion of "childhood innocence." What is
more, Salome's hybrid, sexualized aggression crosses the boundaries of conventional femininity. In her active desire for the Baptist and brazen courtship
of him, Wilde's Salome integrates characteristics and acts in ways that, at the
time, would have been interpreted as "masculine." Freud writes: "The sexuality of most men shows a taint of aggression, it is a propensity to subdue,
the biological significance of which lies in the necessity of overcoming the
resistance of the sexual object by actions other than mere courting." (Freud,
SE, 7 1953 [1905]: 22) Wilde's Jewish Princess comes forth as the – admittedly
radical – embodiment of a new, modern woman who transgresses traditional
gender boundaries. Especially with her mimicry, and parody of the Song of
Songs, she uses the discourse of sexual desire in an inversion that feminizes
Iokanaan. Hence, around 1900, Salome is made to appear so "disconcertingly
arousing because her character unites both the shock that followed the collapse of a bourgeois image of childhood innocence with that of the weak,
sexually passive woman – the femme fragile" (Unseld 2001: 70).

In the biblical legend, Salome and Herodias are characterized not only by their oriental femininity, but also by their being members of the royal family – and Jews by inheritance. "Richard Aldrich, the first *New York Times* reviewer [of Strauss's opera], commented that all of *Salome* was 'a picture set in the time of Jewish decadence and the Roman domination.'" (Aldrich 1907: 9, cit. in Gilman 1993: 198) Like the femme fatale, the "Beautiful Jewess" at the turn of the century was identified with a deviant and threatening femininity; a disturbing femininity that could merge with other anxiety-provoking and (often masculinized) figures, like the "prostitute," the "bluestocking" or the "female criminal." As Sander Gilman notes, "the dark hair and black eyes are the salient markers of this "Beautiful Jewess" [...]. The image of the 'dark' woman, while echoing the Western trope of the 'blackness' of the Jews, is at once and the same time a sign of the femme fatale." (ibid: 202) As is shown in Henri Renault's painting, Salome can also perform as an "uncivilized gipsy".

Further associated with such other deadly mythological figures as Judith, Delilah and Medusa, Salome is nevertheless a figure of fascination who attained prominence as the epitome of ambivalent fin-de-siècle movements and discourses. She was simultaneously the idol of female avant-garde dance, the prototype of striptease and the mythical *pathos formula* (*Pathosformel* in Aby Warburg' sense; see chapter eight) for the modern embodiment of female desire, violence and "perversion." Indeed, many academic interpretations of Wilde's play forcefully perpetuate this very discourse by apparently abandoning their critical distance from the source material. For example, in his book *Idols of Perversity*, Bram Dijkstra writes:

> The spectacle of Salome's bestial passion makes Herod shiver. But the outrages of feminine desire continue. In a passage in which Wilde directly equates semen and the blood which feeds man's brain, Salome, woman, the vampire hungry for blood, tastes the bitter seed of man, deprecates the spirit of holy manhood. (1986: 398)

The more such sexualizing interpretations of Salome focus on the mischievous femme fatale, the more they begin to concentrate on the dance of the seven veils and, as a result, the more uninhibited and lascivious Salome seems to become. Nineteenth-century artists also portrayed Salome as a courtesan: half-naked and in a fantastic costume by Franz von Stuck, or simply as a naked girl. Even:

Fig. 15: Henri Renault: Salome (1870),
Metropolitan Museum of Art.

Public Domain, Wikimedia Commons

Pablo Picasso's 1905 drawing of Salome has her throwing her legs in the air, as described by the Church Fathers, dancing naked while the executioner sits behind her with the head of John the Baptist on a platter, looking at her with admiration, ready to do anything she desires. (Neginsky 2013: 80)

Un-veiling of the Naked Truth

Both the Dance of the Seven Veils, which marks the historical origin of com-
mercial striptease (Sanyal 2009), and the modern notion of being able to de-
mystify the last secrets of feminine sexuality fit in many ways into the popular medical-cultural discourse on hysteria prevalent around 1900. Following George Didi-Huberman's (2003) study on the medical and iconographic
invention of hysteria in the wards of the Salpêtrière, we can find a *tertium
comparationis* for understanding the New Dance by comparing it to another
phenomenon: the occasionally ecstatic performance of "social images of femininity and madness" (Hindson 2007: 103; Dierkes-Thrun 2011: 37). At the time,
hysteria was considered as the principle means of revealing the "riddles of
femininity", yet "hysteria both displays and obscures. It arouses by enshroud-
ing, performs follies of seduction, and reveals itself by concealing. As such, it
stimulates the imagination of the average male and theoretician alike who believe themselves to be capable of disclosing its secret." (Hoven-Buchholz 2008:
359) Salome and Freud's (that is to say, Breuer's) first female patient Anna O.,
whose real name was Bertha Pappenheim, seems to evince a remarkable resemblance to Salome in her self-dramatization of a body that simultaneously
reveals and conceals itself and whose language is indecipherable. In both in-
stances, the body acts as the medium and stage for the unconscious recitation
of a personal language of memories and emotions. As Petra Dierkes-Thrun observes of fin-de-siècle culture, "[h]ysteria functions as a discourse of physical
otherness that is worshiped as a form of ecstasy or madness, a spiritual as
well as physical, perverse experience." (2011: 37) According to Gilman (1993),
the association of the Salome figure with hysteria was also part of her turn-
of-the-century antisemitic stigmatization.

 The parallel cultural discourse of the "criminal" woman was not restricted
to the femme fatale or Salome, and was also prominent in the new literary
genre of the detective novel. Like the figure of the New Woman being pro-
liferated throughout the London social circuit around 1890, "the New Criminal Woman [represents ...] a specifically public form of femininity for a culture that was redefining [...] 'public' and 'private' amid modern social change."
(Miller 2008: 3) In his criminological study "Criminal Woman, the Prostitute
and the Normal Woman", Césare Lombroso (1884) emphasized the codifica-
tion of female violence during infancy. He writes "[...] that children, especially
female children, were more atavistic than adults and closer in temperament
to the prostitute and criminal" (Lombroso, quoted in Kaye 2007: 56). Another

field of discourse in which the protagonist Salome was embedded was, as already indicated, that of homosexuality. Salome's relation to homosexuality was emphasized even more after Wilde's humiliating trial in 1895. This line of inquiry has been pursued by those academic interpreters who aim at locating Wilde's alter ego in Salome and who understand the morally pure John's rejection of her to symbolize Victorian resistance to homosexual urges. In 1985, Elaine Showalter questioned whether "the woman behind Salome's veils [is] the innermost being of the male artist? Is Salome's love for Johanaan a veiled homosexual desire for the male body?" (Showalter 1985: 151) Examining the motifs of shrouding and unveiling in Wilde's work, Katherine Worth argues:

> [U]nveiling was an appropriate image for the activity that Wilde regarded as the artist's prime duty: self-expression and self-revelation. In performing the dance of the seven veils, Salome is then perhaps offering not just a view of the naked body but of the soul or innermost being. (1983: 66)

More recent literary study has been less interested in the secrets concealed beneath the veil than in the veil itself: it becomes a metaphor and a medium for the poetic text. (e.g., Endres/Wittmann/Wolf 2005) As Theodor Ziolkowski (2008) elucidates, the Dance of the Seven Veils, invented by Wilde for his Salome, also refers to older religious traditions. Thus the dance has a mythical precursor in the Sumerian legend of the mother-goddess Ishtar (Inanna/ Astarte) who, in search for her dead son and lover Tammuz, must remove a veil at each of the seven stations of her walk into the underworld, finally to appear naked amongst the dead. In the Greek variant of the story, Demeter's search for Persephone, the daughter stolen by Hades, an archaic "belly goddess" with the appropriate name Baubo plays an important role: Baubo makes the grieving goddess laugh by exposing her vulva. According to Ziolkowski (2008), Wilde, for his part, established a particularly blasphemous link between sex and religion when he has Herod promise Salome the veil from the holy of holies of the Temple as a reward for her dance. The veil, in other words, which covers the Ark of the Covenant:

> The association of Salome's veils with the veil of the sanctuary hints that both veils conceal "the holiest of the holies" – in the one case, the raw sexuality that [...] in the fin-de-siècle represented the destructive female power and, in the other, the Ark of the Covenant symbolizing God's presence in the Temple. (ibid: 70)

The veil, which enshrouds the body of the goddess or the woman in order to stress by staging its ritualized disappearance, has been associated with epistemological, sacred and sexual meaning in many cultures. For example, "in Hebrew the literal meaning of the word for bride (*kallatu*) is "the veiled one". By lifting the bride's veil the bridegroom symbolically exposes her pudenda and, by thus "'knowing' her, he symbolically performs the sexual act" (von Braun/Mathes 2007: 57). In their book *Veiled Reality: Women, Islam and the West*, Christina von Braun and Bettina Mathes (2001) reconstruct not only the complex (religious) meaning of the veil but also trace metaphors and media of an Occidental "search for truth" configured around the "unveiling" of the female body.(FIG Unveiling the truth) Referring to Erwin Panofsky's (1939) research on the figure of Nuda Veritas, Londa Schiebinger (1991) suggests that images unveiling the idealized female form had, by the 17th century, become an allegory for (the pursuit of) scientific truth. As further explained in the previous chapter, however, around 1900 "fetishism" was the buzzword that facilitated the new characterization of Salome's nudity in both symbolist literature and in commercialized mass culture (Fernbach 2001).

The Ambivalence of Orientalism

Drawing on Mario Praz, Koritz (1995) situates her reading of Salome within the context of orientalism. At least since the appearance of Gustav Flaubert's account of Kuchuk Hanem, who arrived on the scene at a time when colonial Europe was virtually obsessed with the veiled oriental woman, sexual fantasies had been focused on the act of unveiling and were set "beyond the reach of the constraints and taboos of European culture" (Graham-Brown 2000: 503). Salome's dance and nudity were subject to the dynamic pressures of mass media marketing, mutating into a fetish by around 1900. Accordingly, Allan's body was obsessively described, detailed, dissected and photographed:

> To drive the point home, pictures of her arms, hands, as well as legs, not to speak of her bare feet, were reproduced in the magazines, where journalists countered Salome's fetishism with their own fetishism of the Salome dancer. (Walkowitz 2002: 15)

The quasi-imprisonment of the female form by the male gaze (Mulvey 1975) corresponded at that time with the eternal "Otherness" of the exotic. Hence, as Edward Saïd maintained, the male conception of the Orient tends "to be static, frozen, fixed eternally" (Said 1998 [1978]: 208). According to Koritz (1995), who again refers to Homi Bhabha, stereotypes of the Orient were indeed fixed but were by no means unambiguous or one-dimensional. On the contrary, they oscillated between the exotic, which is regarded as sensual and erotic, and the mystical, which is depicted as transcendent and infinite. This internal ambiguity of and in orientalism at the turn of the century, Koritz argues, implied potential ways of subverting the Orientalist "fatal-woman figure" (1995: 77). To verify this thesis, she adduces as a central example Allan's choreography "The Vision of Salome." Allan's own view of Salome in "The Vision of Salome" was as a child. In her autobiography, Allan writes "the Princess Salomé, hardly more than a child – fourteen, I take her to have been – surrounded by Galilean maidens who were her attendants, her playmates and her slaves" (Allan 1908: 121). In her childlike innocence, Salome is fascinated by the spiritual message she perceives in the Baptist's call from the cistern. As in the Bible, her mother, Herodias, exploits the child's body as a political tool and has her dance in order as to get rid of John. The dance in the "The Vision of Salome" takes place as a half-real and half-dreamlike event after the Baptist's death: "Drawn by an irresistible force, Salomé in a dream descends the marble steps leading from the bronze doors that she has just flung to, behind her frightened attendants." (ibid: 125) She soon reaches the empty terrace and first repeats the dance she performed in front of Herod. Then the severed head of John the Baptist seems to appear before her and she falls into a kind of somnambulistic ecstasy, "mingled with dread," and dances around the (imagined) head. She feels "every fibre of her youthful body quivering; a sensation, hitherto utterly unknown to her is awakened, and her soul longs for comfort" (ibid: 126).

The story of Salome that Allan "claims to depict in her dance is one of spiritual awakening. Salome is transformed in the dance from an obedient child accustomed to Oriental luxury into a woman anxious to submit to the superior power represented by the Baptist." (Koritz 1994: 66) In Wilde's drama, the dance remains invisible and undescribed. Even if some critics understood the plot of "The Vision of Salome" while watching Allan dance on stage, none of them considered Salome as an innocent child and no critic interpreted the dance around the head of John the Baptist as the story of Salome's spiritual awakening. The association with Wilde and his conviction for homosexuality rendered Salome's connection with sexual transgression and decadence even stronger.

As shown in the previous chapter, the dance of the seven veils first assumed its clearest orientalist shape in Richard Strauss's opera *Salome* of 1905. With the mélange of oriental tones and Viennese waltzes, the composer not only involved Herod and his libidinous guests in the proceedings, but also drew modern audiences in as observers. Strauss simultaneously experimented with the allure of striptease and the thrill of voyeurism. Although Allan did not present herself in her performances as a stereotypical "fatal oriental woman", and although the political subtext of the story remained intangible, many critics and also some suffragists recognized the castrating female power represented in the dancer. Here was a female dancer who danced for the beheading of a holy man, or in trance around his severed head:

> The performance of the dance derives its real allure from the cumulative knowledge of fantasies that combine sexual submission, castration and death. [...] Thus, Salome's death at the end of the opera is a necessary component of her performance. (Hoven-Buchholz (2007: 361)

In its construction of the "Oedipus complex," Freudian psychoanalysis suggested, nearly parallel with the peak of Allan's fame, a way of integrating the male phantasm of castration into "normal" psychosocial development. Every young male must pass through and cope with the threat or fear of castration. In Lacanian psychoanalysis, the status of the phallus as the only visible and therefore verifiable sex indicator is even connected to the perception of "female castration." In *The Four Fundamental Concepts of Psychoanalysis*, Lacan (1998) ponders the precarious question of what might lie beneath the veil of "'nothingness" of the female physique. He considers this precariousness as the driving force behind psychoanalytical-philosophical inquiry seeking to unveil the "mystery of femininity":

> In so far as the gaze, *qua objet a*, may come to symbolise this central lack expressed in the phenomenon of castration [...] it leaves the subject in ignorance as to what there is beyond the appearance, an ignorance so characteristic of all progress in thought that occurs in the way constituted by philosophical research. (Lacan 1998 [1981]: 77)

As explained in chapter five, Freud's generalization of the "castration complex" was also a defensive construction against the antisemitic stigmatization of the "castrated" and thus effeminate Jewish male. In the case of Lacan, there has been much speculation about the misogynistic subtext of his theory of female castration. For both psychoanalysts, the attempt to disempower the agency of women was certainly also in play. As an "absence," "void," or a person who has already been castrated, the normalized female is only a terrifying metaphor, and not an active agent of castration.

Female Visibility, Suffrage and Violence

Maud Allan was not a supporter of the suffrage movement. In the last chapter of her autobiography *My Life and Dancing*, she explained her "old fashioned" position: "to believe that the rightful destiny of every woman is to be the wife and mother, to make the inner sanctuary known by the sweet name of 'Home'" (Allan 1908: 114). As a self-supporting, unmarried woman and artist with public visibility, she attempted to downplay her transgressions of the separate spheres of gender ideology. She knew well enough that her dance and role as the prophet-slaying manipulator of regents Salome epitomized an uncontrollable, threatening femininity which, in wartime Britain, appeared dangerous. Allan's opponents considered her to be the incarnation of increasing female aggression and new female social visibility. Although her "The Vision of Salome" was rejected as immoral by the majority of suffragettes, it inspired some of them to create a symbolic performance. In their choreography of the Salome story, the dummy head of a well-known politician lay in the dancer's bowl (Walkowitz 2002).

The Canadian dancer who played with the decapitated head of John the Baptist on stage in the Palace Theatre must have been especially abhorrent to male British patriots of the Muscular Christianity movement, a group committed to a new, physically potent and puritanical masculinity. This movement combined "physical strength, religious certainty, and the ability to shape and control the world around oneself. [For] muscular Christians, the male body appears as a metaphor for social, national, and religious bodies." (Hall 1994: 7) The ideal of masculine Christianity, which focused on strengthening the male body through physical exercise, was championed in the middle of the 19th century by the liberal author Charles Kinsley and later by the Christian socialist Thomas Hughes. It exerted influence on the Boy Scout movement and quickly transformed itself into a patriotic, church-driven reform campaign. Proponents sought to halt the modern-day feminization of the Anglican Church and to strengthen the Empire: "To describe their new ideal man, his supporters even adopted a new word, the adjective 'masculine', which as Gail

Bederman points out, did not come into general usage until 1890s." (Puttney 2001: 5) What is especially interesting in this context is the fact that Kingsley was also a proponent of British Israelism, a movement that regarded Great Britain as the "New Israel", the nation of the "Chosen Race", and regarded the colonial Empire as the realization of a divine will. As heroic figures of Greek mythology and the Bible were chosen to represent this imaginary, idealized Britain, any public performance featuring early Christian heroes weakened or indeed beheaded at the hands of women would be understood as a heretical and political act. In this context, the very idea of a revived Jewish princess responsible for beheading John the Baptist and playing with his severed head was an attack on the Christian masculinity of the nation.

> The rhetoric of national character was overwhelmingly one of masculinity, while the character of the English*woman* was defined by the perfection of those domestic and maternal qualities felt to be universally present in female nature. (Koritz 1994: 71; original emphasis)

The inflammatory article published in the *Imperialist* on January 26, 1918, and the text that appeared on February 16, 1918 with the title "Cult of the Clitoris", portrayed very specific dangers. Above all, they warned of Salome's "appropriation" by an all-female circle for purposes of feminine self-arousal and masquerades, while also denouncing the corruptive influence of illicit lesbian erotica and seduction on the war effort. Both texts concluded by voicing the respective authors' suspicions that the private performances of Wilde's play served only as the pretense for further acts of subversion.

The biblical and literary figures of Salome were not only intertwined with the intention to provoke impassioned criticism and defensive responses; the dancer Maud Allan was herself identified as the Jewish princess, despite the fact that famous pioneers of dance, such as Loïe Fuller, Isadora Duncan, Mata Hari and Ida Rubinstein, had also performed this role in earlier productions. The identification of Allan with a Jewish woman was no mere coincidence. For Wilde, Salome's ideal embodiment and his original Salome was the Jewish actress Sarah Bernhardt. In June 1892, Wilde started to rehearse his play with Sarah Bernhardt at the Palace Theatre in London:

> Within a month, the Examiner of Plays for the Lord Chamberlain denied his approval for its performance, as it represented biblical figures on the stage. Wilde's anger at this was extreme; indeed, he threatened to renounce his British citizenship and become a citizen of France. And for a moment, this

British theatrical scandal linked the figures of Salome and Sarah Bernhardt. (Gilman 1993: 203)

While some critics emphasized Allan's "Americanness", nationality or ethnicity were of less concern to her audience than her "Oriental" *and* "Western" femininity. As has been mentioned before, Allan used characteristics of middle-class female spirituality and "Oriental" sensuality to position her performance in a liminal sphere between "good" and "bad" femininity. This was accomplished, at least in part, by the way in which Allan subjectively united the infantile, exhibitionist and visionary aspects of the material in her choreography. She succeeded in dissolving the rigidity of then-contemporary visions of the East, especially the dichotomy between a sensual and spiritual-mystical orient. Even as she attempted "to transform what was 'Eastern' into something 'Western', something 'erotic' into something 'spiritual'" (Walkowitz 2002: 14), she simultaneously reproduced the impression of the superiority of the West when it compares itself to the East. Thus Allan's barefoot dance supports the appearance of the Empire's superiority over the "Orient." Using her Canadian/North American body, she succeeded, as her positive reception in the media suggests, in transforming the assumed "vulgarity" of "Oriental dance" into artistic beauty. One critic writing in *The Times* shares the view of many others:

> Now it is obvious that the dancer [Maud Allan, U.B.] could make no movement or posture that is not beautiful, and in fact, her dancing as Salomé, though Eastern in spirit through and through, is absolutely without the slightest suggestion of the vulgarities so familiar to the tourist in Cairo or Tangier. (quoted in Koritz 1995:39)

In some respects, the depiction of Maud Allan in the London press oscillates between two extremes. On the one hand, she is demonic and hypersexual, a "white witch" and a vampire: "One moment she is the vampire [...] next she is the lynx," wrote one reviewer of "The Vision of Salome,"

> [yet] always the fascination is animal-like and carnal [...] Her slender and lissome body writhes in an ecstasy of fear, quivers at the exquisite touch of pain, laughs and sighs, shrinks and vaults, as swayed by passion [...]. She kisses the head and frenzy come[s] upon her. She is no longer human. She is a Maenad sister. Her hair should be disheveled, her eyes bloodshot. (Cherniavsky 1991: 165)

One of the most impressive depictions of a demonized Salome is 1906 painting by Franz von Stuck, who is said to have been inspired not only by Wilde and Strauss alone, but by the expressive dance of Maud Allan. Some rumors even make her the model for his painting.

Fig. 16: Franz von Stuck "Salome" (1906), Lenbachhaus.

Public Domain, Wikimedia Commons

Conversely, the Canadian was esteemed as an icon of pure, spiritual and "healthy" femininity, and not without good reason. After all, Allan's dance combined the most diverse and cosmopolitan of influences. Like Isadora Duncan, she was inspired not only by oriental but, above all, by Greek dance: "I have sought all my attitudes and movement," declared Allan in an interview with Raymond Blathwayt on July 18, 1908, "in the Art Galleries of Europe, on Etruscan vases and Assyrian tablets." (Allan 1908, quoted in Walkowitz 2002: 18) She was, however, also influenced by American popular dance, new gymnastics, body culture and strategies of expression devised by the French choreographer François Delsarte, who was then very popular in North America. Thus Allan certainly integrated thoughts and techniques of the life-reform movement into her Oriental dance: "Freedom through dance," as she writes in her private diary, can be achieved with "great strides, leaps and bounds, uplifted forehead, and far spread arms." (Allan 1908, quoted in Cherniavsky 1991: 123) The particularly hybrid, cosmopolitan quality of her art allowed Allan to traverse the boundary between "popular" and "high" culture in her short but successful career: "[...] at the same time she violated the tacit rule that barred 'respectable' women from the public stage" (Koritz 1995: 31). Allan received her big break in 1907 when she was invited to perform in Marienbad before King Edward VII. The new dance, performed by a Canadian raised in California, certainly had an effect of seismic proportions on London culture. Judith Walkowitz writes:

> Her London performance enables us to track shifting conceptions of gender and the national body through spaces, moments, and [the, U.B.] center [sic.] that bordered the foreign, cosmopolitan, and proletarian district Soho. [...] Allan's gestural system built on available constructions of corporality and subjectivity, but it gave unusual status to a self-pleasuring, embodied, and expressive female self and to the staging of the internal process of consciousness in public. (2002: 2)

1907 was also the year in which the Suffrage Societies staged their first mass demonstration in the streets of London in support of the enfranchisement of women. Many women, including some 1,500 "respectable women", now left the private spaces prescribed for them by political gender roles and burst into the public arena with force, visibility and violence. "In such a climate," as Koritz infers, "the public representation of an aggressively sexual figure such as Salomé would have a high ideological charge". (1995: 37)

A Feminist Salome?

Salome was not just a male creation: "[s]he was also an important resource for women performers and audiences, a vehicle for female self-expression and sexualized assertiveness." (Glen 2000: 98) Especially stars of European modern dance and of American popular theater featured the Dance of the Seven Veils, detached from its narrative context, as a solo piece. Salome's self-revelation set in motion the conquest of the stage by both avant-garde and burlesque dance artists, ranging from Ruth St. Denis and Ida Rubinstein to Anita Berger, and from Gertrude Hoffmann and Valeska Gert to Mae West and Gypsy Rose Lee. In sum, during this period London (and other European) theaters were

> [...] a liberating arena for women. The stage was one of the few places where they could pursue and succeed in independent careers. [...] [On the other hand, U.B.] The theatre's mixing of class and sexuality, and its susceptibility to the suspiciously new, combined to produce a threat to the moral status quo. (Hoare 1998: 29)

As women all across Europe began striking, singers, dancers, and choreographers bringing the male fantasy of the Oriental on stage were received with hostility. Evaluations by female avant-garde performers were also ambiguous: "'Jane Marcus sees Salomé's dance as the New Woman's art form', and yet she believes her dance to be as watered-down and curtailed as 'the tarantella danced by Nora in A Doll's House [...]'." (Showalter 1985: 159) One of the first feminist attempts to transform Salome into a female subject and translate the "Oriental" and sexual exhibitionism into their own hybrid "Otherness" was ventured by the young Russian actress Ida Rubenstein.

In Europe, "Salomania" reached its zenith in the period of Allan's performances. Her middle-brow, spiritualized version of Salome's dance enjoyed 250 performances in 1908 at the Palace Theatre alone. Her stage appearances attracted more women than men. As the liberal *Daily Chronicle* reported in 1908, "at least 90 percent of the audience were ladies. 'It might have been a suffragist meeting [...], the ladies were of all ages, well dressed, sedate'." (Walkowitz 2002: 17) In her cosmopolitan dance, Allan interpreted in new ways the fantasies associated with her and, in so doing, opened up

> [a] set of codes for female bodily expression that disrupted the Victorian conventional dichotomies of female virtue and female vice and pushed beyond such dualisms. Allan used the "Orient" as a register for female sensual expression, but she also built her dance from a range of other cultural forms, including American physical culture, theatrical posing, and modernist strategies of representations." (ibid: 6)

Did Maud Allen really succeed, however, in using the ambiguity of orientalism to escape the discursive prison that typically trapped the figure of the femme fatale and that of the "Beautiful Jewess"? The image of the homicidal, demonic dancer Salome had, already in the 14th century, been famously depicted on facades of European churches as the sinful incarnation of Synagoga, the antithesis of virtuous Ecclesia: "Innumerable churches of St. John depict Salome as the female embodiment of a diabolical Jewish evil, whether in stained-glass windows, sculptures or as the antagonist in stagings of the St. John Passion performed on June 24th." (Hoven-Buchholz 2008: 374; translation Brunotte) As will be shown at the end of this chapter, in 1918 the "witch-hunt" trial of Maud Allan was based on misogynist, homophobic and antisemitic political paranoia. One especially scandalous detail of her production was the appearance on stage during the dance of the decapitated head of John the Baptist. Diana Cooper, a female audience member, wrote in her diary in 1908 that "[...] she was all but naked and had St. John's head on a plate and kissed his waxen mouth" (quoted in Showalter 1985: 162). The cultural association of Allan's Salome with suffragism was intensified in a "British [private] feminist production of Wilde's Salomé by New Stage Players at the Court Theatre on February 27 and 28 1911, unearthed by Judith Walkowitz" (Dierkes-Thrun 2011: 106).

As stated earlier, Salome was a role model, a symbol and mask for women; and this precisely because she was so "perverse", decadent and sexualized. That the Salome epidemic spread to fin-de-siècle America is therefore not surprising. As Glenn shows, the phenomenon of Salomania "provides a remarkably vivid example of the highly volatile interanimations (intersection) of race, ethnicity, and sexuality in early twentieth-century America" (2000: 100). In Europe, the Salome craze on popular stages, "marks a moment in dance history as white dancers used the mythical ['Oriental-primitive'] Salome as a vehicle to elevate barefoot-dance as a serious art form, a drama of the body" (Brown 2008: 178). Yet, as Koritz has explained, the appropriation of the oriental style did not mean that white Western women wanted to come into contact, let alone sympathize, with actual Middle Eastern or North African women. The situation was quite different in the United States, where women of color began to impersonate Salome and her dance. The most famous of these was the dancer and comedian Ada Overtone Walker. "With her version of Salome she claimed a right to black female self-representation and at the same time aligned herself with white modern choreographers and dancers" (Brown 2000: 181).

The Salome Affair in Court: The Pemberton-Billing Trial of 1918

In her autobiography *My Life and Dancing*, Allan seeks to create the self-image of a proponent of the conservative separate-spheres gender ideology. She used the discourse of "good" femininity and rejected all affiliations with women's suffrage. The same is true of her interpretation of the Salome story in "The Vision of Salome." She made the point particularly clear in the first part of her choreography: as in the biblical story, Salome's first dance before Herod "narrates the brutal (psychological) rape of a child by her stepfather and mother" (Böhme 1995: 379). The "Vision" then narrates the story of a second dance. For Allan, this dream dance is purely spiritual, full of beauty and "love." As if in a trance, the girl returns to the deserted scene of the terrible event and begins to dance, only now for herself, in the presence of the severed head. She relives all of the stages and emotions of the evening, only now subject to her own direction. The psychosexual "awakening" approximates a spiritual enlightenment. It leads on to a higher plane of religious awakening, which Allan clearly portrays as the triumph of purist Christianity over the sensuous, "bestial Jewish Orient":

> Now, instead of wanting to conquer, she wants to be conquered, craving the spiritual guidance of the man whose wraith is before her: but it remains silent! No word of comfort, not even a sign! Crazed by the rigid stillness, Salomé, seeking an understanding, and knowing not how to obtain it, presses her warm, vibrating lips to the cold lifeless ones of the Baptist! In this instant the curtain of darkness that had enveloped her soul falls, the strange grandeur of a power higher than Salomé has ever dreamed of beholding becomes visible to her and her anguish becomes vibrant. [...] The Revelation of Something far greater still breaks upon her, and stretching out her trembling arms turns her soul rejoicing towards Salvation. (Allan 1908:127)

Nevertheless, for the audience, the half-naked body of the young woman remained the linguistic and performative medium of this spiritual awakening. Despite the emphasis on spirituality, the sexual overtones strongly influenced the reception of Allan's dance. An artistic interpretation of Salome portraying her as the victim of marital attrition rather than as a demonic perpetrator was neither shared nor understood by the London audience and critics. "When, in 1917, Maud Allan accepted the lead role in J.T. Grein's Salome production for the Independent Theatre Society in London (which specialized in a repertoire of controversial modern plays, especially Ibsen), [...] neither Allan nor Grein seem to have expected trouble." (Dierkes-Thrun 2011: 108) The producer was Jack Thomas Grein, "a Dutchman who had become naturalized some twenty years before, [...] and worked as the well-known dramatic critic of the *Sunday Times*. He now ran the Independent Theatre, which was a dramatic group with no theatre of its own specializing in producing plays considered 'modern', 'psychological' or 'decadent' – most of which were translated from the

German." (Kettle 1977: 16) In 1918 *Salome* was still considered explosive stuff. Wilde's play was banned, but Grein's performance took place in a private theater for an invited audience. Still, as Cherniavsky notes, "the decision to produce Salome in the spring of 1918 was politically unwise." (1991: 240) The private performance of Salome was the straw that broke the camel's back and provoked the slanderous and sexualizing article against Maud Allan in *Vigilante*, insinuatingly entitled "The Cult of the Clitoris" (Kettle 1977).

Against the backdrop of the World War I and the English cultural backlash mobilized by either homophobic or war hysteria, Allan's own non-mainstream interpretation of the figure of Salome could not prevail. On the contrary, the cultural imagination that created the sexually transgressive femme fatale combined with the living memory of Wilde's homosexuality and trial to stir up what amounted to a witch-hunt against Allan. In 1918, "the right-wing newspaper *The Vigilante* and its powerful lobby of conservative conspiracy theorists launched a vicious media attack against Allan, which led to the fateful events of the Pemberton-Billing Trial." (Dierkes-Thrun 2011: 109) As mentioned at the beginning of this chapter, the Independent MP, founder of the Vigilante Society, and member of the Purity Movement, Noel Pemberton-Billing, initiated a campaign against Allan and her performance. For him, she (and Grein) were German spies who sought to infect Britain with homosexual and moral decadence. It was known that Maud Allan was invited to Downing Street by Margot Asquith, "whom her enemies all said was lesbian" (Kettle 1977: 18). However:

> He couldn't accuse Allan of sodomy, so he called the local village doctor, who furnished him with a certain anatomical term. The result appeared in the 16 February edition (1918) of the *Vigilante*, in a boxed paragraph under the heading in bold black type: "The Cult of the Clitoris." (Hoare 1998: 90)

The article under the heading referred to the conspiracy theory of a German (homo)sexual war strategy to infiltrate the English elite. Pemberton-Billing was convinced of the existence of a 'little black book' in the German Kaiser's personal possession containing the names of 47,000 English men and women, mostly liberal politicians and artists, who were willing to join or who had already joined this "perverse" circle. In the box under the heading "Cult of the Clitoris", the *Vigilante* reader was informed that:

> To be a member of Maud Allan's private performance in Oscar Wilde's *Salome* one has to apply to a Miss Valetta, of 9, Duke Street, Adelphi W.C. If Scotland

Yard were to seize the list of these members I have no doubt they would secure the names of several of the first 47,000. (quoted in: Hoare 1998: 91)

It was the first time that a newspaper used such a salacious headline. Like the term "homosexuality" during the Eulenburg trial in Germany and Wilde's trial in London, the term "clitoris," a word previously used only in medical jargon, became known overnight and debated. Allan and her art fell victim to a cultural-moralist power game. She herself was victimized and both her art as well as Wilde's sexualized by a cultural discourse of "anomaly" and "perversion" (Foucault 1990 [1976]) that invented "deviant behavior" and stigmatized transgressive sexualities as a danger to society. When Grein and Allan saw the article, they immediately consulted their solicitors about bringing a libel case against Billing. As Michael Kettle (1977) has demonstrated with the help of detailed cross-examination transcripts, the trial, brandishing medical reports based on discourse from sexology like "sadism," "masochism and "fetishism," became a public stage for the "anomalization" (Foucault) of the defendants. New developments and terms in sexology, mainly from Richard Krafft-Ebing's book *Psychopathia Sexualis* (1894), were used to "cement the assumption that perverse art mirrored perverse minds and bodies and vice versa" (Dierkes–Thrun 2011: 114). This already started with the choice of the term "clitoris" in the sensationalist headline. Lucy Bland observes:

> From late eighteenth-century into early twentieth century, one of the most consistent medical characterizations of the anatomy of the lesbian was the claim of an unusually large clitoris. Not only was the clitoris associated with female sexual pleasure from reproductive potential, but lesbians were also assumed to be masculinised, and the supposed enlarged clitoris was one signifier of this masculinity. In presenting lesbians' bodies as less sexually differentiated than the norm – more masculine – it was inferred that they were atavists – throwbacks to an earlier evolutionary stage and thereby "degenerates". (1998: 184)

After lodging an accusation of libel against Pemberton-Billing on account of his "Cult of the Clitoris" diatribe, Allan was subjected to a personal witch-hunt. During the scandal-ridden public trial, it was not Pemberton-Billing who was the "accused" but the dancer Allan and her enactment of Salome. Not only was Allan identified with Wilde's Jewish Princess, but also Wilde's play (and person) became a central part of the trial. Maud Allan was even forced to read excerpts from the play aloud and commented upon them in court.

At first, Billing was concerned with emphasizing the openly sexual desire of Wilde's Salome. He highlighted it as neither innocent nor spiritual. During the third day of the trial, Dr. Serrell Cooke, a doctor who "had carefully studied Krafft-Ebing's *Psychopathia Sexualis*" (Kettle 1997: 149), became a part of the examination. He commented on the final scene of the drama when Salome has the head of John the Baptist in her hands. First the judge read from Wilde's play:

> Judge: "I love thee yet, Jokanaan, I love thee only… I am athirst for thy beauty; I love thee yet, Jokanaan, I love thee only… ; I am hungry for thy body, and neither wine nor fruits can appease my desire." Is there anything characteristic about that?
> Cooke: Simply love and a wish for sexual desire.
> Judge: But you say that is characteristic of sadism?
> Cooke: Yes, I should think it would be.
> Billing: She has the head in her hand at that time?
> Cooke: Yes, she has it just in front of her, and is addressing the head.
> Billing: The introduction of the head embodies sadism. And the presence of blood?
> Cooke: Exactly; it is the cruel association with blood; but there is something more than that. To clinch the sadism, she says: "I will bite thy lips… I will bite it with my teeth as one bites a ripe fruit.' […] Later in the play she said: 'Ah! I have kissed your mouth, Jokanaan, I have kissed your mouth. There was a bitter taste on thy lips. Was it the taste of love? But perchance it was the taste of love. Love has a bitter taste…"
> In the sadistic woman, particularly, what is known psychopathically as the love bite is exaggerated very often until blood is actually drawn, and with the tasting or the sucking of that blood, intense sexual excitement is going on until sexual orgasm is produced. (all quoted in Kettle: 155)

During cross-examination Allan insisted in vain that, in her understanding of the character as well as in her choreography, Salome's love for Jochanaan and her fascination with John's decapitated head was by no means a simple case of sexual perversion. On the contrary, as she suggested in her own address to the court, "the spirituality of the man has entered into the girl's heart and she wonders why this happens. That is my explanation." (quoted in ibid: 70)[3] For

---

3   Allan dedicated the entire last chapter of her autobiography, *My Life and Dancing* (1908), to misconceptions and misinterpretations concerning "The Vision of Salome."

Pemberton-Billing, who was allowed to take over Allan's cross-examination, she was already "guilty," if only because she knew the meaning of the term "clitoris." As a plea of justification for his article, he argued "that as a medical term, 'clitoris' would only be known to the 'initiated', and was incapable of corrupting moral minds" (Hoare 1998: 95). When Billing repeatedly returned to Salome's alleged sadism, Allan retorted: "I do not understand that she loved him in any other way than with quite pure love as any girl would love a person. [...] Salome fell in love with the holiness and the beauty of this man [...]." (ibid: 74) With no other obvious means of escape, however, Allan fell back on conventional oriental stereotypes to explain the "alienness" of the figure:

> But that is Oriental thought, is it not? [...] It is quite uncustomary for a Westerner to understand the imagery of the Oriental people. [...] I wish the Jury to understand that Salome lived in the Eastern world at a time when our rules were not in vogue, and when to see his head in front of her was nothing. I wish the Gentlemen of the Jury to know that Salome was not a perverse young woman. (ibid: 72 and 74)

Identified as the demonized and medically-diagnosed "pervert" and "mad" Salome, Allan was left with no room to maneuver. As in the case of Wilde, it was the "conflation of art with life and of artistic transgression with moral and sexual perversity – the old problem of mimesis" (Dierkes-Thrun 2011: 110). Consequently, Allan was charged with decadent irresponsibility and accused of every kind of sexual "aberrance", ranging from sadism, fetishism and exhibitionism to, of course, lesbian "perversion". Finally, both Wilde's Salome and Allan were expelled and banished from Anglo-Saxon culture: some accusations highlighted Allan's training in Berlin and Vienna. As Pemberton-Billing repeatedly told the court, "she introduced 'German' dancing into England, a type of dancing that was quite foreign to the British public before her performance." (quoted in Walkowitz 2002: 24) Others equated her "foreignness" with that of a "Jewess." One of Billing's especially antisemitic lines of argument culminated in the overtly racist description of Allan as a spy and supporter of "German-Jewish interests that promoted Salome productions and that were protected by the present government" (ibid). Again as in the case of Wilde, the spectacle of public trial was used to make an example of Allan. At the end the Jury agreed upon their verdict and found Noel Pemberton-Billing "Not guilty" (Kettle 1977: 266) upon the indictment. The courtroom drama in the Old Bailey of May/June 1918 held the attention of the press for six days: "There had not been a McCarthyite witch-hunt trial like this in England for long years – and there has not, mercifully, been once since." (ibid: 311) What kept the London populace on tenterhooks just weeks after the Allied victory, and at the beginning of reconstruction in autumn 1918, harbored existential consequences for the artist who left the court morally "condemned." Once Maud Allan had lost the trial, and despite her once spectacular fame, her successful public career was over. She left England, fell into oblivion, and died in a Los Angeles convalescent home in 1956.

Bibliography

Allan, Maud (1908): My Life and Dancing, London: Everett.

Bland, Lucy (1998): "Trial by Sexology? Maud Allan, Salome and the 'Cult of the Clitoris' Case." In: Lucy Bland/Laura Doan (eds.), Sexology in Culture. Labeling Bodies and Desires, Chicago: University of Chicago Press, pp. 98-183.

Beachy, Robert (2015): Gay Berlin. Birthplace of a Modern Identity, New York: Alfred A. Knopf.

Böhme, Hartmut (1995): "Die Enthauptung von Johannes dem Täufer." In: Geissmar-Brandi/Louis, Eleonora (eds.), Glaube Hoffnung Liebe Tod, Wien: Albertina.

Cherniavsky, Felix. (1991): The Salome Dancer: the Life and Times of Maud Allan, Toronto: McClelland & Stewart.

Didi-Huberman, George (2003): Invention of Hysteria: Charcot and the Photographic Iconography of the Salpêtrière, Cambridge: MIT Press.

Dierkes-Thrun, Petra (2011): Salome's Modernity. Oscar Wilde and the Aesthetics of Transgression, Michigan: University of Michigan Press.

Dijkstra, Bram (1986): Idols of Perversity: Fantasies of the Feminine in the Fin-de-Siècle- Culture, Oxford: Oxford University Press.

Endres, Johannes/Wittmann Monika/Wolf Gerhard (2005) (eds.): Ikonologie des Zwischenraums: der Schleier als Medium und Metapher, München: Fink.

Fernbach, Amanda (2001): "Wilde's Salomé and the Ambiguous Fetish." In: Victorian Literature and Culture 29/1: pp. 195-218.

Foucault, Michel (1990 [1976]): History of Sexuality, vol. 1, New York: Vintage (Random House).

Freud, Sigmund (1953): "Three Essays on the Theory of Sexuality." In: James Strachey (ed.), The Standard Edition [S.E.] of the Complete Works of Sigmund Freud, vol. 7, London: Hogarth Press and Institute of Psychoanalysis, pp. 1-335.

Gilman, Sander (1993): "*Salomé*, Syphilis, Sarah Bernhardt and the 'Modern Jewess'." In: German Quarterly 66.2: pp. 195-211.

Glenn, Susan A. (2000): Female Spectacle. The Theatrical Roots of Modern Feminism, Cambridge and London: Cambridge University Press.

Graham-Brown, Sarah: "The Seen, the Unseen and the Imagined: Private and Public Lives." In: Reina Lewis/Sara Mills (2000) (eds.), Feminist Postcolonial Theory: a Reader. Edinburgh: Edinburgh University Press, pp. 502-519.

Hall, Donald (1994) (ed.): Muscular Christianity: Embodying the Victorian Age, Cambridge: Cambridge University Press.

Hindson, Catherine (2007): Female Performance Practice on the fin-de-siècle popular Stages of London and Paris: Experiment and Advertisement Manchester and New York: Manchester University Press.

Hoare, Philip (1998): Oscar Wild's Last Stand: Decadence, Conspiracy, and the Most Outrageous Trial of the Century, New York: Arcade Publishing.

Hoven-Buchholz, Karla (2008): "Was verschleiert Salomes Tanz? Eine psychoanalytische Interpretation jenseits des Femme-fatale-Klischees." In: Psyche – Zeitschrift für Psychoanalyse 62: pp. 356-380.

Kaye, Richard (2007): "Sexual Identity at the Fin de Siècle." In: Gail Marshall (ed.), The Cambridge Companion to the Fin de Siècle, Cambridge: Cambridge University Press, pp. 53-72.

Kettle, Michael (1977): Salome's Last Veil: the Libel Case of the Century, London, Toronto, Sydney, and New York: Harper Collings Publishers.

Koritz, Amy (1994): "Dancing the Orient for England: Maud Allan's 'The Vision of Salome'." In: Theatre Journal 46: pp. 63-78.

Koritz, Amy (1995): Gendering Bodies/Performing Art: Dance and Literature in early Twentieth-Century British Culture, Michigan: University of Michigan Press.

Krafft-Ebbings, Richard (1894) Psychopathia Sexualis, trans. by Charles Gilbert Chaddock, London: A. P. Watts & Co.

Lacan, Jacques (1998): The Four Fundamental Concepts of Psychoanalysis: the Seminar of Jacques Lacan, Book 11, London: Norton.

Lewsadder, Michael (2002): "Removing the Veils: Censorship, Female Sexuality, and Oscar Wilde's *Salome*." In: Modern Drama 45, issue 4: 519-544.

Mathes, Bettina (2001): Verhandlungen mit Faust: Geschlechterverhältnisse in der Kultur der Frühen Neuzeit, Königstein im Taunus: Ulrike Helmer Verlag.

Miller, Elizabeth Carolyn (2008): Frame: the New Woman Criminal in British Culture at the Fin-de Siècle, Michigan: University of Michigan Press.

Mulvey, Laura (1975): "Visual Pleasure and Narrative Cinema." In: Screen 16/3: pp. 6-18.

Neginsky, Rosina (2013): Salome. The Image of a Woman Who Never Was, Newcastle: Cambridge Scholars Publishing.

Panofsky, Erwin (1939). Studies in Iconology: Humanistic Themes in the Art of Renaissance, New York: Oxford University Press.

Puttney, Clifford (2001): Muscular Christianity: Manhood and Sports in Protestant America, 1880-1920. Cambridge and London: Harvard University Press.

Said, Edward (1998 [1978]): Orientalism, New York: Random House.

Sanyal, M. Mithu (2009): Vulva: Die Enthüllung des unsichtbaren Geschlechts, Berlin: Wagenbach.

Schiebinger, Londa (1991): The Mind has No Sex? Women in the Origins of Modern Science, Cambridge and London: Harvard University Press.

Sedgwick, Eve Kosofsky (1994): Tendencies, London: Routledge.

Unseld, Melanie (2001): "Man töte dieses Weib!": Weiblichkeit und Tod in der Musik der Jahrhundertwende, Stuttgart u. Weimar: Metzler.

von Braun, Christina/Matthes, Bettina (2007): Verschleierte Wirklichkeit: die Frau, der Islam, der Westen, Berlin: Aufbau Verlag.

Walkowitz, Judith (2002) "The 'Vision of Salome': Cosmopolitanism and Erotic Dancing in Central London, 1908-1918." In: The American Historical Review 108/2: pp. 337-376.

Wilde, Oscar (1967 [1894]): Salome: A Tragedy in One Act. (Translated from the French by Lord Alfred Douglas), pictured by Aubrey Beardsley, New York: Dover.

Worth, Katherine (1983): Oscar Wilde, New York: Grove Press.

Ziolkowski, Theodor (2008): "The Veil as Metaphor and as Myth." In: Religion and Literature 40/2, pp. 61-81.

8. "Where there is dance, there is the devil"[1]. Femininity and Violence: Salome as a Maenad

Feminist Appropriations of Greek Antiquity

Using the prominent modern example of Salome's "Dance of the Seven Veils," chapters six and seven discussed the aesthetic and political role of the "new" or "free dance" in the profoundly feminine avant-garde (cf. Brandstetter 2015; Ochaim & Wallner 2021). Chapter eight now focuses again on the multifaceted birth of "modern dance" in female Hellenism/exoticism, in which early 20th century dancers exploited the gestural repertoire of ancient or exotic ritual for their own aesthetic and emancipatory efforts. The chapter connects this artistic avant-garde dance to a critical theory in the study of religion that reflected and accompanied the art form in a unique way. It begins by briefly introducing the classical scholar and archaeologist Jane E. Harrison (1850-1928), who revolutionized the study of ancient Greek religion in ways that stressed the role of images and dance as the most important bridge between ancient female rituals, modern aesthetics and the symbolic performances of the suffragettes. In more than one publication (see especially in my monograph and articles on Harrison, Brunotte 2013, 2017 and 2021), I have shown that Harrison's gender-conscious approach to ancient Greek religion helped her to recognize the importance of the contemporary "new dance" as a key modern medium of all the arts and a conveyor of new "patterns of femininity" (Brandstetter 2015: 25).

Harrison's feminist approach to ancient Greek religion, focused on rituals, emotional patterns, and body images, was also part of the then current "female Hellenism" (Fiske 2008, Brunotte 2013, Prins 2017). This is the term

---

1   "The devil [also] helped her to arouse complacence through her dance and thus to ensnare Herod. Where there is dance, there is also the devil" (quoted in: Rohde 2000: 70).

used by Shanyn Fiske in her book *Heretical Feminism. Women, Writers, Ancient Greece, and the Victorian Popular Imagination* to describe the cultural enthusiasm widespread among authors and performers for the dancing, intoxicated, followers of the god Dionysus, the maenads. Modern female Hellenism had of course a forerunner in what is called the "statue posing" of the Goethe era, as performed, for example, by the notorious Lady Hamilton (née Emma Hart) in Naples (see Schmölders 2014). In "free dance" at the beginning of the 20th century, the performative appropriation of the gestural reservoir of ancient cult dances and exotic or "oriental" dances served as a means for many early avant-garde artists to free themselves from the corset of frozen gender codes and to make new forms of subjectivity their own.

Harrison's appearance in the academic world of Cambridge and in London society was connected not only to the broader development of the first women's colleges at Cambridge, but also to the early women's movement, which asserted both the right to vote and to a share in classical education: "...women were drawn to the cultural prestige of Greek studies as one way to justify their claim to higher education" (Prins 2017: xi). Many middle-class women, some without profound knowledge in Greek language, wanted to appropriate ancient culture through their imagination, their emotions and their bodies, and "tried to make Greek letters dance, figuratively and literally" (Prins 2017: 202). Virginia Woolf was a fan of Harrison's, and Isadora Duncan, the most famous of modern dancer, was also an enthusiastic adherent of this movement. Principally through the study of vase paintings and Greek statues, Duncan endeavored to assimilate Greek antiquity through mimetic acts. She proceeded in accordance with a theory of art rooted in *Lebensphilosophie* and "gave emphasis to the dynamism of expressive potential in the re-enacting and representation of sculpture and painting" (Brandstetter 1995: 28). It was therefore no accident that Harrison not only inspired the ancient Greek costumes of some suffragettes but also helped with the Duncan's choreography (for more details see Brunotte 2013) and shared the female fascination with the incorporation of "rhythm into a moving body, both individual and collective" (Prins 2017: 202) in the Dionysian chorus of Euripides' *The Bacchae*. For Harrison in general, the study of ancient Greek archaeological findings, vase paintings and rituals was directly connected with modern life, dance and every-day experience. In her bestselling book *Ancient Art and Ritual* (1913) she wrote:

If there is to be any true living art, it must arise, not from the contemplation of Greek statues, not from the revival of folk-songs, not even the re-enactment of Greek plays, but from a keen emotion felt towards things and people living to-day, in modern conditions, including, among other and deeper forms of life, the haste and hurry of the modern street, the whirr of motor cars and aeroplanes. (Harrison, 1913 [1951]: 236)

At the same time, Harrison's work on moving body images from ancient Dionysian cults exerted a certain influence on the image researcher Aby Warburg, who was almost twenty years her junior (for more details about this influence, see Brunotte 2013: 119-124). The "art historian, religious studies scholar, and founding father of iconology [also] thought about a body-to-body and image-to-image-in-motion transmission of cultural memory and a gestural archive of embodied emotions. For his *energetic* concept of body, image, and affect-based figures and emotional forms, he coined the term *pathos formula*" (Brunotte 2017: 165; quotation in quotation: Warburg 2009 [1920-24]). In Warburg's *Mnemosyne Atlas*, he assembled an archive of images and scenes, showing an emotional "afterlife of Antiquity" (ibid): the embodied knowledge of emotions of joy, terror, passion or ecstasy. "Undertaken between 1926 and 1929, the atlas of images entitled *Mnemosyne* is Aby Warburg's nearly wordless account of how and why symbolic images of great pathos persist in Western cultural memory from antiquity to the early twentieth century." (Johnson 2012: 4) Of interest in the present context is that Warburg first conceptualized these pathos formulas in relation to the figure of *woman-in-movement*, his "Nympha" or "Ninfa Fiorentina" (Warburg [1900] 2010), and later in relation to the Dionysian frenzy of the intoxicated female followers of the god, the maenads. In her study of modern free dance, *Poetics of Dance: Body, Image, and Space in the Historical Avant-Gardes* (2015), Gabriele Brandstetter therefore makes use of Warburg's theory to analyze the body-images and emotional self-expressions in avant-garde-dance. She maintains that "In turn-of the century dance, theatre, fine arts, and literature, body-images can be isolated and analyzed as characteristic manifestations and transformations of pathos formulas." (Brandstetter 2015: 25)

Harrison, as previously mentioned, was especially inspired by the performative repertoire of the modern dance movement. All her life she acted as an intermediary between the scholarly world of Cambridge and the artistic circles of London. Ritual dance represented for her the decisive link between scholarship and art and art and ritual: "We shall find in these dances," Harrison wrote in 1913, "the meeting-point between art and ritual" (Brunotte 2017a: 174).

Harrison, however, saw the Dionysian maenads, the intoxicated and sometimes frenzied female followers of the god Dionysus, not only as mythical figures from Greek antiquity but also as representations of a "state of mind" (Harrison 1991 [1908]: 390) of normal – ancient *and* contemporary – women. For her, the wild followers of the god of wine, theater and orgies, represented female transgressions of the public order and public gender division. In an essay entitled "Homo Sum," which bore the subtitle "Being a Letter to an Anti-Suffragist from an Anthropologist" (Harrison 1915), Harrison wrote that, while she was not really a political person, her studies of primitive and ancient rituals had aroused her interest in the modern political theater of the suffragettes. Especially the symbolic actions and often ancient-style masquerades of women demonstrating for the right to vote had brought her, coming from the study of ritual, to the conviction that she must become a "suffragist" (ibid.: 114). For her, suffrage was primarily about "a ritualized effort to rewrite the terms of cultural power. She confirms that militant activity is based on the same unity of knowing, feeling, and acting that marked ancient ritual" (Commentale 2001: 483). The aspirations of the suffragettes, according to Harrison, are based on "an awakening the desire to know," that is, "the awakening of the intention to act, to act more efficiently and to shape the world completely to our will" (Harrison, 1915, p. 26).

Salome, Maenads and Female Violence

On 7 December 1909, the newly founded *Cambridge Society of Heretics* invited Harrison to be one of their two keynote speakers. The self-proclaimed "heretics" rejected traditional Christianity and "all appeal to authority in the discussion of religious questions" (Florence 1968: 228), including the exclusively male humanistic tradition and education. A radical anti-clerical scholar like Harrison was therefore a natural first choice as a speaker. "The first woman ever to give university lectures at Cambridge (in 1898), Harrison had become, by 1909, one of the most controversial figures on campus." (Fiske 2008: 2) Her reputation was soon to condense into a veritable heresy scandal when she dared to compare the biblical figure of the Jewish princess Salome to the wild, pagan maenads. The following section is a translation of the corresponding chapter in my 2013 monograph *Dämonen des Wissens. Gender,*

Performativität und materielle Kultur im Werk von Jane Ellen Harrison (Demons of knowledge. Gender, performance and material culture in the work of Jane Ellen Harrison).

In the winter of 1916-17, in the midst of the First World War, an article by Harrison entitled "The Head of John Baptist" in the prestigious journal *The Classical Review* sparked heated scholarly, theological, and political debate in Cambridge. In her text she promised a completely new and radically untheological approach to the dance of Salome, which led to the decapitation of John the Baptist. In the Gospels of Matthew and Mark, in which these events are reported, the Jewish princess does not yet have her later famous name and is referred to only as the daughter of Herodias or simply "the girl." As Chapter six argued in detail, the "girl" in the Greek text is a mere instrument in the hands of her hating and power-hungry mother. It is Herodias who planned her daughter's dance and who later urged Salome to demand the head of John the Baptist "on a platter" as her reward. "The girl dances. Only two words are devoted to the event. John's head is in fact the payment. [Nevertheless] this passage in Mark shows the rising tension and the trophy – death itself – to which dance can lead." (Baert 2014: 13) In the long pictorial tradition of the motif her dance is normally depicted separately from the beheading. However, as Barbara Baert demonstrates using pictorial examples from 13th and 14th century Europe, there exists a "second branch of images in which the dancing Salome holds the platter with the head above her head." (Baert 2014: 18) In those depictions it is, however, still not certain whether Salome bears the head on the platter to hand it over to Herod. Yet even in Wilde's tragedy (and all other modern adaptions of the Salome story) the severed head is not present on stage while during the dance. Salome never dances *with* or *around* the head. In her article Harrison questions this sequence of events. Right at the beginning of her essay, she announces that she will take a fresh look at the story of Salome and John the Baptist:

> No one, I suppose, reads the story of the daughter of Herodias and the head of John Baptist without a sense of sudden jar. In the Old Testament it might stand; in the New its licentious savagery seems an outrage. But for the familiarity of Holy Writ we should probably long ago have asked what lies behind. (Harrison 1916/1917: 216)

In her subsequent interpretation of the story Harrison claims not only to read the New Testament historically and critically, but also claims that Salome danced with or around the head of John the Baptist. Thus she positions the legend of the death-bringing dance of the Hellenistic Jewish princess in the context of pagan fertility rituals and ancient Greek female expressions of ecstatic transgression and violence. The dance of the girl is located in the Bacchic context. Harrison establishes a motivic parallel between the frenzy of the maenads, who first kill and dismember Pentheus in a cruel animalistic manner and then display his severed head, and the dance of Salome for or *with* the head of John the Baptist. In her anthropological interpretation of the *cult*, however, Pentheus and John the Baptist become nothing more than embodiments of demonic life forces which, de-individualized and recurrently sacrificed, represent *zoë* (universal life). Behind this, there appears more and more the concept of a cyclical becoming and passing away, in which all male gods and heroes ultimately merge into a single figure of the "Eniautos daimon". As before, now too Harrison advocates in her article the thesis of the existence of a "year daimon", an embodiment of slain and resurrected life, which

> should include [...] the whole world-process of decay, death, and renewal. I prefer "Eniautos" to "year" because to us year means something definitely chronological, precise segment as it were of spatialized time; whereas *Eniautos*, as contrasted with *etos*, means a *period*, in the etymological sense, a cycle of waxing and waning. (Harrison 1912: xvii)

Harrison transforms the dance of Salome and the beheading of John the Baptist, which she or her mother Herodias demands as a reward for the performance, into a cyclically recurring vegetation ritual. Through this naturalization of the dance *and* the decapitation, which in the Bible are part of the prehistory of Jesus's work, the narrative is stripped of its Christian uniqueness and holiness. It now appears as a variant of myths wandering vastly between Orient and Occident, which also follow a pattern of action that, according to the author, refers to a "primitive ritual":

> John the Forerunner has kept some savage elements expurgated from the sacred legend of his Prototype, and these elements rightly understood are not so repulsive as they seem. The loathsome story of the Head and the dance is redeemed at once from its squalour of amorous licence and dressed in a new ritual dignity. (Harrison 1916/1917: 216)

Harrison's heretical desecration of the biblical text takes place in two specific ways. On the one hand, she compares the dance of Salome around the head of John the Baptist with the maenadic death dance of Queen Agave, as passed down in Euripides' *Bacchae*. After she and other women tear her son Pentheus limb from limb in Dionysian ecstasy, Agave dances triumphantly with his severed head as with that of a slain animal, like a trophy. For Harrison one thing is certain: "*The dance of Herodias' daughter* **with** *the Head of John Baptist is, mutatis mutandis, the ritual dance of Agave with the head of Pentheus. It is the dance of the daimon of the New Year with the head of the Old Year, past and slain.*" (ibid.) On the other hand, though the scholar of religions may seek to remove the drama from the murderous events – the mutilation of Pentheus, the beheading of John the Baptist – by seeing them as part of a recurrent vegetation cult of growth and decay, her conception of the "maenads" speaks a different language and links the scenes of murderous aggression to contemporary gender struggles.

Harrison understands the maenads both as mythical inventions of the poets and at the same time as very real women: "These Maenads are as real, as actual as Satyrs; in fact more so, for no poet or painter ever attempted to give them horses' ears and tails." (Harrison 1903: 388) She describes the frenzied followers of Dionysus, who have abandoned their homes, as "simply 'mad women'" – women of all origins and ethnic groups, possessed and intoxicated by their god: "The Maenads are the women-worshipers of Dionysos of whatever race, possessed, maddened or, as the ancients would say, inspired by his spirit." (ibid) Even if scholars sometimes describe the maenads, who went to the mountains every other year to celebrate their rapturous nocturnal festivities in honor of the god Dionysus, as pure fiction and a product of art, the ancient sources speak more of their actual existence: "There must have been a time," writes Dodds, "when for a few hours or days the maenads [...] really became what their names suggest – frenzied women whose human personality was temporarily supplanted by another." Dodds 1970 [1951]: 132) Every woman, Harrison emphasizes, can become a maenad and so break through the structure of the social and gender order for a short time. That she does not thereby lose sight of the upheavals in the gender code of her own time, and that the ancient Greek maenads may have served as a projection surface for her own liberation fantasies, is made evident from comparative remarks such as the following. Referring to the maenad chorus in the *Bacchae*, she writes: "The chorus in the *Bacchae* call themselves 'swift hounds of raging madness', but the title was not one that would appeal to respectable matrons." (Harrison 1903: 389) As Linda Shires's analyzes (1992) have shown, maenadism already became a metaphor for the emancipatory aspirations of women at the time of the French Revolution. The term "maenad" could of course appeal to such "odd women" as Harrison, whose friends sometimes called her "the last mae-nad found running" (in Versnel 1993: 24), because "the odd woman" was not the only sign of burgeoning "[s]exual anarchy", as Elaine Showalter (1990: 19) has written. The increased public appearance of unmarried and working women also shook traditional notions of femininity. In Harrison's eyes, the maenad is above all "an actively terrifying and transgressive figure during Dionysic wor-ship" (Prins 1999: 47). We can only speculate how far the positive emphasis on maenadic fury and transgression reflects Victorian and modern debates and events and whether it can even be read as an allusion to the sometimes violent actions of the suffragettes.

In this context it is worth considering that the formative power of trans-gressive female violence, as it was expressed in the ancient scene of Orpheus' death, seems to feed a dynamic visual memory. It was not by accident that Warburg, in his lecture "Dürer and Ancient Italy" ("Dürer und die italienische Antike") given in Hamburg on October 5th 1905 (Warburg 1905 [2010]), placed Dürer's drawing *The Death of Orpheus* at the center of a small accompanying ex-hibition on the survival (afterlife) of a Dionysian antiquity. Especially in this Dürer lecture he emphasized the threat of Dionysian pathos when it is ex-pressed in extreme emotions and formulas – not of joy and liberation – but of murderous violence. "The concept of the *pathos formula*, used first by Warburg in this lecture and now widespread, seeks to give linguistic expression to this knowledge." (Stolzenburg/Ketelsen 2012: 9) Based on groundbreaking archival research the German art historian Charlotte Schoell-Glass reconstructed and examined the influence that antisemitism has had on Warburg's cultural the-ory and his *Kulturwissenschaftliche Bibibliothek* (Schoell-Glass 1998; 2008). For her the change of emphasis on the afterlife of Dionysian formulas in his lec-ture on "The Death of Orpheus" from liberation to threat, is closely connected to Warburg's perception and assessment of anti-Semitism." (Schoell-Glass 2008: 43) His term "afterlife [Nachleben] of antiquity" was firstly focused on the reuse and revival of ancient pictorial formulas in new historical circum-stances, storing and expressing emotions and affects. However, Schoell-Glass (ibid.: 6) argues:

If the European tradition of antiquity is sometimes latent, sometimes ac-tive, yet always an effective force in preestablished imaginary, then this is parallel in an equally ancient and similar accessible tradition of Christian anti-Semitism, a yardstick of that barbarism within civilization that can be activated at any historical moment and can equally be transferred to other minorities.

Fig. 17: Albrecht Dürer: "The Death of Orpheus" (1494), Hamburger Kunsthalle, Kupferstichkabinett.

Her interpretation of Warburg's concern with the Renaissance recovery of images and scenes of violent murder from classical mythology – especially the *pathos formula* of "The Death of Orpheus" draws a parallel between Sigmund Freud's notion that civilization is only a thin veneer "that simply obscures our view of the wildness lying hidden beneath" (ibid: 53). Warburg's art historical thoughts about the Renaissance revival of "animal frenzy" in man confronted him as shockingly contemporary. (see also Levine 2018). For her hypotheses Schoell-Glass ties in with Anne Marie Meyer's questions and reflections from 1988. The latter noted: "Exactly what was the relation between Warburg's research on paganism in the Renaissance and his mediations and fears about Judaism (and Jews) remains of course the problem." (Meyer: 452, quoted in Schoell-Glass: 4). Following Emily J. Levine it was his influential biographer and successor, Sir Ernst Gombrich, who served from 1959 until 1976 as the director of the London Warburg Institute, who towered over the image of Warburg. "Gombrich whitewashed not only Warburg's scholarship and depression but also his Judaism." (Levine 2018: 118). In contrast to this sanitized Warburg image, Schoell-Glass asserts that antisemitism was the primary explanatory background of his work. In her book first published as a German habilitation in 1998 she showed how accurately he collected reports and accounts of antisemitic pogroms in Eastern Europe (cit. p. 21, 81) always looking to find "modern parallels" of ancient or pagan Dionysian scenes of violent murders. Following Schoell-Glass's research and using her archival discoveries, Matthew Rampley (2010: 321) argues:

> This violent myth – Orpheus was torn to pieces by frenzied maenads – attested to an aspect of classical culture usually overlooked by art historians. [...] However, it is also clear that the *indirect* referent of such texts was modern anti-Semitism, with which Warburg exhibited an enduring preoccupation. Specifically, he saw anti-Jewish violence was as the expression of deep-seated psychic current, and the sporadic outbreak of such aggression in the present continued a primal impulse evident in the monstrous narratives of ancient Greek and Roman myth.

Obviously these connections were not drawn neither seen by the archaeologist and classic scholar Jane E. Harrison. It is even not certain to what extend she analyzed and even understood the violent myths about the ancient maenads as more than symbolic role models for contemporary women. Interestingly, however, maenads also recur in caricatures and depictions of violent suffragettes; in addition to the posture, these images feature above all the umbrellas which were often carried by suffragettes as, as it were, phallic symbols, but which were also frequently used as weapons. A picture of an attack by several women upon a man lying prostrate on the ground is particularly reminiscent of the weapons and agitated slaying gestures of the maenads.

Yokie Prins suggests that the maenad renaissance in early 20th century culture had several contemporary points of reference at large. Thus the Victorian imagination not only doted on the dangers that the multiplied appearance of unmarried and independent New Women could represent for public morality, but also went so far as to invent the discursive horror figure of the modern "wild woman." This was accomplished with lasting effect in the title of an anti-feminist pamphlet that Eliza Lynn Linton published in 1891: "The Wild Women as Social Insurgents." Linton warns her fellow citizens of the growing influence of unmarried women, whom she puzzlingly describes on the one hand as "unsexed" and on the one hand as "oversexed": "Our Lady of Desire, the masterful *domina* of real life – that loud and dictatorial person, insurgent and something more preaches the 'lesson of liberty' broadened into lawlessness and license." (Linton 1891: 596)

Interesting here for the context under consideration is also the mystifying merger of this new pattern of femininity with that of the murderous *femme fatale*. In this the dancing maenad celebrated her special successes as a movement image and goddess of an unleashed artistic modernism. In her doppelgänger-like proximity to the dancing Salome, who knows how to rule even a king, the figure of the mad maenad (s) could also become a model for the suffragettes. *Salomania* thus condensed fascinating fears that were associated with completely different new visibilities of women: the suffragettes demonstrated most clearly how the biblical story of Salome could be read in political terms. This not only through their political theatre and sometimes violent public self-stagings in London, but also and above all through their very own political choreography of the Salome material, in which the dummy head of a leading politician might lay in the dancer's bowl. (Walkowitz 2003: 14).

On the other hand, as Brandstetter (1995/2015) first showed, the figure of the maenad or more generally that of a young woman (Warburg's Nympha) in "wild movement" was linked at the beginning of the 20th century with idealizing notions of the working woman, who traversed public space in brisk steps. In Eugen Wolff's work *Die jüngste deutsche Literaturströmung und das Prinzip der Moderne* (The Most Recent Trends in German Literature and the Principle of Modernism) (1888), the "freely moving woman" confronts us as programmatically modern *and* as an allegory of modernism:

Thus a woman, a modern, [...], that is, a working woman [...], for example on the way home to her beloved child, for she is not a virgin, [...] is a *knowing*, but *pure* woman, [...] and wildly moved like the spirit of the time, that is, with *fluttering garments* and *flying hair*, with *onward-moving* gestures [...] – that is our new idol: *modernism!* (Wolff: 1988 [1888]: 70)

The maenad appeared in the fine arts across Europe as an aesthetically appealing "figure for mobility that cannot be contained" (Prins 1999: 49), very prominently, for instance, in the paintings of Lawrence Alma-Tadema. "In later paintings, Alma-Tadema represented maenads in a wide range of movements and poses: sprawled on the floor, dancing madly, or playing musical instruments." (ibid.: 50) Many contemporaries, however, saw the maenads, who penetrated more and more into the cultural awareness thanks to the *Dionysian* turn in the discourse about antiquity inspired by Friedrich Nietzsche and Walter Pater, as the very embodiment of violent feminine rebellion.

Harrison, dispensing with any further explanation, first put the biblical dancer in a Hellenistic-pagan context by equating the bacchante Agaue and the Jewish princess, and then declared Salome to be a sister of the ancient Greek maenads. She thus crossed the line of taboo for more than only the theologians of her time.

A look at the iconographic tradition and the writings of the Church Fathers (!) would have furnished Harrison with a good deal of evidence to corroborate a thesis that was so scandalous at the time. As will be shown, this would require a minimal shift in focus away from the death of Pentheus and to the slaying of Orpheus. The latter scene of violence condensed, as Warburg showed, both in terms of motif and iconography, a dynamic *pathos formula* that continued to have effect even beyond Christianity and into modern art. The Church Father Clemens of Alexandria interpreted the figure of Orpheus as a prefiguration of Christ and the scene of the poet's murder served as a model for the representation of the death of Christian ascetics and martyrs. This image transfer "is [also] used for one of the most prominent forerunners of Christ, John the Baptist" (Lindner 1987: 29). The Greek Church Father John Chrysostom, on the other hand, denounced Salome's "sinful dance" and her "even more sinful wages for the dance" as the work of the devil, for "Where there is dance, there is the devil" (Chrysostom (2000 [356]: 70). In the 12th century, Theophanes Ceramaeus, in his commentary on Salome, directly equated her dance with that of a maenad. In this Christian remolding, the Bacchic ecstasy was at the same time strongly sexualized:

[And] she danced like a bacchante [corybant], shaking her hair, twisting in an unseemly manner, stretching her arms, baring her breasts, alternately

throwing up her feet, revealing her body by the rapidity of the swirling movement and even exposing her pudenda to view. (Ceramaeus in Daffner 1912:
41)

Around 1900, however, the mainstream of contemporary depictions of Salome
in England and France focused not on her proximity to the ancient maenads
but above all on her orientalization. As shown in Chapter one and seven, a
complex expression of unleashed femininity thus emerged in the figure of
the Jewish princess, in which motivic and iconographic tropes of the beautiful but dangerous Jewess and the oriental-exotic woman were superimposed
on each other. It should not be forgotten that then contemporary scholarship
still considered Dionysus the "foreign god" and his train of followers of Asian-
oriental origin (even if he comes back to his hometown Theben). The invention of a feminized antiquity associated with the name "Dionysus" brought
forth, as has been seen, a new language of desire. Moreover, the figure of the
ancient maenad, seen as "the very embodiment of feminine rebellion and un-
ruly female sexuality", preoccupied Victorian culture in the debate about the
"question of women's rights" (Prins 1999: 49).

Harrison's article triggered not only vehement scholarly and theological
but also political repudiations (See Fiske 2008: 149-188). It was seen as an
attempt to interpret Christian cult-celebrations and soteriological figures as
plagiarism of pagan rituals or even to replace them with a "savage ritual." As
will be shown, in this the university establishment of Cambridge in 1916/17
thought it discovered an attack on one of the fundaments of the English nation. Of particular interest is the coincidence of a Salome revival of a different kind, which has been discussed in Chapter one, because corresponding to
the scholarly rediscovery and discursive production of a Dionysiac antiquity,
which crossed the boundaries between the occidental and oriental traditions,
were the choreographic artistic reinventions of ancient forms of movement.

Both ancient revivals, that in cultural and religion studies and that in
the arts, coincided in their fascination for dancing, women and their "moving accessories", as Warburg called the fluttering hair, veils and robes of
the dancers (cf. Didi-Hubermann 2005: 331). In the fragments of his *Ninfa
Fiorentina* project, Warburg also spoke directly, in the analysis of Ghirlandaio's
frescoes in the Florentine Church of *Santa Maria Novella*, of a survival of the
ancient nymph(s) in the form of Salome, for

... even the pious Church Father's zeal [...] failed to expel them, yes, failed
even to prevent their living on in church art, because apparently as a bona

fide biblical figure, as a dancing Salome [...] she treads light-footed through the art of the early Renaissance. (Warburg 1901 [2010]: 227)

Here, at the conclusion of this chapter, the argument comes full circle again, because around the same time the dramatically moving body of the dancing maenad or nymph, to which Warburg and, as we have seen, Harrison added Salome, also became an early model for avant-garde dance. (see Brandstetter 2015) In this, as previous chapters have discussed, the Europe-wide and then also America-wide *Salomania*, which revolved around the Dance of the Seven Veils, played a major role. And now, Maud Allan and her *Vision of Salome* came briefly, and in a surprising way, into the focus of scholarly discussion.

Fig. 18: Maud Allan with the Head of John the Baptist (Postcard 1906-1910).

Public Domain, Wikimedia Commons

In her unconventional interpretation of the Salome material, in which the dancer dances around the decapitated head of the Baptist, Allan closely linked the unveiling of female nudity with deadly violence. The dancer's choreography thus confirmed Harrison's radical interpretation. In the venerable *Cambridge Review*, Harrison had even gone so far as to use the Canadian dancer as a reference for her scholarly reading:

> To speak of a dance with the Head is to put the loathsome performance of the modern dancer – that is Maud Allan – in place of the Gospel story. I have lately met more than one person who – such is the power of suggestion – had actually made the transition – actually believed the dance with the Head was part of the Gospel story. [...] Yes, both S. Matthew and S. Mark tell us that the head is not the motive of the dance, but its guerdon. Yet by an odd chance the modern dancer hit on the horrible truth – the original dance was with the Head, was motivated by the Head. (Harrison 1916/1917: 216-217)

The use of the distancing adjective "loathsome" to characterize Allan's dance did little to disguise the scandalous fact that a Cambridge classicist gave a controversial choreographic transformation of ancient material the same weight in her interpretation as she did to the evidence of ancient vase paintings or religious source texts. Moreover, a scholar of Newnham College, the second women's college at Cambridge, thus made the biblical dancer from the court of Herod the Jewish sister of the violent pagan maenads. In the form of the *pathos formula* of Salome's dance and that of the intoxicated maenads, in both cases deadly, Dionysian myth is overlaid with biblical narrative. This overdetermination of threatening female "wilde movements" in Harrison's interpretation is better understandable also as a commentary on current events: The rediscovery of ancient expressive repertoires current around 1900 in literature, in the "new dance," and among the suffragettes, may be regarded as the *tertium comparationis*.

Bibliography

Brandstetter, Gabriele (1995): Tanz-Lektüren. Körperbilder und Raumfiguren der Avantgarde. Frankfurt/M.: Fischer.

Brandstetter, Gabriele (2015): The Poetics of Dance: Body, Image and Space in the historical Avant-gardes. NewYork: Oxford University Press.

Brunotte, Ulrike (2013): Dämonen des Wissens. Gender, Performativität und materielle Kultur im Werk von Jane Ellen Harrison, Würzburg: Ergon (Diskurs Religion 3).

Brunotte, Ulrike (2017): "The Performative Knowledge of Ecstasy: Jane E. Harrison's (1850- 1928) Early Contestations of the Textual Paradigm in Religious Studies." In: Grieser, Alexandra K./Johnston, Jay (eds.): Aesthetics of Religion. A Connective Concept Berlin/Boston: de Gruyter, pp. 195-220.

Brunotte, Ulrike (2021): "Jane Ellen Harrison (1850-1928). Gewendeter Kolonialdiskurs, *Material Religion*, Ritual und Suffrage". In: Höpflinger, Anna-Katharina/ Jeffers, Ann/ Peozzoli-Oligiati, Daria (eds.): Handbuch Gender und Religion (2. edition), Göttingen: UTB (Vandenhoeck-Ruprecht), pp.219-232.

Ceramaeus, Theophanes (1912 [12th century]: "Über die Enthauptung des ehrwürdigen Künders". Quoted in: , Daffner, Hugo: Salomé. Ihre Gestalt in Geschichte, Dichtung, bildender Kunst und Musik, München 1912: p. 41

Chrysostomos, John (2000, [350-407]): "Wo eben ein Tanz ist..." In: Rohde, Thomas (ed.) Mythos Salome: Vom Markusevangelium bis Djuna Barnes, Leipzig: Reclam, pp. 68- 70.

Didi-Huberman, Georges (2005): "Bewegende Bewegungen. Die Schleier der Ninfa nach Aby Warburg". In: Endres, Johannes/Wittmann, Barbara/Wolf, Gerhard (eds): Ikonologie des Zwischenraums, Paderborn: Wilhelm Fink Verlag, pp. 331-360.

Dodds, Erec Robertson (1951): The Greeks and the irrational. Berkeley: University of California Press.

Glenn, Susan A. (2000): *Female Spectacle*. Cambridge/MA: Harvard University Press.

Harrison, Jane E. (1916/1917): The Head of John Baptist, in: The Classical Review 30/31(8), pp. 216-219.

Harrison Jane E. (1991 [1903]: Prolegomena to the Study of Greek Religion, New York: Princeton University Press.

Harrison, Jane E. (1915). "*Homo Sum. Being a Letter to an Anti-Suffragist from an Anthropologist.*" In: Harrison, Jane E.: Alpha and Omega. London: Sidwick & Jackson, pp. 80-115.

Harrison, Jane E. (1951 [1915]. Ancient Art and Ritual. London: Williams & Norgate and New York. Henry Holt.

Johnson, Christopher D. (2012): Memory, Metaphor, and Aby Warburg's Atlas of Images. Ithaca, NY: Cornell University Press.

Levine, Emily J. (2018): "Aby Warburg and Weimar Jewish Culture: Navigating NormativeNarratives, Counternarratives, and Historical Context." In: Aschheim, Steven/Liska, Vivian (eds): The German-Jewish Experience Revisited. Boston/Berlin/New York: de Gruyter, pp.117-134.

Lindner, Ines (1987) Die rasenden Mänaden. Zur Mythologie weiblicher Unterwerfungsmacht. In: Ilsebill Barta (ed.): Frauen, Bilder, Männer, Mythen. Kunsthistorische Beiträge. Berlin: Dietrich Reimer Verlag, pp. 282-303.

Linton, Eliza Lynn (1891): "The Wild Women as Social Insurgents." In: The Nineteenth Century 30 (October), pp. 596-605.

Laura Mulvey: "Visual Pleasure and Narrative Cinema". In: Screen 16 (1975), No.3, pp. 6-18.

Ochaim, Brygida/Wallner, Julia (2021) (eds.): Der absolute Tanz. Tänzerinnen der Weimarer Republik (Ausstellungskatalog Georg Kolbe Museum), Berlin: Georg Kolbe Museum.

Prins, Yopie: Greek Maenads, Victorian Spinsters, in: Dellamora, Richard (Hg.): Victorian Sexual Dissidence, Chicago 1999, pp. 43-72.

Prins, Yopie (2017): Ladies' Greek: Victorian Translations of Tragedy, Princeton University Press.

Rampley, Matthew (2010): "Aby Warburg: Kulturwissenschaft, Judaism and the Politics of Identity." In: Oxford Art Journal, 33.3, pp. 317-335.

Schmölders, Claudia (2014): Das griechische Gesicht des Tanzes. Eine Faszinationsgeschichte von Lady Hamilton zu Isadora Duncan. In: Hans-Georg von Arburg et. al.(eds.), Physiognomisches Schreiben. Stilistik, Rhetorik und Poetik einer gestaltdeutenden Kulturtechnik. Rombach: Freiburg i. Br.: Rombach, pp. 207-224.

Schoell-Glass, Charlotte (1998): Aby Warburg und der Antisemitismus. Kulturwissenschaft als Geistespolitik. Frankfurt/Main: Fischer

Schoell-Glass, Charlotte (2008): Aby Warburg and Antisemtism. Political Perspectives on Image and Culture. Detroit: Wayne State University Press.

Shrines, Linda (1992): "Of Maenads, Mothers, and Feminized Males: Victorian Readings of the French Revolution." In: Shrines, Linda (ed.): Rewriting the Victorians: Theory, History, and the Politics of Gender. New York: Routledge, pp. 147-165.

Showalter, Elaine (1990): Sexual Anarchy: Gender and Culture at the Fin de Siècle, London/New York: Penguin Books.

Stolzenburg, Andreas/Ketelsen, Thomas: "Aby Warburg in Köln. Ein Vorwort." In: Hurtig, Marcus, Andrew/Ketelsen, Thomas (eds.): Die entfesselte Antike. Aby Warburg und die Geburt der Pathosformel, Katalog zur gleichnamigen Ausstellung im Wallraff- Richards-Museum & Fondation Corboud, Köln 2012, pp. 7-12.

Versnel, Hendrik S. (1993): Transition and Reversal in Myth and Ritual, Leiden/New York/Köln; Brill.

Warburg, Aby (2010 [1901]): "Florentinische Wirklichkeit und antikisierender Idealismus." In: Treml, Martin/Weigel, Sigrid (eds.): Aby Warburg. Werke. Frankfurt/M.: Suhrkamp, pp. 211-233.

Warburg, Aby (2009 [1920-1924]): "The Absorption of the Expressive Values of the Past," (engl. translation der Einleitung zum Mnemosyne Atlas, by Matthew Rampley). In: Art in Translation $\frac{1}{2}$ Berg journals: pp. 273-283.

Warburg, Aby (2010 [1900]): "Ninfa Fiorentina." In: Treml, Martin/Weigel, Sigrid, Ladewig, Perdita (eds.): Werke. Frankfurt/M.: Suhrkamp, pp. 187-198.

Warburg, Aby (1998 [1893]: "Sandro Botticellis "Geburt der Venus" und "Frühling". Eine Untersuchung über die Vorstellungen von der Antike in der italienischen Frührenaissance." In: Ders.: Bredekamp, Horst et al. (eds.): Die Erneuerung der heidnischen Antike. Gesammelte Schriften, Bd. I 1,2. Berlin 1998: Akademie Verlag, pp. 1- 60.

Wolff, Eugen (1988 [1888]): "Die jüngste deutsche Literaturströmung und das Prinzip der Moderne." In: Wunberg, Gotthart/Dietrich, Stephan (eds.): Die literarische Moderne. Dokumente zum Selbstverständnis der Literatur um die Jahrhundertwende, Freiburg i. B. : Rombach Wissenschaft, pp. 27-8.

Acknowledgments and Print Proofs

Three of the chapters in the present book were based on shorter contributions to our joint ReGNOO-conferences and workshops. A longer version of "Queering Judaism and Masculinist Inventions: German Homonationalism Around 1900" was presented as the keynote lecture of the research network's conference in October 2014 at Humboldt University in Berlin under the title "The homophobic Argument. National Politics and Sexuality in Transregional Perspective," and a shorter version at the conference "Contested Privates: Religion and Homosexuality in Public Discourse" at Utrecht University in 2017. The chapter "The Jewess Question" is based on a lecture I gave in July 2018 at a workshop at the *Selma Stern Centre* entitled "Kolonialismus und Judentum in Deutschland" and on an invited lecture and workshop at the Meertens Institute of the *Royal Netherlands Academy of Arts and Sciences* (KNAW), Amsterdam, on 23 January 2018. "All Jews are Womanly, but no Woman is a Jew" is a revised and shortened version of an earlier peer reviewed book chapter that appeared in the anthology *Orientalism, Gender, and the Jews* (de Gruyter 2015). "The Jewess Question" is an expanded text based on the final published version of the article "The 'Beautiful Jewess' as Borderline Figure in Europe's Internal Colonialism," which appeared in the peer reviewed journal *ReOrient. The Journal of Critical Muslim Studies*, vol. 4, No. 2, Spring 2019. "Queering Judaism and Masculinist Inventions: German Homonationalism around 1900" was first published in 2020 in a volume edited by Marco Derks and Mariecke van den Berg entitled *Public Discourses About Homosexuality and Religion in Europe and Beyond*. It was a result of a five years research project "Contested Privates: The Oppositional Pairing of Religion and Homosexuality in Contemporary Public Discourse in the Netherlands" which was funded by the NWO. "Seeing, Hearing and Narrating Salome: Modernist Sensual Aesthetics and the Role of Narrative Blanks" is a slightly revised version of an earlier article which appeared in *Figurations and Sensations of the Unseen in Judaism, Christianity and*

Islam (Bloomsbury 2019), edited by Birgit Meyer/Terje Stordalen. I would like to express my gratitude to the NWO for the financial support of the five years of our joint research and the international network on "Gender and Sexuality in (Neo-)Orientalism: An Entangled History of European and Middle Eastern Identity Discourses." (ReNGOO). I would also like to thank the respective editors and publishers for granting permission to reprint these articles. And finally I would like to thank Jonathan Uhlaner for the excellent proofreading of all chapters and the translation of chapter four, five and eight.

Notes on the Author

Ulrike Brunotte is still affiliated to Maastricht University as Senior Researcher. Until her retirement in September 2021, she was an Associate Professor at the Faculty of Arts and Social Sciences, a Research Fellow at the *Center for Gender and Diversity*, both Maastricht University (The Netherlands) and an adjunct Professor for *Kulturwissenschaft* at Humboldt-University Berlin. From 2013 to 2017 she was chair of the international research network "Gender in Antisemitism, Orientalism and Occidentalism." Her research focuses on sexuality-, gender- and masculinity studies, North American (puritan) religion, literature and modern antisemitism. Her publications, as author and editor, include, *Imagined Orientals? Antisemitism, Colonialism and Modern Constructions of Jewish Identity* (Ergon 2017); *Orientalism, Gender and the Jews: Literary and Artistic Transformations of European National Discourses* (de Gruyter, 2015); *Dämonen des Wissens. Gender, Performativität und materielle Kultur im Werk von Ja-*

ne Ellen Harrison (2013, Ergon, Diskurs Religion vol. 3) and *Zwischen Eros und Krieg: Männerbund und Ritual in der Moderne* (Wagenbach, 2004). Together with Jürgen Mohn (University Basel) she is editor of the book series "Diskurs Religion" (Ergon, since 2010).

Historical Sciences

Sebastian Haumann, Martin Knoll, Detlev Mares (eds.)
Concepts of Urban-Environmental History

2020, 294 p., pb., ill.
29,99 € (DE), 978-3-8376-4375-6
E-Book:
PDF: 26,99 € (DE), ISBN 978-3-8394-4375-0

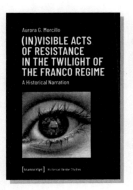

Aurora G. Morcillo
**(In)visible Acts of Resistance
in the Twilight of the Franco Regime**
A Historical Narration

January 2022, 332 p., pb., ill.
50,00 € (DE), 978-3-8376-5257-4
E-Book: available as free open access publication
PDF: ISBN 978-3-8394-5257-8

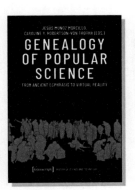

Jesús Muñoz Morcillo, Caroline Y. Robertson-von Trotha (eds.)
Genealogy of Popular Science
From Ancient Ecphrasis to Virtual Reality

2020, 586 p., pb., col. ill.
49,00 € (DE), 978-3-8376-4835-5
E-Book:
PDF: 48,99 € (DE), ISBN 978-3-8394-4835-9

**All print, e-book and open access versions of the titles in our list
are available in our online shop www.transcript-verlag.de/en!**

Historical Sciences

Monika Ankele, Benoît Majerus (eds.)
Material Cultures of Psychiatry

2020, 416 p., pb., col. ill.
40,00 € (DE), 978-3-8376-4788-4
E-Book: available as free open access publication
PDF: ISBN 978-3-8394-4788-8

Andreas Kraß, Moshe Sluhovsky, Yuval Yonay (eds.)
Queer Jewish Lives Between Central Europe and Mandatory Palestine
Biographies and Geographies

January 2022, 332 p., pb., ill.
39,99 € (DE), 978-3-8376-5332-8
E-Book:
PDF: 39,99 € (DE), ISBN 978-3-8394-5332-2

Harald Barre
Traditions Can Be Changed
Tanzanian Nationalist Debates
around Decolonizing »Race« and Gender, 1960s-1970s

2021, 274 p., pb.
45,00 € (DE), 978-3-8376-5950-4
E-Book:
PDF: 44,99 € (DE), ISBN 978-3-8394-5950-8

**All print, e-book and open access versions of the titles in our list
are available in our online shop www.transcript-verlag.de/en!**